THE HORSEMAN'S WORD

Blacksmiths and Horsemanship in Twentieth-Century Scotland

THE HORSEMAN'S WORD

BLACKSMITHS AND HORSEMANSHIP in TWENTIETH-CENTURY SCOTLAND

TIMOTHY NEAT

Birlinn

DEDICATION

To the Smiths and to the Horsemen
And to my friends Alec John and Duncan Williamson

First published in Great Britain in 2002 by Birlinn Ltd
West Newington House
10 Newington Road
Edinburgh EH9 1QS

www.birlinn.co.uk

ISBN 1 84158 094 5

The publishers acknowledge subsidy from

towards the publication of this volume

British Library Cataloguing-in-Publication Data
A catalogue record is available on request from the British Library

Designed by Carnegie Publishing Ltd, Lancaster
Printed and bound in Spain by Book Print, S.L., Barcelona

Frontispiece – 'Two horses, plough, man', East Scotland, c.1930. (CHS)

CONTENTS

ACKNOWLEDGEMENTS

I am deeply grateful to all those people who have helped create this book. In particular I thank the blacksmiths and horsemen: A.G. Mackenzie (Achnagarron), David Wilson, Jock Mackenzie, Sandy Moncrieff, Jim Aitkin, Iain MacInnes, Jock Anderson, Walter Robinson, Arthur Elliot, Adam Murray, Willie McIntosh, Charlie Barron, James Stewart of Balmuir Wood and James Stewart of Alford; also Alistair Livingstone Baron of Bachuil, and Alec McIntosh of Edinburgh. Their openness, friendship and generosity continue the great tradition and their photographs are beautiful.

I would also like to thank my long-term friends, colleagues and supporters Hamish Henderson, Duncan Williamson, Stephanie Wolfe Murray, John Berger; and especially Jean Mohr of Geneva for permission to use his magnificent cover photograph and his great series of images of Charlie Barron and Lucia Lancerini, taken for the film *Play Me Something* in 1988. Special thanks also go to David Hayes and the Landmark Visitor Centre at Carrbridge for use of photographs from the Strath Spey forests, notably from the collection of Mr and Mrs J.D. Smith. Also I thank the Clydesdale Horse Society for permission to use a selection of their superb photographs, and Nec Teymur for his photograph of the Anatolian horsemen with scythes; also Clive Richardson, a great horseman, from the North of England; and Carcanet Press for permission (in kind) to quote extracts from the poetry of Hugh Macdiarmid. The Birlinn editorial staff have been, as usual, most understanding and helpful; Neville Moir in particular.

Across thirty years my thanks go to the School of Scottish Studies at the University of Edinburgh; to Norman Christie of Brechin, Willie Milne of Cuminestown, Jimmy Stott of Fyvie, Henry Thomson, farmer Binne of

Broich, William Chalmers of Turriff, Morrison of Shapwells, and Morrison of Meagie. I also thank John Tickner, Davie Adams, Sharon Cregier, Gary Robinson, Mark Steven, Campbell Sandilands, Lorn McIntyre, and the *People's Journal*, Dundee. And, as always, deep thanks to my wife and family.

Photographs are copyright and codified as follows. Jean Mohr (JM), the Clydesdale Horse Society (CHS), Timothy Neat (TN), Davie Adams (DA), A.G. Mackenzie (AG), Campbell Sandilands (CS), Landmark Visitor Centre (LM), Sandy Moncrieff (SM), Hamish Henderson (HH), The School of Scottish Studies (SSS), Jim Aitkin (JA), Polly Pullar (PP) Francis Neat (FN), Jock Anderson (Jock), Walter Robinson (WR), Alec McIntosh (AM), Private Collection (PC), Clive Richardson (CR), Jane Turriff (JT), James Stewart (JS), Charlie Brown (CB).

PREFACE

This book is the last of my *Highland Quintet* – five illustrated volumes exploring traditional life in the Highlands of Scotland in the twentieth century. *The Horseman's Word* presents portraits of horsemen, blacksmiths, farriers and others whose lives have been shaped by contact with horses. Today, these men play only a peripheral role in the economic and cultural life of Scotland but they remain heirs to some of mankind's oldest traditions and throughout history their agricultural, economic, cultural, social and military roles have been of great importance. The men profiled here are worthy of high honour in the story of Scotland.

The most important technological development in the prehistory of man was his adoption, use and control of fire. This happened about one million two hundred thousand years ago, probably first in South Africa. The light of fires gave early man protection from predators, and the warmth of the fireside nurtured mankind's innate social and cultural propensities. Much later the latent energy in fire put man on the escalator of technological progress and it was 'the smith' who acted as the prime intermediary between this energy and the course of modern man's evolutionary development. Control of fire led to metallurgy; metallurgy led to the control of horses; horsemanship has been the basis of the military and political power that has shaped Western civilisation over the last five thousand years. Horsemen and men of fire are the subject of this book.

Fire gave our primitive ancestors access to deep caves and greater protection against carnivores. It widened sources of food supply and increased the proportion of meat in the humanoid diet. These things encouraged hunting and an ever-increasing dexterity of hand and eye, and social interaction round

Dave Greenhill of Leuchars entering David Wilson's smithy, Balmullo, with a Clydesdale filly for shoeing, 2000. (TN)

the fire gave humanity time – to think, to feel and enjoy life. The single focus point of the life-giving fire gave mankind a new sense of perspective – just as revolutionary as Brunelleschi's 'invention' of linear, scientific perspective at the beginning of the Italian renaissance (man is the fire-making, art-making animal). He who controlled fire had power and, over millennia, the 'firemen' became shamen and both spiritual and martial leaders. Their modern equivalents remain influential exemplars in society, as W.B. Yeats wrote of Major Robert Gregory:

> Soldier, scholar, horseman, he . . .
>
> What other could so well have counselled us
> In all lovely intricacies of a house
> As he that practised or that understood
> All work in metal or in wood,
> In moulded plaster or in carven stone?
> Soldier, scholar, horseman, he,
> And all he did done perfectly
> As though he had but that one trade alone.

It was an English palaeontologist, Bob Brain, working in the Swartkrans caves outside Pretoria in South Africa, who was responsible for discovering the burnt remains that have proved mankind's dependence on fire goes back much further than had been thought but even before Brain made his crucial 'first fire' discoveries, in 1984, he had published a book entitled *The Hunters or the Hunted?* in which he advanced the theory that early man was not the savage 'cannibal' often depicted but a relatively gentle, ape-like, species on whom prehistoric African cats had preyed with great success. This gentle, early-humanoid species (our species) only prospered after it gained control of the 'magic' power of fire. He subsequently proposed that the most dangerous of early man's predatory enemies was the *dinofelis,* the false sabre-toothed tiger, and that this highly successful carnivore savagely constricted man's early development until control of fire, quite suddenly, turned the tables. This, Brain believes, was the crucial step in the subsequent 'ascent of man'.

His theories acknowledge the 'men of fire' as central characters in the history of mankind. After years of hesitation, most leading anthropologists now accept the veracity of Brain's decision to place 'fire, communality and "wits"' as the forces at the heart of mankind's unparalleled development. Thus the family tree of the blacksmith must be recognised as one of the oldest and significant in the human story.

Man's digital dexterity and linguistic abilities seem to have been the prime influences upon the development of our big human brain, but our human-being – as social-cultural animals – goes back to the 'technology' of the hearth, to the magic of a fire in a circle of stones. Fire was, from the beginning, not just useful but wonderful. It came to earth via lightning in thunderstorms, it came with rain, it came refracted through diamonds scattered amongst rocks and riverbank tinder. In the beginning fire was a 'found' object – preserved and maintained. Five hundred thousand years were to pass before man began to make fire to order. After that, for as long as the earth was presumed to be the centre of the universe, fire remained the pre-eminent determiner of human history. It was necessary and magical and it is not surprising that the story of Prometheus, the man who stole fire from the gods, is one of the archetypal, horror myths of mankind. This story is much older than the Homeric world from which 'our' legend comes. It goes back to times when lack of fire really meant death, or a society's return to anarchic brutality – symbolised, in the story, by the ravenous devouring of raw human liver which clearly represents the reality of the barbarous world from which fire had allowed mankind to escape.

For thousands of years many of the world's best religious thinkers and writers have addressed the dark barbarism against which man has struggled to create temporal happiness and 'civilisation'. And it is interesting that it was Brain's book on hunting that drew the documentary writer Bruce Chatwin to South Africa to Brain's field camp, on the very day when the first crucial finds, pushing back the date of man's first use of fire by 700,000 years, were made. For Chatwin, as a novelist and as a man, this was a revelatory moment. Excavating with Brain in South Africa, encouraged Chatwin to develop ideas about 'the Prince of Darkness'; his theory that mankind's primordial terror of the false sabre-tooths that prowled the darkness beyond the light of the fire, has been passed down, these million years, to us – as ingrained, imprinted fear of the dark and 'the other'. This archetypal fearfulness has given man, and in particular men, an inbuilt sense of there being a permanent 'enemy' whom they must always be ready to face and vilify – whether there is a present and concrete reason for such vigilance, or not. Mankind, Chatwin believed, has evolved a conditioned need for enemies, a Prince of Darkness, against whom individuals, continually, seek to defend themselves and their tribe, with all necessary ruthlessness. This enemy is both real and imagined. He is the eternal scapegoat; an evolutionary throwback ensconced in contemporary human behaviour; ever ready to propel the media, politicians and demagogues towards hysterical, bloody violence – today as much as ever. One of the great virtues of the horseman and blacksmiths portrayed in this book is that they know both the beast and the fire – and address both with calmness and knowledge; one eye on the social good, the other on simple, practical function.

From the time of its first use the mystical character of fire was controlled by various kinds of 'fire-shamen'. As the Neolithic period (8,000–2,000 BC) merged into the Copper and Bronze Ages some of the magic of the fire-shamen began to pass into the hands of men best described as smiths. The rise of new castes of military, political and religious leaders, however, immediately let to determined efforts to dilute and control the status and power of the fire practitioners. Though their mystical and practical usefulness remained as great as ever, dynastic self-interest and intellectual conceit ensured they were kept in their place – as craftsmen only.

Another Greek legend gives psychic form to the human consequences of this ancient division of labour – the story of Vulcan, Venus and Mars. Vulcan, blacksmith to all the gods, was married to Venus, the goddess of beauty. He was lame but made the weapons with which Mars, the handsome god of war, wins glory. Vulcan (the boffin) stays at home; he is the archetype for Freud's theory of the artist as cripple – he buries sexual failure in work and more work. Mars is the man of action, the film-star, the war hero returned; he seduces and runs off with the willing Venus. This legend encapsulates the fundamental frameworks within which all divided, hierarchical societies function – to the advantage of their established elites. Vulcan is the Class D/E operative – practical, dirty, tired, disabled; habituated to the process of labour. Mars is the Class A officer/executive – thrusting, aristocratic, expectant of rewards and hungry for praise; the man who, from birth, is educated to aspire to managerial control and take risks, even though, across the span of history, he risks less to his life's health than Vulcan the labourer.

The origin of the Greek word for 'civilised' is 'to be recumbent' – thus to be civilised one needs time – for relaxation, high thoughts, gardens, palaces, the pleasures of sex, art and exploration of all kinds. These are things that Mars had plenty of, these are things that the labouring masses, across history, have always had little of. But no civilisation exists in a vacuum and leisure, normally, has to be earned. All civilisations are the product of hard work, concentrated attention and effort – whether in the vineyard, the kitchen, the study, the forge or the workshop. Success on the battlefield is nothing without them. Civilisation has always been a product of collaboration but the rewards of civilisation have never been equally shared – and Vulcan, the lame cuckold, personifies the phenomenon. Whether Vulcan was a cripple before he became a smith, or was crippled in the course of his work, is not explained in the legend – he might even have been 'broken' by his wife's desertion – but, whatever the origins of his disablement, his story, the story of the smith, remains full of historical and artistic resonances – wonderfully painted by Botticelli and Velasquez, wonderfully turned into music by Wagner.

The reduction of the smith, within civilised societies, to the role of skilled or semi-skilled labourer might have been the end of a very old song. But was not. The dark magic of the smithy retained its strange ancient powers – underground. Like hope, something eternal springs when man meets fire. The smith has continually transformed himself – making ever new kinds of tools and appliances, fuelling spaceships, building Formula One racing cars.

David Wilson, President of the National Association of Farriers, at work, Balmullo, 2000. (TN)

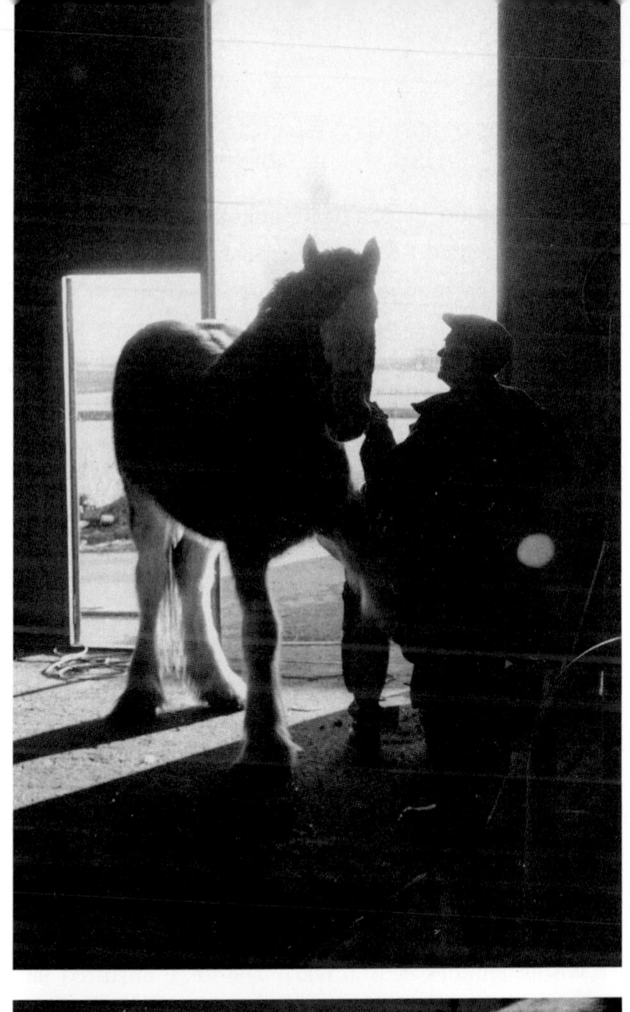

And fire retains a magnetic hold on the human heart and mind: who can doubt the continuing link between the lighted television sets that glow in the corner of the world's living rooms and the luminous forge in the smithies in which the modern world was created. Who can doubt the link between the lighted stage at the heart of every theatre and the campfires which so long flickered, in their thousands, across the plains of Africa and in mouths of caves from Gibraltar to the Caithness coast – where mankind found shelter and protection from the outside world and set out on the march towards civilisation.

* * *

The original development of metallurgy is believed to have begun in the Balkans, about seven or eight thousand years ago, and it seems likely that the smiths were from the beginning both modernisers and fierce advocates of 'tradition'. They knew their knowledge and skills were in demand and from the beginning formed themselves into something like 'closed shops': separating themselves and their secrets. This has remained true over the centuries and even during periods of extraordinary change, like the Industrial Revolution, the smiths remained secretive – bastions of conservative traditionalism, their knowledge passed down within families by oral relay. The forge nurtured talk and remembrance, physical strength and inquisitive minds. In addition the combination of great heat and great labour necessitated the downing of large quantities of liquids; these were often alcoholic. Thus, many smithies became hostels where music and song flourished. These would usually be the traditional folksongs of the locality but two particular kinds found natural homes in the smithies – martial and nationalistic songs, and bawdy and licentious songs. The anvil was a place of meeting and makars, of rumour and rebellious self-assertion (another reason why the social establishment sought to keep the smiths and their contacts in place).

In Scotland, a vital ballad tradition has remained notably strong amongst the horsemen and blacksmiths and a huge repertoire of song, music, riddle and proverb is still to be found amongst the men of the smithies (including the poetry of shepherds, the songs of cattle-drovers, and the martial balladry of returning soldiers).

The darkness of the smithy provided each village with a theatrical space. Everybody enjoys watching someone else working. The physical realities of iron, water, fire and horses awakened sensory responses. In most stable communities the tradition of bawdy resides most deep-rootedly and poetically amongst the oldest social groups and, in Scotland, the Tinkers, the smiths, the horsemen; criminals, whores and upper classes – bawdy, traditionalism continues:

Rosebery to his lady says,
        My hinnie and my succour:
'O shall be do the thing you ken,
        Or shall we take our supper?'

Wi' modest face, sae fu'o' grace,
        Replied the bonnie lady:
'My noble lord, do as you please,
        But supper is nae ready.'

G. Legman, author of *The Horn Book* (1964), points out that this short song, about the aristocratic, Roseberys (normally sung to the tune of *Clout the Cauldon*), goes back to a fifth-century Greek text attributed to Philagrius which can be translated thus:

A young man said to his randy wife
Wife what shall be do?
Shall we rise for breakfast noo
— or the love of Aphrodite?

As you prefer my love, my sire
— but we've not a bite to eat!

The pedigrees of erotic songs are frequently old. They flow on, like permanent underground streams, whilst songs that flow on the surface are prone to flood, drought. Authoritarian religion has traditionally taken a hard line against eroticism, equating it with licence and satanic practices. Fear of sexuality and the pleasure principle have nurtured, in Scotland, a very presbyterian 'Prince of Darkness'. In 1671, George Sinclair reported in *Satan's Invisible World Discovered,* 'Anent some Prayers, Charms, and Avis, used in the Highlands'.

> As the Devil is originally the Author of *Charms and Spells,* so is he the Author of most Bawdy songs, which are sung (at the Witches Sabbat). A reverend Minister told me, that one who was the Devil's Piper, a wizard, confessed to him that at a Ball of Dancing, the Foul Spirit taught him a Bawdie song to sing and play, as it were this night, and ere two days past all the lads and lassies of the town were lilting it through the street.

But that tradition lives on in similar rumbustious folksongs, like the epic *Ball of Kirriemuir*, a vigorous, endlessly adaptable, subterranean song from the heartland of Scotland's horse country. Liberty, sexuality and whisky gan thegither! And Legman identified various links between repression and vitality in the politics of Scottish history.

> In the British Isles, Scotland and Ireland retained longest a certain freedom – at both the folk-level, and in Scotland at the level of scholarly recording – in connection with the folk songs of sexual passion ... And there operates in Scotland (as elsewhere), a most important sociological law, which, although examples of it are not difficult to observe, I do not recollect having seen in print. And that is the petrifying but protective influence of great military defeats on those nations which have nevertheless managed to survive these defeats. As the Scots are themselves the first to recognise, the whole cultural and political life of Scotland is still attuned, basically, to no later historical period than the mid or late eighteenth century, except in the neo-Marxist atmosphere of Glasgow and the industrial area, which has entirely leapt the nineteenth century, into the present, owing to the challenge of the industrial blight. Cultured Scotsmen today still brood over their defeat by England – under the flattering pretence of the 'Union' of the two kingdoms ... The whole aspect of their culture has in every case been petrified in the form and image of the moment of their defeat. Yet far from being harmed by this immobilisation of their development, it is that immobilisation that has preserved them as national and cultural entities. They have outlived, or hope to outlive, their traditional oppressors – most of whom have already disappeared from the stage of history, as the 'defeated' people have not – but they are still angry, still aggrieved, still bursting with the pride of their separateness, and who would not throw off their proud distinctiveness and brooding cultural petrification, even if they could ... For it is by clinging to their insularity, to their private cultural folklore and folk-religion, to their myths and legends, and especially to their dialect speech and songs, that all these 'defeated' peoples know well that they have best and solely protected themselves from destruction and disappearance in the past, and hope to protect themselves still. For exactly the same reason, the victor nations fight the folklore, the folk-habits and even the foods, the language and the religion of the defeated, and are impatient to see all such 'peculiarities' disappear and be assimilated under the wave of 'progress' and modernisation, however little these latter may respond to any human need, even in the victors themselves.

The Scots poet, Hamish Henderson, helped formulate Legman's ideas and theories but Legman deserves a recognition he was not given in his lifetime. Folk values can be provincial, sentimental and regressive but the best, in countries like Scotland, stand as permanent markers – against the mechanisation of life, the elevation of pretension, the subordination of minority groups. They stand against the fractured discontinuity of modern, urban, industrialised living.

> There is no horizon there. There is no continuity between actions, there are no pauses, no paths, no patterns, no past and no future. There is only the clamour of the disparate, the fragmentary present. Everywhere there are surprises and sensations, yet nowhere is there any outcome. Nothing flows through, everything disrupts. There is a kind of spacial delirium . . . this is what one sees in the average publicity shot, or a typical CNN news bulletin, or any mass-media commentary. There is a comparable incoherence, a comparable wilderness of separate excitements, a similar frenzy.

Those words, by the writer and art critic John Berger, update Legman's perceptions with contemporary force and no occupational group embodies the reality of the value of social and physical continuance better than the horsemen and smiths. Contrast the chaotic vision Berger conjures with the necessary quiet of the horseman and the rhythmic calm of the working smith. A sense of oneness is bred into them – man, animal, earth, air, fire and water are recognised as being, as it were, of one flesh. (It was with good reason that George Orwell made the carthorse his hero in *Animal Farm*.)

Horsemanship is an ancient art shaped across at least 6,000 years. Some processes have changed but the principles have remained much the same and in the novel *G*, which won the Booker Prize in 1973, Berger writes:

> To be mounted is already to be master, a knight. To represent the noble (in the ethical as well as the social sense). To vanquish. To feature, however modestly, in the annals of battle. Honour begins with a man and a horse . . . To get well away with the hounds is intrepid. To be ingenious. To be the respecter of nothing but the pace ... To hunt is the opposite of what it is to own. It is to ride over. To dart in the open. To be as men free as the straight-necked dog-fox is as fox. To meet is to ride with others, who whatever their character know something of these values and help to preserve them. All opposed to these values appear to be represented by the invention of barbed wire. (The wire that millions of infantry will die against – on the orders of their mounted generals.)

Barbed wire and senseless orders have no place in good horsemanship. We now find ourselves governed by an institutionalised majority that will imprison all those who hunt foxes with hounds! As surely as the law once secured civilised equalities, the law now institutionalises corrupt human behaviour – it is quite all right for local authority workmen to go out to gas, snare, shoot and trap foxes but to chase them with hounds, to their death or escapement, is barbarism!

A great deal of the best and worst of European civilisation, across thousands of years, is summed up in Berger's sentence, 'Honour begins with a man and a horse'. The Parthenon Frieze, The Bamburg rider, Donatello's *Gatamalata*, Marshall Haig mounted above the city of Edinburgh, the Knights of the Teutonic Order. The beautiful, the religious, the chivalrous, the dutiful, the terrifying, the powerful, the sexual, the brutal can all be portrayed through imagery of the manpowered horse. 'Cast a cold eye / On life, on death / Horseman pass by' is the epitaph on the grave of W.B. Yeats. In *G*, Berger describes his hero, a modern Don Juan, with these words:

> On his hands is the smell of horse and harness. Its components derive from leather saddle soap, sweat, hooves, horsehair, horsebreath, grass, oats, mud, blankets, saliva, dung, and the smell of various metals when moisture has condensed upon them. He brings one of his hands to his face to savour the smell. He has noticed that sometimes a trace of it lingers till evening – even when he hasn't ridden since early morning. The horse and the harness smell is the antithesis of the cowshed smell. Each can only be properly defined by reference to the other. The shed smell means milk, cloth, figures of women squatting hunched up against the cow's flank, liquid shit, mulch, warmth, pink hands and udders almost the same colour, the absolute absence of secrecy and the names of the cows: Fancy, Pretty, Lofty, Cloud, Pie, Little-eyes …
>
> The horse and harness smell is associated for him (G) with the eminent nature of his own body (like suddenly being aware of his own warmth), with pride – for he rides well and his uncle praises him, with the hair of his pony's mane and with his anticipation of a man's world.

Horsemanship, like the Bible, originated in an essentially masculine world and the Book of Proverbs, one of the oldest books in the Bible, contains a wonderful parable about horsemen, their knowledge and the demands their skills will unleash on the world.

> The horseman hath two daughters crying, Give, Give.
>
> There are three things that are never satisfied,
> Yea, four things say not, it is enough;
> The grave; and the barren womb;
> The earth that is not filled with water;
> And the fire that saith not, it is enough …
>
> There be three things that are too wonderful for me,
> Yea, four things that I know not:
> The way of an eagle in the air;
> The way of a serpent upon a rock;
> The way of a ship in the midst of the sea:
> And the way of a man with a maid.

Those very Druidic sounding verses might have been delivered out of the mouth of an Aberdeenshire horseman and they carry a stark poetic wisdom that remains current amongst horsemen in the twenty-first century. And, not surprisingly, the oral literature of the horseman cult, known as 'The Horseman's Word', remains infused with verbal richnesses that would have thrilled Shakespeare and Burns. This ambiguous phrase, 'The Horseman's Word', serves as the umbrella-title under which many horsemen organised themselves, for centuries, and through which they collated and handed down the art/science of horsemanship. Semi-secret horse societies were once wide-spread across Britain and particularly powerful in north east Scotland. They were bodies of men that acted as a primitive trade union, as a cooperative veterinary service, as a repository of traditional knowledge, and as folk clubs – long before that revivalist phrase came into being. The ceremonial liturgies published in this book are cultural and literary documents of considerable importance. They come from a variety of sources but their existence is another example of the seminal folklore contribution made by Dr Hamish Henderson of the School of Scottish Studies in the University of Edinburgh.

* * *

The German artist Paul Klee once said that in making a drawing, he liked 'to take a line for a walk'. My method in writing this book has been somewhat similar. A wide-ranging group of men have looked back on their lives and together we have brought facts, thoughts, songs and stories, in a new form, to the page. The Irish painter, Jack Yeats, once said 'you can organise an event, but if it turns out as you planned, it won't be an event!' He loved the spontaneous, the vital, the ever-enduring, and in taking readers for 'a walk' in these books, I hope, I combine events, thoughts and ideas – to recreate something of 'the event' that every life is, every visit to the stable, every day at the forge.

This final volume of my five books on Highland life moves, I hope appropriately, well beyond the geography of the Highlands. All five volumes are collaborations – between the subjects, the writer, and the reader – combining factual history, oral remembrance and opinion. Each book has a strong visual component, orchestrated so that word and image, form and content, complement each other. It is a method, I believe, that reflects the nature and culture of the people portrayed and, for that reason, I conclude with an extract from J.M. Synge's preface to *The Playboy of the Western World*. It brilliantly encapsulates the world within which Synge worked at the beginning of the twentieth century in Ireland and it has been my wish to do something similar, in Scotland, at the dawn of the twenty-first.

In writing *The Playboy of the Western World*, as in my other plays, I have used one or two words only that I have not heard among the country people of Ireland, or spoken in my own nursery before I could read the newspapers. A certain number of the phrases I employ I have heard also from herds and fishermen along the coast from Kerry to Mayo or from beggar-women and ballad-singers nearer Dublin; and I am glad to acknowledge how much I owe to the folk-imagination of these fine people. Anyone who has lived in real intimacy with the Irish peasantry will know that the wildest sayings and ideas in this play are tame indeed, compared with the fancies one may hear in any little hillside cabin in Geesala, or Carraroe, or Dingle Bay. All art is a collaboration; and there is little doubt that in the happy ages of literature, striking and beautiful phrases were as ready to the storyteller's or playwright's hand, as the rich cloaks and dresses of his time. It is probable that when the Elizabethan dramatist took his ink-horn and sat down to his work he used many phrases he had just heard, as he sat at dinner, from his mother or his children. In Ireland, those of us who know the people have the same privilege. When I was writing *The Shadow of the Glen*, some years ago, I got more aid than any learning could have given me from a chink in the floor of the old Wicklow house where I was staying, that let me hear what was being said by the servant girls in the kitchen. This matter, I think, is of importance, for in countries where the imagination of the people, and the language they use, is rich and living, it is possible for a writer to be rich and copious in his words, and at the same time to give the reality, which is the root of all poetry, in a comprehensive and natural form. In the modern literature of towns, however, richness is only found in sonnets, or prose poems, or in one or two elaborate books that are far away from the profound and common interest of life. One has, on one side, Mallarme and Huysmans producing this literature; and on the other Ibsen and Zola dealing with the reality of life in joyless and pallid works. On the stage one must have reality, and one must have joy; and that is why the intellectual modern drama has failed, and people have grown sick of the false joy of the musical comedy, that has been given them in place of the rich joy found only in what is superb and wild in reality. In a good play every speech should be as fully flavoured as a nut or an apple, and such speeches cannot be written by anyone who works among people who have shut their lips on poetry. In Ireland, for a few years more, we have a popular imagination that is fiery, and magnificent, and tender; so that those of us who wish to write start with a chance that is not given to writers in places where the springtime of the local life has been forgotten, and the harvest is a memory only, and the straw has been turned into bricks.

The Playboy of the Western World gives life to all that Synge envisaged in his preface but it is also a great work of art that expands our understanding beyond the frame the writer set himself in his preface. Synge's characters inhabit not just rural Ireland and the house next door but also a mythic world of Greek gods and Celtic heroes – and us. His play documents particular events on the Aran islands but it is also a group self-portrait of Ireland and her people across the ages. Complex layers of symbolism shelter beneath the vivid energy of his characters and they gain force by doing so: this force wells from both the conscious and subconscious being of the marvellous people presented in that play – and this quintet of books.

Timothy Neat
Wormit, Fife
24 June 2002

Overleaf:
'Autumn, ploughing time, parading the pairs', East Scotland, c.1914.
(HH, DA)

Part One

Blacksmiths and Farriers

David Wilson

A Photo Portrait of
Scotland's World Champion Blacksmith

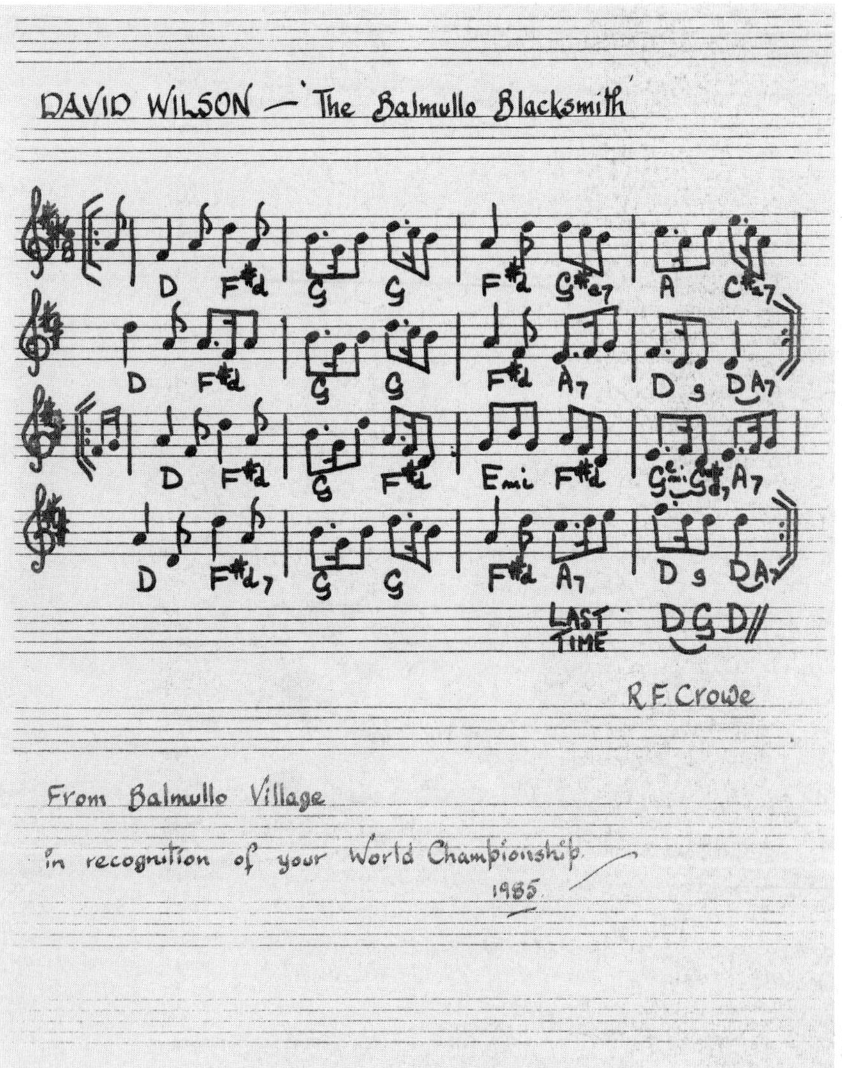

Opposite: The young David Wilson fishing with his wife Mairi in the Highlands.

Left: 'The Balmullo Blacksmith' written to celebrate David Wilson – World Champion Blacksmith, 1985, by R.F. Crowe.

Following pages: David Wilson, sixth generation farrier and blacksmith, with his grandfather, outside Kilmany Smithy, 1950. David Wilson – first car; and hard at work with his longtime partner, Jock MacKenzie of Ayton, (DW); shoeing Alan Greenhill's filly, Balmullo, 2000. (TN)

DRM 724

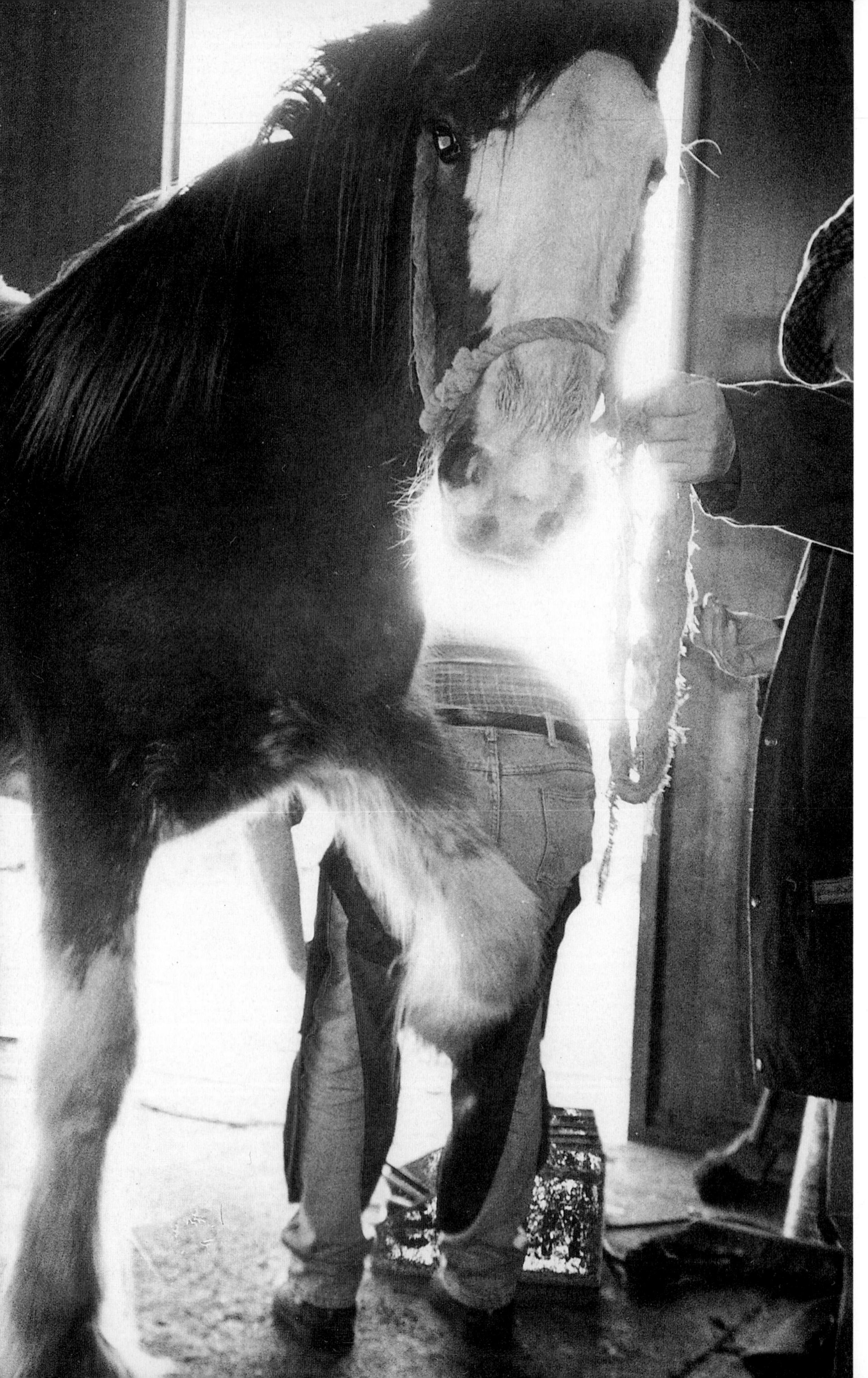

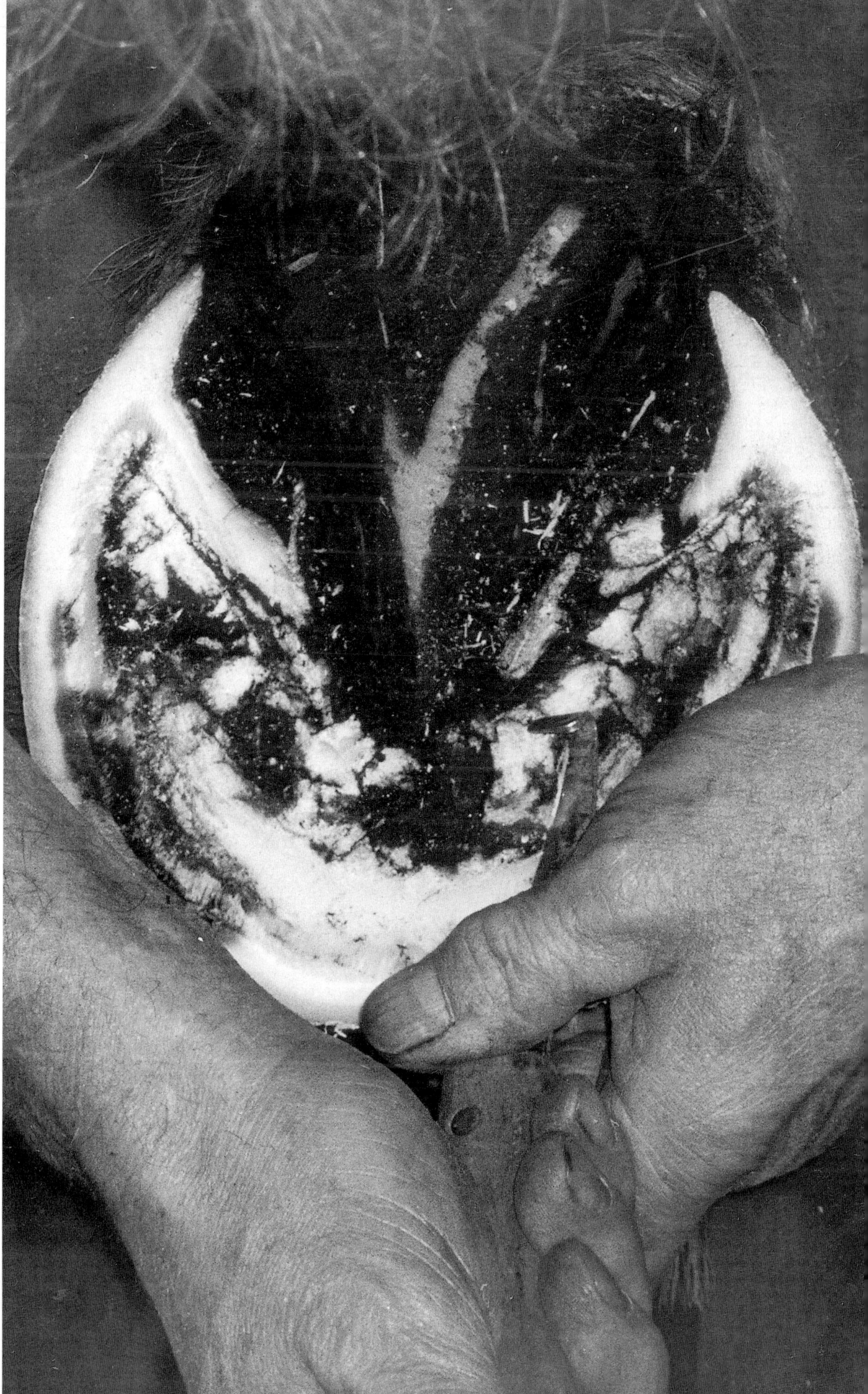

MUSTAD
1985
WORLD CHAMPIONSHIP BLACKSMITHS' COMPETITION
HORSESH
1985
WORLD CHAMPIONSHIP BLACKSMITHS' COMPETITION
EGG BAR SHOE
WORLD CHAMPIONSHIP BLACKSMITHS' COMPETITION
POT LUCK FORGING
1985

A.G. MacKenzie

Achnagarron, Ross-shire

One of the finest men I knew was Mr William Urquhart of Kildary. He was still working as a smith at the age of ninety years. I remember him as a very kind old man with a long white shaggy beard. His hearing had been affected by years at the anvil, his eyes were good but he wore glasses when I knew him. He was a man of great contentment; I've heard it said he slept with ease and had nothing to grieve about. 'What more could a man want but his work and his health?' I remember him saying that to my father, here, in the smithy at Achnagarron ... There was a piece about him in the *Ross-shire Journal* and my father kept it. When asked about his birth he said:

> Looking backwards, 10 May 1843 does seem a long time ago. It was on that date, eight days before the disruption, that I was born at Lemlair, near Dingwall. My father was a blacksmith before me. Those were the days of the large families. I had seven brothers and two sisters, and of the lot, only two are alive. One of the former lives in Vancouver, and I have a sister resides in Winnipeg. My uncle, Kenny Bain, was the first Ross-shire settler in Manitoba. He went out from Foulis, to Picton, shortly after the Battle of Waterloo but sold out on being told of the rich lands in Manitoba. He came home just once, when he was over eighty years of age and although he'd been sixty years away from Ross-shire, he was still fluent with the Gaelic. How he and my father embraced each other!
>
> Like all ambitious people I went south for work. That was in 1869, two years after my marriage. I settled in Glasgow and I did well, earning as much as thirty-eight shillings a week in the tempering department

Sandy Achnagarron (Alexander Mackenzie) of Invergordon, Easter Ross; archetypal, Highland Blacksmith, c.1903. (From a contemporary postcard. TN)

of a big firm. It was hard work but the hardest job was to hide my ignorance! So I attended night-classes and lectures. I studied arithmetic, book-keeping, natural philosophy, anatomy and many other subjects. But changed ways, changed days. Today, to my mind there is far too much enjoyment – in the way of amusement. I often wonder what my old Sunday School superintendent, William Tulloch, would say. He was another Waterloo veteran – and a very godly man.

The thing I must tell you about is the Ross-shire rifle invented by Sir Charles Ross. Six years before he was born, I was down in Buckinghamshire and I saw a very unusual type of gun. It was a good gun but flawed by a certain lever that, when struck, put the whole gun out of action. So, over the years I thought about this gun and when Sir Charles, then a youth at the Parish School, visited me in the smithy and I learned of his natural interest in firearms – I told him about my ideas and the end result was his famous Ross rifle. It was here in my smithy that the wooden, brass, and iron models were made. I taught him the rudiments of engineering, he used my anvil and my lathe and when at the finish he could not find a satisfactory magazine spring, I made him

Sandy Achnagarron with his wife Mary Cameron, their daughter Madge and her husband the smith, William Tuach, plus grandma and granddaughter, c.1905. (AG)

one. He got samples in from Germany and France but in the end it was my spring did the trick and that spring was never improved upon. I got my idea from a mole-trap but, of course, my experience of tempering had a lot to do with the success of that gun . . .

In my long life I've seen much. On the Mountgerald Estate I saw a cart with wooden wheels, solid wood wheels set on their axle and ploughs with a wooden board. And it was I that drove the first steam plough in Ross-shire. That was seventy years ago, when the Marquis of Stafford, later Duke of Sutherland, took one up to Tarbat.

That was William Urquhart. He worked with my father. The smiths have always been inventive people. Many a good engineer came out of the smithies. I like to keep and collect old implements myself, old tools, and I like to renovate and repair machinery no longer used. Even when I was a boy I was interested in the old people and the old ways. Man, they say, is a tool-making animal! He certainly was around here. When you look back, you can see how important man's control of fire was – fire, metal, horses – they were the foundations of all our technological inventions.

Tradition was very important to the smiths, that's how you learned – by doing what was handed down. There was a tradition of apprenticeship. Most of the smiths would have an apprentice. Around here the smiddy at Contin was a great place for training. It was hard work and the discipline was hard but there was always a bond between the older men and the younger men. I've got a letter sent by the father of an apprentice to my own father – when that boy died. That young apprentice died and after the body had been sent up to Caithness for the funeral this letter came. It's dated 19 February 1931 and the paper is trimmed with the black of mourning. The address is Invergordon Cottage, Strathy East, Thurso.

> Dear Sir – on behalf of my mother and relatives, I should like to say a word of thanks for what you have been to, and done for, our son and brother John. Especially would we thank you for all you have been to him during his sojourn among you, we are satisfied, Sir, that within the hospitable precincts of your works, 'Jock' had found a home from home, and, if that were needed, his letters here would bear ample testimony to the fact that he never tired of telling us how kind you all had been to him, when first he came among you, and in person he looked upon you, Sir, as an ideal and model employer.
>
> That you treated him well and were pleased with his services, is in itself a lot to be thankful for, but how then, Sir, shall we thank you for your kindness and practical sympathy, when the end came. Fate has dealt us a blow from which we shall never recover, but your genial presence for the last sad rites here, was a source of pride to us, and you

Dodie Achnagarron, blacksmith, farrier and Freemason; c.1920. (AG)

may rest assured, Sir, that each and every time we think of dear 'John' we shall think of you, his last earthly master, who was to him a guide, philosopher and friend.

Kind regards & deepest gratitude – George MacKay.

Now, that boy, John Mackay, was not killed in the smiddy, we never had a death in here, he was killed at a football match. He got a kick in the kidneys and he died. That was in 1937. I was hardly more than a baby and I don't remember him but my mother used to tell me how much that boy liked me, when I was young. And lodging here with us he would look after me and, she said, the last thing he did at Achnagarron was give me a spoonful of sugar. That was before he set off for the football match. I'm very pleased to have the Caithness letter because it tells you something about the people of the north, something about Achnagarron and something about my father. Achnagarron means 'the place of the horse', so this must be very old horse country. There is a personal brotherhood amongst the smiths and a working brotherhood. My father was on good terms with everybody. That was the natural way of it for him. All the smiths here would give each other a shove up the back to help out. Even if a man was needing something himself, he would send it across to another, the moment he was asked – knowing no fellow would ask for something unless the need was clear. There was no dog-eat-dog here, even when the tractors came in and different smiths became specialists in the different makes – Massey Ferguson, International, Fordson Major, Alice Chalmers – we still helped each other out.

Many was the time my father sent me over to Ken MacKenzie's smiddy. I can see myself now. I'd stand in the door, in the light, and he'd look up from his work at the anvil, or from shoeing a horse and he'd say, 'What you needing, boy?' I was young and that was the word he always used, 'boy'! And then, not waiting for an answer, he'd say, 'Ah, just go in and help yourself'. You see, he knew that I'd know what I was looking for – so I was the best man to look! And he had work to do. No money would ever change hands and before I left he'd always ask, 'And how's your father, A.G.?' Trust was the natural thing in those days. The smiths had a pride in themselves and their work, and so you had trust. It goes right back to the time of Solomon. 'Enough, enough, good fellow,' he said, 'Thou hast proved that I invited thee, and that thou art all men's father in art. Go, wash the smut of the forge from your face and come and sit at my right hand. The Chief of my workmen are but men – but thou art more!'

So it happened at the Feast of Solomon and so it continued here. The smiths would be there at the harvest home and they had their place in the Masonic Lodge. I'm not a mason but my father he was very keen. He did a lot of work for the Masons and they presented him with the first television set

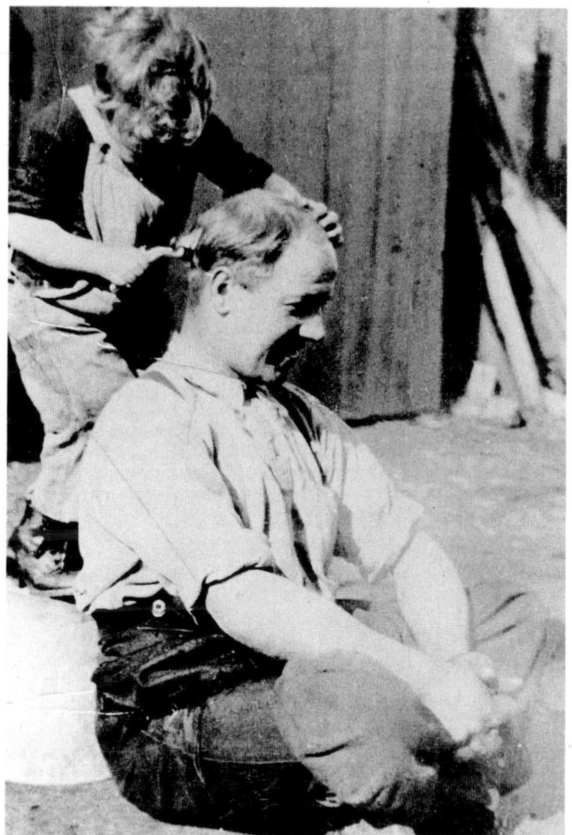

Left: A.G.Achnagarron, as a small boy, trimming the hair of one of his father's smiths, Kenneth Ross (killed in action in France, 1940). (AG)

Right: A.G. Achnagarron, in retirement, 1999. (TN)

that came in here. That was in 1954. I have a photograph of that presentation. My father's name was John MacKenzie but everyone called him Doddie, Doddie Achnagarron, that was because when he was a boy he had a bad stammer and when he tried to say Johnny it came out like Doddie and the name stayed with him till the day he died. Doddie Achnagarron. I have a paper from the Blacksmiths, Forge and Smithy Workers Society that tells you something about the pride of the smiths in the work they did. My father used to know it by heart:

> And it came to pass when Solomon, the son of David, had finished the Temple of Jerusalem that he called unto him the Chief Architects, the Head Artificers, the Cunning Workers in Silver and in Gold, and in Wood and in Ivory, and in Stone – yea all that had aided in rearing the Temple of the Lord; and he said unto them, 'Sit ye down at my table, I have prepared a feast for all my chief workers and cunning artificers, therefore stretch forth your hands; eat, drink and be merry. For is not the labourer worthy of his hire? Is not the skilful artificer worthy of honour? Muzzle not the ox that treadth out the corn.'
>
> Now, when Solomon and all the chief workers were seated, the fatness of the land and the wine and oil thereof were set upon the table,

Horsemen, smiths and horses taking a breather outside Achnagarron smithy, c.1930. (AG)

there came one who knocked loudly on the door and forced himself in, even into the festal chamber. Then, Solomon the King was wrath, and said, 'Who and what manner of man art thou?' The man answered and said, 'When men wish to honour me they call me Son of the Forge, but when they desire to mock me, they call me Black Smith: and seeing that the toil of working in the fire covers me with sweat and smut, the latter name, O King, is not inapt and in truth thy Servant desires no better.' 'But', said Solomon, 'why come you rudely and unbidden to the feast, where none save the Chief of the Workmen of the Temple are invited?' 'Please ye, my Lord, I came rudely,' replied the man, 'because Thy servants obliged me to force my way, but I came not unbidden, was it not proclaimed that the Chief Workmen of the Temple were invited to dine with the King of Israel?'

Then, he who carved the cherubim said 'This fellow is no sculptor', and he who inlaid the roof with pure gold said, 'Neither is he a worker in fine metal' and he who raised the walls said, 'he is not a cutter of stone' and he who made the roof cried out, 'he is not cunning in Cedar wood; neither knoweth he the mystery of uniting strange timber together'. Then said Solomon, 'What hast thou to say, Son of the Forge?

Why should I not order thee to be plucked by the beard, scourged with a scourge, and stoned to death with stones?'

Now, when the smith heard this he was in no sort dismayed but went up to the table and snatched up and swallowed a cup of wine, and said, 'O King, Live for Ever! The Chief men of the Workers in wood and gold and stone have said I am not one of them, and they have said truly. I am their superior. And they are all my servants.' Then he turned round and said to the Chief of the Carvers in Stone, 'Who made the tools with which you carve?' And he said, 'The Smith' and he said to the Chief of the Masons, 'Who made the chisels with which the stones of the Temple were squared?' And he said, 'The Smith' and he said to the Chief of the Workers in Wood, 'Who made the tools with which you hewed the trees on Lebanon and formed them into the pillars and the roof of the Temple?' And he answered, 'The Smith!'

My great grandfather MacKenzie lived at Drumsmettal in the Black Isle and he was the father of three sons, Alexander, Colin and Ian. He was a crofter as far as I know. Alexander was my grandfather, he was born in 1848. In 1860, when Alexander was ready to leave school, his father went across to the Contin Smithy and asked the smith if he would take the boy on as apprentice. The smith looked at my grandfather and asked him, 'Is he a big lad?' My grandfather looked around the smithy and pointed at the boy working the

A fine spread of corn ricks at Dalmore, by Achnagarron, 1930s; their form and placement is similar to that of homesteads in an Iron Age village. (AG)

A selection of nine antique horse brasses and one modern, reproduction (bottom right). (TN)

forehammer and he said, 'about as big as him'. The man he pointed out was big and very strong and the smith slapped his hand and said, 'send him over with a bole of meal and he can start next Monday'.

So, the next Sunday evening Alexander set off. Sandy rode on the family pony, his two younger brothers walking beside him. At the top of the lea rig, Alexander got down from the pony, said farewell and walked on. The two brothers turned and rode home together. That was big Sandy's start in the world. It was sixteen miles to Contin but that was no distance in those days. My grandfather served his time at Contin, then went down to Inverness to work in the new locomotive works. For some years he was there, earning sevenpence-halfpenny an hour. In 1874 the company decided to cut the rate to sixpence an hour. At the very same time Achnagarron, here at Alness, came up for let – so he took it and he struck out on his own. When he went to give in his notice, the locomotive people said, 'No! Don't go. We'll make you foreman – we'll do this, do that . . .' But the die was cast and Alexander came here and he married Mary Cameron of Alness. Once he was settled he got the name Sandy Achnagarron and that was him set for his lifetime. They had a family of three daughters and one son. Madge, who married William Tuach, he was another smith; Anna who married Donald MacKenzie and went to Canada; and Alice who died unmarried in 1922. And, of course, the boy was John my father, Doddie Achnagarron.

I never saw my grandfather but he was a big man and a strong man and a very generous man. He liked a dram. He worked very hard. And soon enough my father joined him in the smiddy. In 1916, because it was believed my grandfather could manage the smiddy on his own, my father was called up into the ranks. He stood there on parade in the square in Inverness, for the very first time, when he was called out – to be informed of his father's death – and ordered home. My grandfather had been out at Ord farm, shoeing horses. On the way home he stopped at Station Road, Invergordon, to see his daughter Madge and her husband Bill Tuach. They had a dram or two. Maybe he was upset – with his son going away to the war. Madge went out with him and saw him check the gig lights and she watched him away down the road, she watched him till the gig disappeared round Slaughterhouse corner. Big Sandy was never seen conscious again. Coming back to Achnagarron that night something happened. What it was we'll never know. Did he drop his whip and go back and an army lorry hit him? Did he fall from the trap? Whatever it was, pony and trap came home alone. His wife followed the road back and found him lying, dying by the side of the road; he was alive but unconscious and passed saving. They brought him back here to Achnagarron and a day or two later he died.

The death of my grandfather brought my father home. Doddie Achnagarron came back to the smithy and whilst still on leave from the army he started working the forge. The farmers here knew he was good and they got up a petition; they said they couldn't function without a good smith, and Doddie Achnagarron was released from the army to work in the smiddy. So, maybe, the death of the father saved the life of the son – we'll never know. But one thing is clear, although my father never saw the trenches it was a long hard war that he had here. After finishing work each day in the smiddy, serving all the farms in the area, at four o'clock he had to go out and shoe twelve army horses, five days every week, until the end of the war. That was hard work.

The amount of work a good smith got through in a lifetime, in the old days, is difficult to imagine. I've worked out that this smithy, in the thirty years after 1916, planted 6,283,200 nails in the farm horses alone, that's excluding the army horses, and any navy horses that might come in, all the riding horses, and what passing trade came in off the road. We had twenty-four farms and 170 horses to shod at Achnagarron. That's 680 shoes on the go at any one time. That makes 7,480 shoeings per year. In thirty years that makes 224,400 shoeings and that demanded well over 6,000,000 nails! Of course,

A.G.Achnagarron with one of his large collection of tractors, 1999. (TN)

that was just the farrowing, the horse work – we had plenty of fire work, mechanical work and engineering besides that. At a distance you can't see it but, at the time, you just did it.

There's a rhythm to work and the best thing is to keep at it – and when you rest, there's a rest not a stop. We never stopped. Work with the hammer has its own momentum, like a great liner – you can't stop or turn round and the best thing is to plough on. And for us a break was another job, a change of job. Down in Aberdeenshire most of the smiddies had a separate shoeing shed but up here we always shod in the smiddy – so maybe a change of job was easier for us. At Achnagarron we had two two chapping men, two men making shoes. And a good chapping man did a great deal of work – he was there in the front line and if he was working well everybody would follow on behind. Bar iron weighed in at 2.34 lbs per foot. Each Clydesdale shoe took between seventeen-and-a-half and eighteen-and-a-half inches of iron. The chapper would usually be an apprentice, he tended the fire – it was all blowing with bellows in those days. He cut the iron in lengths, he beat iron. He took the moulds for the shoes. It was his job to bend the iron and beat the shoes into a boomerang, into the horseshoe shape.

It was the journeyman, or the smith, who took the shoe out of the fire. They would be often enough the same up here. The apprentice would then stand at the forehammer and help the journeyman make the shoe and hammer the heel. By the time the smith was finishing off, the apprentice would be back at the fire – checking the other shoes weren't burning. The shoe would then be swedged with a grove to take the nails – he chapped all that and he chapped holes for the nails. Then it was back to the fire and other moulds put on for another set of shoes. Round and round it went – we always kept the pot boiling, so to speak, at Achnagarron but that was true everywhere. It kept you very fit and the smiths got hands and forearms like nobody else. Look at my grandfather's hands in the photograph – get hit by them and where would you be? The weight is there in the bone and the strength is there in the muscle, especially the muscles of the forearm. Our aprons would be old binder canvas more often than leather, and ours were always just down from the waist. I never saw a full-length apron in Achnagarron.

The first shoe made would be right hand, the second shoe would be left hand and on you go in pairs. Four pairs in a set, thirty-three sets made in a day. The two chappers would be told, and they knew this very well, make thirty-three sets of shoes and you can go home. A pair was two, a set was four, thirty-three sets was a day – one hundred and thirty-two shoes.

It was very rare for a smith to do other than fire work, fire welding, sharpening pegs, making hinges for gates, rings, sharpening hammer teeth, laying socks, drilling socks for the plough, laying culters, sharpening culters – that's the knife that precedes the plough and it did what the disc does today on the

Handmade ploughs outside Newmill smithy, Angus, c.1925. (CS)

big power ploughs. The journeymen here were never off the fire, except in the spring of the year when they might take a rest from the fire and go into the sun and dig the garden. That was a break; we'd work hours at the forge then dig the garden and get some seeds planted before a new horse came in or an order came out from my father. Kenny Cameron was journeyman here – and the gardening he did was done for his sister, she being a widow like. But most of the year we worked all the time.

The names of the farms here were Rosskein, they had six horses, Kincraig four horses, Tomich five, Invergordon Muirs four, Inverbreakie five, Ord five, Balintraid five, Broomhill five, Inchfair three, Kindease four, Newmore six, Rosebank three, Culcairn four, Nonikiln four, Millcraig four, Milnafua two, Newfield one, Dalmore seven, Northfield one, Ruskmere one, Collemere, Heathfield two, Mossfield one, and ourselves here at Achnagarron, we had two horses.

And that reminds me, after the death of Sandy Achnagarron, falling from his gig in the road, we heard a story of the second sight. On the night of his death an old lady was lying bedridden, up at Coilemeal. Neighbours had to go in to turn her once in a while and two women were up there that night; whether they put on fresh clothes or removed soiled clothes from her, I don't know – but, that night that bedridden woman, suddenly foretold 'Mrs

MacKenzie, Achnagarron, will be a very sorry woman this night'! Now there were two old ladies up at Coilemeal at that time, one was a granny Reid and one was a granny Graham – but who was who, who was dying and who heard the prophesy, I don't now remember, but those words were spoken long before any news of my grandfather's accident was out – and it's always said, here, to have been an instance of the second sight.

My great grandfather Cameron was a shoemaker in Alness. He had the power to stop bleeding but that's a very different power. My father told me of a time when he was a boy – one of the men in the smithy was badly cut. The bleeding wouldn't stop. Whilst one of the men fought to staunch the flow of blood another checked the time, he asked the man to repeat his full name and say whether he was baptised or no – and then they sent my father on his bike to the shoemaker, my great grandfather, with all the facts set out in his head. My father told Cameron about the bleeding, he told him the name of the man, that he was baptised, and the time on the clock in the smithy at the moment the accident happened. Cameron looked at his own clock and said, 'The bleeding has stopped – note the time!' And when my father got back to the smithy, he was told that the bleeding had stopped. And when my father asked at what time the bleeding stopped it proved to be at exactly the time at which the old shoemaker had spoken. His son was Kennie Cameron, the journeyman who dug the garden. As a young man he went out to work on the Panama canal. No wonder he liked digging in the sunshine.

There was another family with healing powers lived up in the Kinehive area. That family had had these powers from way back but in the end the family came down to two brothers and a sister. And it was the sister who had the healing powers. Now, the thing was she could only pass them on to a man, but not to a brother. It was the same with a man, he could only pass the power on to a woman but not a sister. So, when she grew older she wished to hand the gift on and the person she chose was the Revd Samuel MacIver, the Free Church minister at Kilmuir. Unfortunately, it seems he was too frightened to accept the gift, thinking that people would think he was involved with witchcraft. So that gift died with the last woman who had it. Having made her choice and been refused, she could not pass the gift to another. So that was it.

The old ways stuck here a good long time. The best place for dances was in the granary at Newmore, Mrs Robertson. The granary up there was built so it could both serve as a store and as a place for the Harvest Home and dances. The ceiling was low but designed to ensure that a man of six foot six could stand erect and dance in every corner of the room. And the floor was beautifully smooth. Workmen were not allowed to go into the granary without removing their boots, nor climb the stairs unless they were barefoot or shod in some kind of slipper or sandshoe. The shovels to sift and turn the grain were made entirely of wood and moved over the floor like curling stones! The floor, the stairs and the granary were all kept perfect and spotless – that was good for the grain and great for dancing.

The custom was to hold a Harvest Home each year in the Newmore granary. All the farm workers and their families were invited; also the blacksmith, the joiner, the mason, the plumber and everybody who contributed to the life of the farm. Mrs Robertson's two daughters were married in the granary. Unfortunately, those Harvest Homes finished during the Second World War. After that it was just Hogmanay parties, or New Year's parties, depending on the day of the week and the fall of the Sunday. Great parties they were – people would be walking from Invergordon and Alness. There were no taxis, and no drunks, no unpleasantness, no fights. Sometimes somebody might come with a half-bottle but people would walk it off climbing up to, or walking down from, Newmore. Great nights we had up there and that went on till 1951, the year the Highland Show at Aberdeen was washed out by floods. That year the granary got burned to the ground – along with the Newmore barn and the small stable. When a new granary was built, it was designed to hold grain solid all year – and the dances and Harvest Homes lost out to economy.

Every parish had its own ways and a pride in their own. My father told me once of an Aberdeenshire man who came up here to the Lord Lovat estate at Beauly. To work. Well, he was a real Aberdeenshire man and he was forever letting it be known – that the men down there could do everything and nobody could better an Aberdeenshire man and he happened to be one himself! This went on month after month and it didn't slow up, so it began to irritate the Lovat men and especially it irritated the foreman there, Willie Smith. He didn't batter the man but one day without warning he gave in his notice. It was November time, the time of the carting of turnips, and he went down to Aberdeenshire – where he was unknown to man and beast, and very great men they were! Well, Willie took a job as a ploughman and coming in fresh he was well down the line at the horses. First he worked at the turnips and anybody could do that. Then he was asked if he could plough. Of course the gaffer said yes – but it was a terrible mess he made of it! Deliberately, and as soon as the high horseman saw the mess he was making – he sent Willie back to the turnips.

Time passed and Willie got talking with the smith and he saw that he was developing a very nice plough and Willie made a deal with the man – that he would have the plough for the next ploughing match – and nobody else was to know. Together the men worked on the sock and the culter and it was a fine job that they made. Then Willie went to the farmer and asked for a good pair of horses to take to the ploughing match and when the horsemen heard the Beauly man was in for the ploughing match they had more than a laugh at his expense. Well, the day came and Willie dressed up his horses and harnessed them to the brand new plough and set off – making a beautiful line.

A Speyside smithy, 1930s. (LM)

The men stopped laughing when they saw how he handled the team and how he turned to come back. And when he stopped at their end he took off his belt and hung it there between the bridles of the two horses and on that belt Willie had fixed all his ploughing medals, medals from the Highland Society and medals from meets all over the north. Then he got on with the job. It was a beautiful job that he made and he won the first prize and the best of the cups. And that same day Willie gave in his notice and came back home to the north. He put the Aberdeenshire loons in their place and the first thing he did back in Beauly was to go up to that Aberdeenshire ploughman, and he showed him the cup and the new medal on his belt and he said, 'Never tell me again of the better work of the Aberdeenshire men, or I'll skin your arse with a horse-whip!'

Some things you see, some things you hear and some things you remember for ever. At school, the teacher I best remember was Mr MacDonald, Gaelic Mac, the headmaster. He taught class 6 and 6A, those were the classes for pupils who had not passed 'the qualifying exam' and had no intention of going on to Invergordon Academy. In those days you wrote on slates and in your school bag you carried a small tin with a damp cloth for cleaning the slate. On and off through the year we'd take the slate home for a wash, and we'd scrub the frame white as a willow wand. We were proud of our slates and half terrified of Gaelic Mac. He was a fiend with the tawse.

Tests and examinations were held in the headmaster's room. One day we were in there for dictation. Gaelic Mac was a tall man, very tall and very heavy and his breathing was the loudest I heard. After the dictation he got us to stand back to back in two lines whilst he checked for spelling mistakes and grammatical errors. He didn't like what he saw. I was nearest the door and he told me I had a whole raft of mistakes! I knew what was coming and I thought about making a run for it. Then he announced everyone had mistakes and I thought thank God for that! And I stayed. Suddenly he stamped his foot and went to Miss Ramsay's room to get her strap. We knew what was coming. There was nothing we could do but wait. I was first. Four blows I got, two on each hand. Because of his height and his weight, the blows came with such force I nearly couped over. Then he moved down the lines, strapping the whole class, boys and girls. By the time Gaelic Mac had finished almost every kid there was crying and rubbing their hands and Gaelic Mac himself was half dead! The foam was coming out of his mouth.

After that it was playtime and out we all trooped to the tree in the corner of the playground. We used to talk about taking revenge on the tyrant but in the end there was no need – Gaelic Mac had a massive heart-attack, just a few weeks later. He had to retire and after that Mr John Ray from Invergordon took over. Although we hated Gaelic Mac, he wasn't all bad. On 28 August, the Duke of Kent was killed when a flying boat from Alness crashed into a mountainside in Caithness. I remember the news of that and I remember the funerals. The RAF mortuary was at Teaninich, that was a farm owned by Bob Falconer. The day of the funeral was a good weather day and the school windows were slightly open. About 1.30 p.m. we heard the pipes, far away. For a long time the music never seemed to get any nearer. The pipe band and the RAF men were coming in slow time. This proved fortunate because the class interval came before they did and we all went outside to see them come by. Suddenly the pipe major appeared at the corner of the hedge, mace reversed. All of us stood completely still and silent. Nobody told us to do that. The pipe band slow-marched with drums covered in black. The RAF guard marched slow with their rifles reversed. Two tractor units followed, pulling artic. trailers (they were usually used for carrying the Sunderland flying boats). One trailer had seven coffins aboard and one had six. Each coffin was draped in the Union Jack. The cortege was long, but not one child moved until the last car and last person had disappeared over the bridge at Dalmore. All that happened just before Gaelic Mac had his attack and I remember him coming round to every class to congratulate the pupils on their excellent behaviour.

When I was young, before my father died, they called me 'young Achnagarron'; after that I became A.G. Achnagarron, Alexander George. Small things you remember – on a Sunday afternoon, when he'd finished his meal, my father would wander up to the old crossroads by the church, to have a smoke, leisurely fashion, and chat with passers-by. One day, A.B. Davidson, grandfather of the present A.B. Davidson, whom we call Ack, came along in his car and together they went for a run up to the Marl – so called because of the rushes and water which stood there and still do. A.B. wanted father to take a look at two colts that belonged to his son, John Davidson of Inverbreakie; one was a big horse and one was small. He was about to send them to the horse sale in Dingwall and their feet needed dressing. My father said, 'the little horse is the better horse'. A.B. exploded, 'Nonsense!' he said. Well, in time the two horses came into the smithy for dressing. My father eyed them up a second time and he was still unhappy about the big horse so after he'd dressed the feet he asked that horse be run up and down the road. And he got the Inverbreakie man to turn it this way and that. He didn't say a word. He'd said what he said and he wouldn't say more – but it clear he was unhappy with that horse. Well, off to Dingwall that horse went and it made ninety guineas! That was ninety-four pounds ten shillings, and that was a lot of money for a horse in those days.

That was a Wednesday. When my father heard news of the price he said, 'John Davidson doesn't know how lucky is!' On the Saturday, my father was stood at the half-door of the smiddy looking out, just before dinner, when up the road came John Davidson. He asked my father what he'd thought was wrong with the big horse. My father said, 'I said the small horse was the better horse, I didn't say anything was wrong with the big horse.' John Davidson then repeated his question and my father repeated his answer. He knew something was up. John then produced a letter, a letter from the man in Perth who'd bought the horse. Four vets had examined it and found it unsound and that horse was at that moment on a train coming back up the line to Inverbreakie. The horse was a 'shiverer'. The cold of the journey down into Perthshire had brought on the symptoms – but my father had sensed things wrong with that horse, as soon as he saw it. A good blacksmith would often know more about the health of a horse than the horsemen themselves. For farm men the horse was a friend and a tool but for the blacksmith the horse was more like a patient. Like a good doctor, the good farrower was always on the lookout for a sign or signal.

A similar thing happened with Major Ian Forsyth, Balintraid. He had a filly everybody thought was going to sweep the board at the Tain Easter Show. The day the filly was brought in for dressing, the smiddy was busy with the Newmore horses – so father put her in the big shed to wait. When the Newmore horses were shod, my father thought he'd have a smoke and a good look at 'the show winner' from Balintraid. He didn't like what he saw and he asked Francie MacKay, who'd brought the filly in, to move her back by the rein – and all her faults showed up to perfection. She was another 'shiverer'. Father said he wouldn't touch the horse until the Major had seen her. Francie sent a boy by bike, there were no telephones on the farms in those days, and up he came by car. Forsyth was furious and, by that time, the filly had calmed down and seemed all right. The Major went for my father, thinking he was just showing off his knowledge or maybe trying to get him to withdraw his 'winner' from the show. He was walking round in circles in rage. My father leaned back and lit up his pipe. And then he suggested the Major take out his pipe – and that they should both have another look at the filly, in ten minutes. Well, when Francie reined backed that filly a second time the fault was there for the whole world to see. That filly was never shod. The Major asked the boy to take her home by the back road and soon enough she was sold on to the Tinkers. What they did with her nobody knows.

The blacksmith didn't always get the thanks he was due and the farmers could sometimes be hard men to deal with. Before the war the smiths made most of the machinery on the farms as well as doing all the shoeing. There wasn't the big importation of machines you get today. In those days we got steam-engines, thrashing mills, reapers and mowers from the south but everything else we made ourselves – ploughs, harrows, horse sub-soilers, turnip-sowers, all that kind of thing as well as tools and implements. The farmers didn't like to pay more than they had to – and we weren't always the men to charge what we should. I remember Malcolm Fraser, the last farmer at Culcairn, coming in asking the price of a turnip-sower. 'Nine pounds,' my father said. 'Too dear!' said Fraser, 'I'll get one up at the displenishing sale, when Cruikshank goes out of Rosebank.' Well, the sale came and the turnip-sower, one year old, went to James Falconer of Teaninich for thirteen pounds! He was going into Pitglassie farm and needed a sower straight away. Of course, it wasn't long before Fraser was back at the smiddy saying he'd take the sower for the nine pounds, 'for the asking price', he said. 'Sorry,' said my father, 'the price of sowers is up! Thirteen pounds for a new one like this and seventeen pound for a third hand, like they've got at Pitglassie.' And he sold the sower for thirteen pounds.

One occasion when he did make some money was when the big foundry in Falkirk went on fire and all their patterns were burned. They paid my father a hundred pounds to send down all the rollers, boxes etc. that he had in store – so they could make new patterns.

We were lucky with injuries at Achnagarron. We had no men killed by a horse, we had no amputations. My father lost a quarter of an inch off the end of his thumb. That was the day my mother went away to Edinburgh for a break and a holiday. She left by train at nine o'clock. At eleven o'clock my father was sharpening a chisel on the buff, that's the carborundum stone, when one of the bushes on the countersunk shaft above his head began to squeak. Father looked up, the chisel slipped on the stone and his thumb went between the chisel and the stone – and the top of his thumb was away! Luckily, no bone was taken. Although there was a lot of blood and it took a long time to get Dr Mackenzie up here, he dressed and stitched the wound and it healed well.

Luck was also on my side the time my hand went into an electric sewing drill. Three bones and two joints on one finger were stripped before my father heard my bawling! He came running and he wrenched the bayonet-fitting apart – just in time to stop the real damage starting. Iodine was the cleanser. My arm was in a sling for three weeks. The worst thing was, three months later, I was working on a binder when I hit my injured finger with a hammer. That caused the greatest pain I've ever felt. My finger swelled up like a balloon. I went to Dr Robertson. He said, 'O, boy, those bones were dry! It's dry and brittle bones most feel the pain! But there's nothing I can do. All I can offer is painkillers. Only time can heal a double wound like that.' Well I took two of the painkillers straight away and another two four hours later – but that was all and here I am.

There are things you just have to put up with. The fighter-bombers come in very low over the Cromarty Firth. I was saying, the other day, to a farmworker who came in – it's a good job all the horses are dead. Low flying like that would frighten work horses, here in the smiddy and out in the fields. The Clydesdale is a placid beast but they can rear, they bolt, they can shy and the weight in their foot makes their kick something special. The worst thing like that concerned some toffs, shooting. A man was clearing a sheaf, stuck in his binder, when a shot went off just over the hedge – the horse bolted and the cutter took off the man's foot. Clegs can bolt a horse, wasps, hornets, or a swarm of bees; cutting corn, it was always up to the horseman to see a binder was out of gear before going in to sort out any problem.

My son used to go over to New England for the cranberry season – but he's back now. He's taken over. He knows the business, horses, smithing, machinery but it's a different business now. He's more like a salesman and I'm more like a retired machine restorer – antique machines, the yard's full of them. Metal gets in your blood, just like horses. I still work every day. Any day you come, you'll see me under some machine's that taken my fancy. Achnagarron, the place of the horses, is now a place of arc-welding torches but it's still no more than a blacksmith's shop and I'll be a farrier till the end of my days.

Under a spreading chestnut tree
    The village smithy stands;
The smith, a mighty man is he,
    With large and sinewy hands;
And the muscles of his brawny arms
    Are strong as iron bands.

His hair is crisp, and black, and long,
    His face is like the tan;
His brow is wet with honest sweat,
    He earns whate'er he can,

And looks the whole world in the face,
    For he owes not any man.

Week in, week out, from morn till night,
    You can hear his bellows blow;
You can hear him swing his heavy sledge,
    With measured beat and slow,
Like a sexton ringing the village bell,
    When the evening sun is low.

And children coming home from school
    Look in at the open door;
They love to see the flaming forge,
    And hear the bellows roar,
And catch the burning sparks that fly
    Like chaff from a threshing floor.

He goes on Sunday to the church
    And sits among his boys;
He hears the parson pray and preach,
    He hears his daughter's voice,
Singing in the village choir,
    And it makes his heart rejoice.

It sounds to him like her mother's voice,
    Singing in Paradise!
He needs must think of her once more,
    How in the grave she lies;
And with his hard, rough hand he wipes
    A tear out of his eyes.

Toiling, – rejoicing, – sorrowing,
    Onward through life he goes;
Each morning sees some task begin,
    Each evening sees it close;
Something attempted, something done,
    Has earned a night's repose.

Thanks, thanks to thee, my worthy friend,
    For the lesson thou has taught!
Thus at the flaming forge of life
    Our fortunes must be wrought;
Thus on its sounding anvil shaped
    Each burning deed and thought.

That's from New England: Henry Wadsworth Longfellow. That's very much as it was here when I was young.

Sandy Moncrieff

MOST NOBLE GRAND – NEWBURGH

While glittering planets gold the night
While toys the earth with time.
While sun and moon and stars are bright
Odd fellowship shall shine.

Those are the words on the Newburgh Oddfellows' banner. There will be more than 600 Oddfellows in this town. Newburgh is a place of very ancient settlement and it's always been a frontier town. We stand on the south bank of the Tay, looking north to the Highlands – four miles east of the confluence of the Earn and I would say, the geographical division created by the Clyde/Earn/Tay has been, historically, more important than the Forth/Clyde line or the Antonine Wall. At Abernethy we've got one of only two Pictish round towers standing in Scotland. William the Conqueror made his pact with the leaders of the North at Abernethy – and the ridge above us here is studded with Iron Age forts and Bronze Age tombs. Across the Tay those green hills, above Inchture, were the main seat of Caledonian power before the kings moved down to Scone – were the Tay bends round on the other side of Perth. The river's still tidal here but not at Scone; it's here that the Firth suddenly narrows; this was always an important place – for salmon, for boats coming in, for ferryboats crossing, and for the defence of both sides. We've got Megdrum island moored, permanently, in mid-stream. We lose the sun in the winter months but everything else has to come in through here – year round. We're still a port and we're a Royal Burgh – in fact there's nothing new about Newburgh at all.

The Newburgh Caledonian Oddfellows Lodge is dedicated to

Opposite: Sandy Moncrieff, Most Noble Grand Master of the Newburgh Oddfellows Lodge, climbing the stair of the Newburgh Tolbooth to check the clock that rings out the New Year, 1999. (TN)

Left: Sandy Moncrieff as a young blacksmith outside his flat in Newburgh, Fife, c.1955. (SM)

Right: Sandy Moncrieff, Most Noble Grand, with the Newburgh Oddfellows' Scroll, 1999. (TN)

upholding tradition and looking after the rights and well-being of the people. I've been a member for over fifty years. It was officially founded in 1827 but the origins of the Order and the ceremonies here go back long before that. The main thing is the walk on Old Year's night. First comes the Outside Guard with drawn sword. Last comes the Most Noble Grand. On horseback, behind the Outside Guard comes the latest recruit into the Brotherhood – riding backwards, bareback on a piebald garron. Some people think a garron's a breed of horse, but it's just the Gaelic word for a gelding – a castrated horse or pony of any kind. He'll be a youngster. He wears one mask on his face and another on the back of his head; so, as he rides he looks both ways – like the god, Janus. No reins for the new initiate, he has to grip the garron with his knees and steady himself with his hands on the haunches. In the mask he's disorientated, if that horse was to take off – he'd have to grab the tail or fall off pretty soon. But of course that won't happen – we always have someone at the head of the horse and we choose a steady, good-tempered creature. He's the chosen man, the last man of the year and he rides for everyman inducted through the year. It's a process whereby we can take the muck out of them – clean out the stables. We like the new man to make a fresh start. It used to be a donkey that carried the new man, now we have the garron, a light working horse – the kind that carried Robert the Bruce out to meet Bohune at Bannockburn.

We gather in the Old Tolbooth. After the initiate has been brought out and set on his horse the rest of the Oddfellows come out – some in their robes and the rest in fancy dress costumes. Mostly monsters, ghosts and freaks to celebrate the change of the year. We like the first, second and third prizewinners to lead the way – but with all the chasing into the crowd the whole gang often enough gets mixed. We have a competition for the best, and most original, costume. I'm the judge and last year the winner was a hobby horse with a table of cards. Very good indeed. The band leads us away – the monsters breaking out to rampage into the crowd, chasing the kids, herding them here and there, terrifying them in a friendly kind of way. Some will be frightened but many will stand and outface them; I like to see kids shout back and join in the chase. It's all high spirits and good nature.

After the fellows in fancy dress comes the silver band playing 'Hearts of Oak', stopping here and there to salute the good people of Newburgh. They play 'For He's a Jolly Good Fellow'; 'Rule Britannia'; and 'The Bonnie Woods o' Craigie Lea'. After the band come the office-bearers dressed overall – as priests and knights, and as kings and bishops carrying swords, pikes, emblems, banners and the Oddfellows' cisk. Then, first out last in, comes the Most Noble Grand. Three times for three years I was Most Noble Grand. It's all democratic, you get proposed and seconded, then elected by popular vote. As the senior Oddfellow I'm last out first in. At the end of the walk I go through the ranks and the procession follows on behind, back into the Old Tolbooth which is our meeting place and quarters. We leave at seven o'clock and we're back in before eight. That's long enough on a cold winter's night. We march to the bottom of the High Street, up the top and back again to the Tolbooth. Then at midnight we ring the New Year in.

What's it about? It all goes back to religion. It commemorates, today, the rights and wrongs of the past – and it sees out the Old Year. I would

The Ancient Chest of the Newburgh Oddfellows, the back of old Tolbooth, 1999. (TN)

Sandy Moncrieff presiding at the high dais, in the meeting room of the Newburgh Oddfellows Lodge, 1999. (TN)

say it goes back to Druid times, it certainly goes back to the days of Lindores Abbey – to the time of the monks and the Age of Chivalry, it goes back to the Protestant reformation, it goes back to first holding of the Newburgh Highland Games – which go back to the Battle of Black Earnside, a long running battle in which the Newburgh men joined William Wallace to defeat an English army led by the Earl of Pembroke, in 1298. Pembroke had marched west from Ferryport-on-Craig, that's Tayport today, in an attempt to regain Scotland for Edward Longshanks after Wallace's victory at Stirling Bridge. Black Earnside was a four-day battle and many of the Newburgh men fell, as did their leader, Balfour of Denmiln. Many a Newburgh man lies in the earth of Black Earnside but they won an important victory and it cleared the way for Bannockburn sixteen years later. I've no doubt that the Oddfellows go back a long way – but our charter and the Order of Oddfellows – here in Newburgh – only go back to 1827. When you're singing 'Hearts of Oak' on the walk you know you're singing a tribute to Lord Nelson and the men who went out from here to fight in the Napoleonic Wars. In our rituals sea-ropes, chains and swords play their part. And there's still a strong tradition of Newburgh men going away to sea. We built boats here for hundreds of years, we had plenty of blacksmiths here when I was young. I was a blacksmith myself.

As far as we know, the Order of the Newburgh Oddfellows was founded out of the Dundee Oddfellows – but we soon became independent and, today, we're the only Oddfellows left in Scotland. We're affiliated to nobody, we just look after ourselves and the Burgh, but that's no bad thing –

and we keep the old traditions going. You see as the nineteenth century went on the Oddfellows became a Friendly Society, a Benefit Society. There was no National Health in those days, there was no Social Security, no pensions – except from the army or navy, so Benefit Societies were set up, across the land, to help their members should they fall ill, or get injured, or die. Every Oddfellow paid something in every week, a penny very likely, and the money would go back to the members, according to need.

They've still got Oddfellows down in England. The Manchester Oddfellows is a very big organisation. They've got 300,000 members worldwide. We've thought about affiliating ourselves with them but we haven't. That would bring us benefits and insurance cover but these days our people here have got the National Health Service and most can now afford their own insurance. So, we don't think we'd gain much by joining up with the Manchester Oddfellows. We're just a very ancient kind of social club and we may as well keep our independence.

What happened to the other Oddfellow Lodges in Scotland others might tell you. We know there were Oddfellows in Arbroath because the father of Mrs Taylor, the electrician's wife, shook the hand of an Oddfellow up in Arbroath, in the fifties. That proved the point. And Mrs Robertson, who now lives in Newburgh, though she comes from Dundee, has told us that the Dundee Lodge took in women members. Because of that she suggested we take women Oddfellows in here. She didn't tell us that the Dundee Lodge had gone the way of all flesh! But, we knew, the Dundee Lodge no longer existed – and we thought that women might very well have been one of the reasons for its demise! So, we said, 'No, no, no! We can't have that! No, no, no! No women in the

Sandy Moncrieff in the Newburgh Oddfellows Lodge, 1999. (TN)

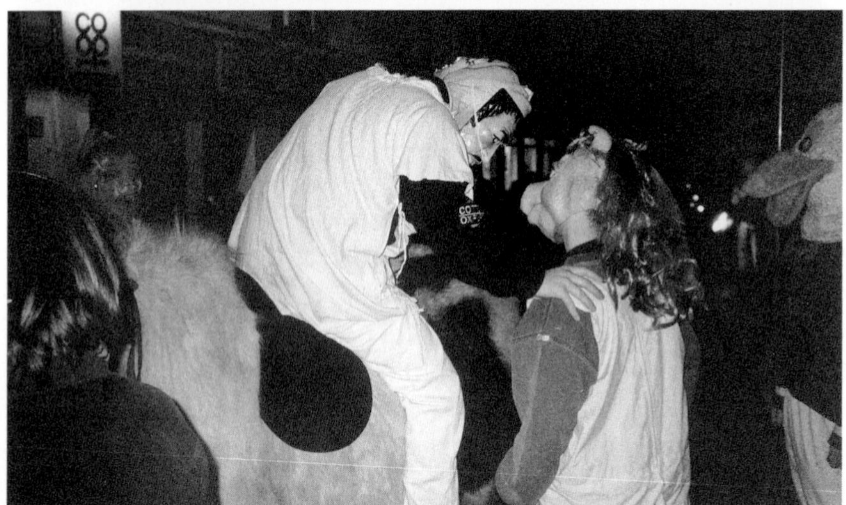

The Old Year Night's Oddfellows Parade, Newburgh, 1999. (TN)

Newburgh Lodge.' Very nicely we said it but we said it loud and clear. That was the democratic opinion here. That decision left me with the heavy end of the stick – but people know I've always stood up for the burgh and everybody in it, regardless. I'm not against the women but – I am for the Lodge – as it was and as it is. Well, following our refusal of the request for female Oddfellows, a lame wave of protest went the rounds. The *Daily Record* phoned me up asking about the problem. Now, I might have gone for the publicity, stirred things up and got a lot more people in here for the walk but I just said this, 'We have no problem! It's a storm in a teacup!' And the issue died away. Fortunately. Why should we kill tradition in the name of equality? Why should we finish things off to be fair? Everything's equal in death and the grave, little's equal in life and love. I'm not keen to attempt to mix the colours of the rainbow. Grey's a habit best left to the Germans.

It's not much that we Oddfellows do but it's something and it's very old! We have a wee bit fun at Hogmanay and that's about it. We light our torches and carry the flame – one hour on Old Year's night. The year may die but why should we. We are what we are. We have more than half of the men of Newburgh still with us and we keep up the spirit of the town. Out we go, come rain or snow, and we're well satisfied – even if two thirds of our members are watching and standing out in the street. I'd like everyone of them to join in the march – but we don't insist they do. As long as a good group carries on the tradition, I'm happy. Our costumes are proof of how old our traditions are – cardinal's hats, the patriarch's mitre, banners from crusading times. The Glengarry bonnet, worn by the Outside Guard, is another historic object and very valuable. We have our cisks, our robes, ancient signs and ancient symbols. I try to get them lodged in here, in the head – in the heads of the youngsters. I want them to know the meaning of symbols and remember them and carry them on. They have meanings which shouldn't be forgotten.

When I'm judging the costumes for the fancy dress – I'm looking for topical costumes but with the ancient signs implanted here and there. We're separate from the Masons but some of our signs stand in common and on our walk, the Masons come out to give refreshments and greet the Oddfellows. Some of the Oddfellows are Masons but most are not and we have no direct connections. I'm not a Mason myself. Our symbols include – the crossed keys, the hand on the heart, the sun, the stars and the moon, the hourglass, the all-seeing eye, the upside-down cross, the bell, and the sealed lips. Our office bearers consist of the Most Noble Grand and a Brother Secretary who sits beside him on the bench. Then we have a Vice Grand and a Right-hand Supporter who swears in the initiates. By the bench stands the Inside Guard. The Outside Guard stands outside the hall, on the stairwell with drawn sword. Each initiate is brought in from the ante-chamber by one of the brothers. They may come as three, or singly, in twos or fours, it just depends. The brothers

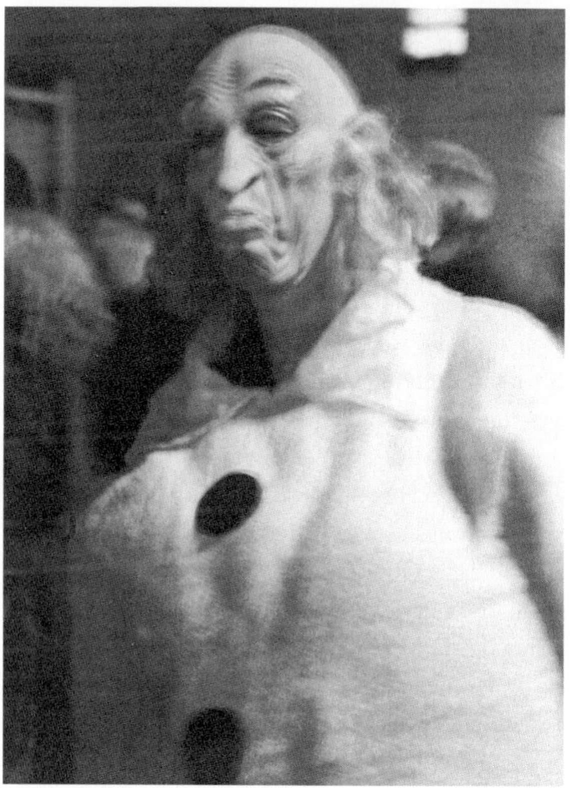

will be seated round the walls on bench seats. And the hall can sometimes get packed full. There's a lot of meaning in what we do – but there's no religion in Oddfellowship today. No religious dispute or bigotry is allowed in the Newburgh Oddfellows – no way.

The Oddfellows used to organise a Burns Night Supper. That's one tradition that has died out in recent years but when we meet we still like to have poem or a song. One of the brothers, Alex MacDiarmid, made up a poem about the walk. I remember some of it:

Once a year, on old year's nicht
The Oddfellows are a richt braw sicht –
It really is a nicht tae remember
That last long nicht o' each December.
There's wan sitting the wrang way roun on a horse!
An then to mak matters fully worse
A parade sets oot ahent a banner
And mony will say it's a funny manner
Tae gae gallivanting roun the toun –
In fancy-dress or coloured gown.
The first fower hae placards round their neck!
What does it mean? But what the heck!
They'll be prizewinners, I'll be bound,
An' mak themsels a fair few pound.
Then come the rest all lookin' grand
Dancin' aboot in front o' the band.
It's no ofen we hae dancers in oor street
Gien a' the locals an visitors a treat!
The torches fairly blaze up in the dark
But watch it lads, they dinnae spark! ...

Once an Oddfellow always an Oddfellow and the Newburgh men have carried our fellowship all over the world. I was on the bus in Australia one day, I'd gone out to visit my brother, and the driver leaned across to my brother and he asked him whether I was a member of any Lodge in Scotland. When my brother told him I was Most Noble Grand of the Newburgh Oddfellows that driver was very happy. He really was happy. It's a worldwide brotherhood. The principles are simple but none the worse for that. I won't disclose what the ritual is but it locks Oddfellowship inside the skull, inside the head, and that helps one all one's days to know what true, true fellowship is all about – human brotherhood.

Here's another poem I like, about Lindores Abbey, and it gives you a clue as to what we're all about. It was written by one J. Stirling in 1838 and it's called 'Lindores Abbey'.

Newburgh High Street, Old Year's Night, 1999. (TN)

They were kind tae ilk bodie that cam tae Lindores –
Tae the puir an' the blind and the lame at Lindores,
Wi' handfu's o' meal an' platefu's o' kail,
An' the stranger was sure o' a hame at Lindores.

That's it. Fife was a big place for abbeys. Lindores had a big abbey, it's just about three miles from here and we have Newburgh Abbey, and Newburgh was originally the new burgh of Lindores. There was another abbey up at Balmerino, there was St Andrew's Cathedral, there was Arbroath Abbey, Dunkeld . . . Most of the supplies and visitors to Lindores Abbey would have come in here, by boat, to Newburgh and many a train of pack horses would have wended their way from here up to Lindores. The two old inns are the Abbey Inn and the Ship Inn. Newburgh is a 'lang toon' with the high street running parallel with the shore for more than a mile – that suits the procession very well.

Although Oddfellows were officially founded in 1827, I have no doubt our procession goes back long before – to before the Reformation and it carries the weight of the two Christian traditions as well as the older pagan traditions. I joined the Oddfellows in 1946, that's fifty-five years ago. I should have joined in 1945 but the then Most Noble Grand was still away in the navy and he didn't get demobbed until 1946. It's been like a family to me ever since. I've never got married, 'naebodie wad tak me'! I live a quiet life away on my own but I've always enjoyed helping out and keeping the community going. Newburgh went through hard times in the twenties and thirties; then there was the war, then in the fifties the linoleum factories started closing, now the salmon netting's gone right down to nothing. So, for many people in Newburgh life's been one long struggle. I hope I've done my bit to help things on. I know the Oddfellows have helped the folk here.

I was born on 21 December 1925. The longest night of the year. My father was Moncrieff, a joiner to trade, my mother was Janet Sinclair. The thing I remember about school was – running away! I didn't like school. I was always wanting to get home. I was determined. I remember the chases, the teachers coming after me! They didn't always catch me but, in the end, they broke me in – like a horse and soon enough I learned to take the bit and enjoy it. I was there at the school until the outbreak of war, then I left to join my uncle, Dave Moncrieff, in the smithy. He was a blacksmith and farrower. He needed an apprentice and down I went to join him. He'd bought the place from MacFarlane and before him it was McKinley. You were supposed to be sixteen before you started work on the horses but I jumped straight in. There were just the two of us. The first job I had was on the forehammer. That's a big hammer and it's called the forehammer because you're working in front of the anvil. That got you fit and that got the sweat running. Then I went on to removing the shoes and dressing the feet.

I remember the first horse I shod myself, a big Belgian horse, awfully short legs on him compared to a Clydesdale – but he was strong and I was light and he put me straight in the shoe box, head first! But I learned. When you take up the hoof, the horse likes to lean down on you and you have to be ready. 'Up again you go,' I'd say, 'you rascal! Up again you go!' That was up to a ton of horseflesh. You had to show who was master. You had to be firm but it's best to be gentle. The horses here liked us – they enjoyed coming in to be shod. It gave them a break from their slog in the fields. There was one horse used to regularly run away from his farm – down to us at the smiddy. He'd come down, have a drink and stand about! He'd come in – have his dram at the bar, so to speak – and go away refreshed, good as gold – me leading him back to the farm. That shows we didn't ill-treat the horses coming in.

When I was seventeen-and-a-half I took the train to the Caird Hall in Dundee, for my call-up medical for war service. I got passed 'grade A1', but as soon as the orderly heard my occupation was agricultural blacksmith he said, 'What the bloody hell are you doing in here! Get out!' He was laughing like! Pretending he was angry because he knew blacksmithing was a Reserved Occupation. Keeping the horses working, keeping the farm machinery going – was crucial in those days. Because of the U-boats very little food was coming into the country. We had to increase home production and the smiths were crucial to the war effort. I knew all that but when my call-up papers came I didn't want to stand back or be found wanting so away I went to Dundee and back home they sent me. There were still six or seven smiddies working in Newburgh and every man worked six days a week. And through the summer months we'd

Sandy Moncrieff (left) awarding the winners of the Two Man Cobble Race, Newburgh, c.1980. (SM)

be out helping harvest on Sundays – hay and corn. It was three horses on the binder, two on the big carts; all the stooking and lifting was done by hand. We enjoyed that – sitting out for our dinner under the tree. It made a change from the smithy. Twenty years I worked at the forge but, by the mid-fifties, the horses were done, the tractors were in. Some of the farrowers kept going as welders and mechanics but most of us had to get out. I went into the factory to work as a forklift driver and that's what I did till I retired. Time marches on.

Strong is the smith
He can split iron
But stronger is death
Than the smith or his Lord.

I always enjoyed the crack in the smithy – the stories, the rhymes, the songs. We had a story handed down from the days when sailing ships were still coming into Cameron's, the tattie merchants, down on the pier. A sailor got very drunk and he was hauled away to the Tolbooth, the police station, where the Oddfellows meet. Next morning he was up before the court. Sentence was passed. He was fined half a crown. 'Half a crown!' the sailor shouted, 'That's terrible! Half a crown in Newburgh! I would nae hae gae half that in

A carved wood panel from Balmerino Abbey, showing a medieval procession very similar to the Newburgh Oddfellows Parade. Panel is held by the National Museum of Scotland. (TN)

the pool o'London!' 'Laddie', said the magistrate, 'We've got laws in Newburgh, London kens naethin' aboot! Awa ye gang – afore I croon ye!'

I've not worked as a farrier for thirty years now but I often think of an old song I heard, sung by a Tinker. I don't know what it's called but this is how it goes. I like it.

O bide, lady bide, there's no place you can hide
For the old blacksmith will be your man
And there's no place you can hide.

So she turned into a turtle dove
And flew right through the air
And he turns into a great goshawk
And chased her here and there.

O bide, lady bide …

So she turned into a little fly
And flew around the air
And he turned into a swallow
And chased her here and there.

O bide, lady bide …

So she turned into a big brown hare
And fled across the land
And he turned into a grey greyhound
Saying, 'I will be your man!'

O bide, lady bide …

So she turned into a nice bedspread
And spread across the bed
And he turned into a white blanket
And took her maidenhead.

O bide, lady bide, there's no place you can hide

For the old blacksmith will be your man
And there's no place you can hide.

I suppose you could say I've always had too many fingers in too many pies. I joined the committee of the Highland Games in 1946 and I'm still on that. I'm on the Community Council here. Every year it's me that organises the Riding of the town marches. Our Games go back to the Battle of Black Earnside and I like to say that they're the oldest, continuously practised, sports event in Scotland. They're held on the third weekend in June, in honour of the fallen. A week after Newburgh comes the Ceres Games. They commemorate the battle of Bannockburn – which took place sixteen years after our victory at Black Earnside. It was me that extended our Games, so they now cover two days. We have the coble races on the Friday evening and the full Games on the Saturday. By doing that we double the crowd. A coble is the boat used for salmon netting, it's heavy and very stable. We have the British

Double Handed Championship and the Under Twenty-ones Championship. We hold the events on the West Shore Pier and I'm the starter. They're two-man, four-oar boats – traditional salmon cobles. They used to be over eighteen feet but today we just have the sixteen-foot boats. When the salmon fishing ended, I arranged that we bought the old cobles for the Burgh and they're used every year for the races. We still have good prizes. Fifty pounds for the fastest heat. We know that the boat race goes back to 1880 and we believe our horse races go right back to the battle. The main race is out to the halfway tree on the Abernethy road, and back.

In September we have the Riding of the Marches. We call it that even though no horse goes out these days. It's just a walk. We go out as soon as the ground is clear of crops, but never on the Battle of Britain weekend. We walk seven-and-a-half miles. Starting at the East Port we go down the Coach Road, round Parkhill and cross the burn. We go away up Burnside to the cemetery, follow along the back of the cemetery, then straight to the Railway Marker, up the hill to the Black Cairn, along Winnie Bank, across the top fields to Ninewells Farm, up the hill – until you see Loch Mill, along the face of the hill and down to Hare's Flat; then back onto the coach road; then to Ghillie's burn and Woodrow Flat where we take refreshment – pies, teas and things like that. From the shore at Ghillie's Point, we throw a stick out onto the water. The idea being that the stick will float out and sail down our northern march – which runs down the middle of the Tay. After that, it's up Tay Street

The George Hotel, Newburgh, decorated for the Summer Games, c.1930. (SM)

to the Abbey Inn where I give out my wee bit speech, opposite the fountain.

It's a good day out and it keeps the old traditions alive. It gives youngsters a good idea of the burgh they're part of. We've only ever had one problem. It's in the hands of the Court of Session in Edinburgh – there's a couple up there at Broomfield don't like us coming through their ground. Once a year! Our rights are small enough these days – so we'll fight so as not to lose them. Whilst Oddfellowship exists, whilst sun and stars and moon still shine we'll seek to maintain our ancient rights! At every stage we've won so far – now they've made a final appeal. I wonder why people want to live in a community if they don't want to be part of the community. 'A man's a man for a' that the world o'er' – we don't like to see division, exclusion, airs and graces. This is a working town and the place is here for one and all.

People may think that the Oddfellows are a useless anachronism but we bring together ideas as well as the people. The dispute about bringing women into the Oddfellows seems to me unnecessary. I like variety. The men and women of Newburgh can go out together every night of the week and many of them do. I believe in the equality of men and women but that doesn't mean that women have to do everything men do, or become Oddfellows. It may be a good thing that women should become ministers of the Kirk but I don't think it would be right to force all monasteries and nunneries to be bisexual places.

There is a time and there is a place. For instance – I think it's better, and cheaper, to keep public toilets separate for men and women.

So, there we are, I'm in favour of the Oddfellows continuing the way we've always been. There's plenty of room for new things and there will be more and more new things, just as there are bound to be less and less old things, genuine old things, in the future. I certainly hope there'll be no attempt to force us to change, or have us banned in the name of democracy. The King of France outlawed and murdered the Knights Templar but I wouldn't say the Newburgh Oddfellows were a danger to church, state, or womankind. In fact, I believe we are a pillar of what should be the best values of the Kirk and state. And we carry on traditions that have been very important, not just to Newburgh, but to the history of Scotland. You'll know that the Knights Templar played a crucial part in the battle of Bannockburn. That was just seven years after they sought and were given refuge in Scotland, and nine years after the first of the Newburgh Highland Games!

I'm very interested in history and I've read quite a lot about the Knights Templar. At the beginning of the fourteenth century, France was ruled by Philip the Fair, a man who can only be described as a tyrant and a megalomaniac. In July 1306 he ordered the arrest and expulsion of every Jew in France. On Friday 13 October 1307 he ordered the liquidation of the great and historic Order of the Knights Templar. Fifteen thousand men were arrested, their lands and property were seized, they were killed, tortured and imprisoned on all kinds of charges. A number of them managed to flee westwards into Portugal, into Britain and Ireland, and especially into Scotland. Robert the Bruce had been excommunicated by the Pope so they found succour here and the story we have is that the appearance of the mounted Knights Templar, with their pennants and standards flying in the wind above Bannockburn, turned the tide of that battle and the history of Scotland. They were the battle-host.

People ask what happened to them? It's not easy to say. The Knights Templar retained some power in Portugal for at least four centuries after their suppression in France. There they played a big part in driving the Moors out of Spain. Their headquarters were at Tomar, where there is a chapel where the knights attended mass on horseback. And after that the knights join in the festival of the *Tabuleiros*. All the children dress up as mice and scatter through the streets. The women of the town dress up in towering headdresses decorated with flowers and loaves of bread then chase the children and frighten them. Collections of money are made and beef, bread and wine are given to the poor. Of course, there's always a band and a big parade through the streets, so it's just like Old Year's night in Newburgh! Only with us, it's the men dressed as women and monsters that chase after the children.

Old traditions get changed but they carry on. Where our walk actually comes from we'll never know and if we did – maybe we wouldn't let on. But there's no doubt that Lindores Abbey is still very important to the people of Newburgh – and Balmerino Abbey is just seven miles downriver. They've got a Spanish chestnut tree growing in the garden there that's more than 500 years old. It stands in the grounds amongst the tombstones that go back to Cistercian times. Some of the old Balmerino woodcarvings got taken down to the Royal National Museum of Scotland in Edinburgh. One of them shows a procession – there's a man riding an old horse, looking backwards over his shoulder – and there's someone pulling the tail of the horse – and down below various strange figures are leaping and rushing about! So I ask you – what does that scene remind you of? I won't tell you what it reminds me of. Some things must remain secret! But, I'll tell you this, when I rang in the New Millennium from the belltower of the Old Tolbooth and I looked out onto the High Street, crowded with hundreds of people as far as I could see, I thought to myself, 'I hope the Oddfellows keep this up – for another thousand years!' And I was so happy then, knowing that we'd carried things through.

While glittering planets gold the night
While toys the earth with time.
While sun and moon and stars are bright
Odd fellowship shall shine.

Overleaf:
Horsemen preparing a stallion at the Perth Stallion Show, 1999. *(TN)*

Part Two

Horsemen

The High Horseman of Angus

'Now, is the brother a blind man?' That was the first question with which the horsemen of the ancient Pictish county of Angus addressed an initiate of their secret horse society – the Horseman's Word. Initiation was a dramatic and memorable event, once practised across much of mainland Britain, but nowhere was the ceremonial more ancient, traditional and authoritative than in Angus and the north east. Local horsemen would gather at an appointed place, a barn, byre, stable or steading at some distance from any farmhouse or place of habitation. The ceremony would take place at night, with a full moon for preference. Inside the appointed place the High Horseman would be already seated, waiting for his horsemen to bring the apprentice before him. He will control and preside over the whole ceremony.

The apprentice, the youngster, the new man is brought forward blindfolded and stripped to the waist. He has been manhandled to the steading by a group of attendant horsemen, deliberately disorientated by pushing, pulling and spinning, so he arrives at the byre with little idea as to what's going on or quite where he is. Into the byre he comes, his arms pinned to his side and is suddenly stood still in front of the High Horseman, whom he can't see. A lamp burns. The other horsemen gather round. Silence is called. Then, the High Horseman speaks; he is clad in the heavy clothes of a working horseman – with the cloven hoof of a goat up one sleeve.

High Horseman: Now – is the brother a blind man?
Men: Yes
HH: What does he want here? To get, or give instruction?
Men: Rather more to get than to give.

Opposite:
Norman Christie, Grand Master of the Horseman's Word, East Scotland, c1930. (HH,SSS)

HH: What does your blind man want?
Men: To be the same as yourself.
HH: What way came you here?
Men: Through crooks, and through crooks and straights, as the nearest road led us.
HH: Well, boy, what age are you?
Boy: Eighteen years.
HH: What brought you here?
Men and Boy: To find the secret.
HH: Did anyone send you here?
Boy: No.
HH: Did you come of your own free will?
Boy: Yes.

The horsemen now stand back from the boy and the High Horseman rises to demand the oath. The blindfold is removed.

HH: Now boy – this is a very solemn oath we require of you. Hold up your right hand. And place yourself in a position neither sitting, nor standing, bowing nor bending, naked nor clothed, and say this after me.

The men get the apprentice to *kneel* before the High Horseman; they raise his right arm and lead him, phrase by phrase, through the oaths of the Horseman's Word.

HH: Firstly.
I do most solemnly take upon me
The vows and secrets of horsemanship
Before God and witnesses
And may God
Help me to keep my secrets as a horseman
Which I shall account for at the last day.
Boy: I do.
HH: I shall always conceal
And never reveal –
To father nor mother
To sister or brother
To wife or to wench
Nor to any babe that sitteth upon my knee
Nor any he or she –
Any signs shown
Any oaths taken
Nor any secrets of Horsemanship.

Boy: I do.

At this moment the High Horseman moves forward to physically lower the raised arm of the apprentice. He steps back to continue:

HH: Secondly.
I further vow and swear
That I shall not give it
Nor see it given
Under the sum of one hundred and ten pounds
And a bottle of whisky being paid down
– As I know I did myself
And these brothers beside me being present.

Thirdly.
I further vow and swear
That I shall not give
Or see it given
To a youth under the age of eighteen years
Nor to any man above forty five years of age
– Nor to any tradesman
Unless he be a blacksmith.

Fourthly.
I further vow and swear
That I shall not give
Nor see it given
Unless the number of brothers being present are
Three, five, seven, nine, eleven
– All strictly tried and duly examined
And proved to be the same as myself.

Fifthly.
I further vow and swear
That I shall not give it or see it given
On any part of the Lord's Day
Nor within twenty four hours of it
Nor on a Fast Day
Nor on a market day.

Sixthly.
I further vow and swear
That I shall attend all Brothers' calls
Summonses and signs
Within the distance of five miles
Within warning of twenty four hours

Excepting – my master's service
– my wife in child-bed
– sickness in my family
– Going for a doctor or a house on fire.

Seventhly.
I further vow and swear
That I shall not give the oath
Nor see the oath given
To a drunkard or a liar
Nor to a madman
Nor to a revealer of secrets
Nor to anyone I am suspicious of
Nor to anyone who would bad use his horses with it.

Eighthly.
I further vow and swear
That I shall not give nor see it given
To a farmer, nor a farmer's son
Unless they are serving the same as myself
– Nor to a grieve that is not working horses
Nor to a woman at all.

Bothy loons, Aberdeenshire, c.1930. (HH/DA)

The men of the bothy, Aberdeenshire, c.1930. (HH/DA)

Ninthly.
I further vow and swear
That I will not ill-use my horses with it
Nor any other man's horses
Nor woman's horses
Nor see ill done without reporting it
Or telling them they are doing it wrong –
Even if I know them to be brothers of mine.

Tenthly.
I likewise vow and swear
I will always conceal and never reveal
The Secrets of Horsemanship
To any but a Brother
Not even until he is strictly tried and duly examined.

> Eleventhly
> I likewise vow and swear
> That I shall not – cut it or carve it
> – paint it or print it
> – write it or engrave it
> On anything that is movable at all
> Or unmovable under the canopy of Heaven
> Nor do so much as a single letter of it
> In the air –
> To cause it to be known.

After this, the Horseman's Creed is spoken by all present, lead by the High Horseman:

> So help me Lord to keep my secrets and perform my duties as a horseman. If I break any of them – even the last of them – I wish no less than to be done to me than that my heart be torn from my breast by two wild horses, and my body quartered in four and swung on chains, and the wild birds of the air left to pick my bones, and these then taken down and buried in the sands of the sea, where the tide ebbs and flows twice every twenty four hours – to show I am a deceiver of the faith. Amen.

Once the apprentice is formally initiated, the horsemen introduce the new horseman to the secrets of the order. Later a 'ceilidh' would emerge out of the formal ceremonial – everyone drinking the whisky brought by the apprentice – and others as necessary. A series of toasts would be drunk with the High Horseman leading the assembled men in recitations in which the traditional principles of horsemanship would be affirmed and the importance of the Brotherhood of Horsemen reinforced – in poetry, song, riddles and secret lore.

HH: Here's to the E.N.O.
If you can tell me the answer to these four –
I will risk you with all I know.
Ans: ONE!
HH: Here's to the three.
You the three
Me the three
O reveal that to me –
In three small words.
Ans: HORSEMAN'S OATH.
HH: Here's to the poles that cut the wind
The two before
And the one behind.

Ans: TWO EARS, TAIL.

HH: Here's to the horse with the four white feet
Here's to the horse with the sprangled mane
Here's to the man who trained the first horse
– Pray, tell me his name?

Ans: JULBE VANE.

HH: Here's to the living before
The dead between
The body and the soul behind.

Ans: HORSE, PLOUGH, MAN.

HH: So, I toss an apple over an orange
And I drink to you in friendship's terms.
If you are the man I take you to be
You'll drink up your glass and answer me.

Ans: I toss an apple over an orange
And drink to you in friendship's terms –
I am the man you take me to be
So – for your sake – I'll drink to thee.

HH: Here's to the horse as stubborn as a mule
Here's to the child can put him to school –
He knows his capitals E.N.O.
Ready to start and ready to go.

Men: Here's to the Horseman
A horseman of might –

Ploughing match, Strathmiglo, Fife, November 1999. (TN)

He trains his horses to the dead of the night.
He trains them to walk and he trains them to stand,
He learns them to obey the word of command.

The Horsemen now toast the New Horseman and reaffirm their own allegiance:

Here's to them that brought me in
Here's to them and many others –
Here's to them that brought me in
And changed my name from friend to Brother.

HH: For his sake I'll drink this glass
– and for His sake I'll drink another!

Various other toasts are then proposed and drunk:

HH: Here's to the horse with the four white feet
Here's to the cord that binds him:
Here's to the Brother when he meets Another
Will from top to bottom – sound him!

Here's to the horse with the four white feet
Tied firmly to his manger.
He comes to the crack of his master's whip –
He does not do that for a stranger.

Here's to the difficult horse!
I bring him down with one blow.
When he rises he smiles
Asking which way to go!

Here's to the horseman
And the horseman's bairns –
The woman with the lovely charms
Who loves to be in the horseman's arms.

Here's to the horse with the star on his brow
Here's to the mare with the bell on her breast.
They are easy to harness
They are fleet in the yoke –
It's a good going horse that works with a nod.

Here's to the four poles that go in a row
Cutting the wind wherever you go.
One day if you wish
In my position to be –
Come now and name them
Once over to me.

Men: Four Bars.

HH: Here's to the big black nudge
Beneath the old oak tree
Where first I learned
The meaning of the E.N.O.E.

Here's to the lad that can always conceal
– And keep a thing hidden!
Brings both his horses at the crack of whip
– And stand like a stone when bidden.

Men: And here's to you – as good as you are
And here's to me – as bad as I am.
For as good as you are
And as bad as I am
I'm as good as you are
As bad as I am.

HH: Here's to the whip and the bridle
Here's to the spur and the saddle
And here's to the bonnie lad
Who carries the key of the stable.

> Here's to the jolly plough boy –
> That'll follow the cart and the plough lads.
> That'll neither ill-use or abuse
> But uses yet in time –
> Who neither fears a horse's look
> Nor yet a woman's wean.

> Now, help me O Lord to keep my secrets and perform my duties as a Horseman. If I break any of them – even the last of them – I wish no less to be done to me than that my heart be torn from my breast by two wild horses and my body quartered in four and swung in chains and the wild birds of the air left to pick the flesh from my bones and then taken down and buried in the sands of the sea where the tide ebbs and flows twice ever twenty four hours – to show that I was a deceiver of the faith. Amen.

The apprentice was then given the key to the stable and a final toast was drunk. The horsemen might then continue celebrating or wend their way home to be ready for work in the morning. The particular dramatic impact of the ritual would depend upon the characters involved, circumstances and local tradition but as with a conventional religious service the heightened language and ceremonial set a framework for an impressive and meaningful event. And, even a lacklustre ceremony would, psychologically and socially, prepare each new horseman for a lifetime's commitment to the Brotherhood of which he now became part.

The Brotherhood of the Horseman was a form of primitive Trades Union and a quasi-religious and mystical cult that distilled and passed knowledge within a half-professional, half-tribal group. It gave courage and confidence to youngsters coming in to work and was, undoubtedly, an organisation that did a great deal of good. The High Horsemen and oldtimers kept reams of information about potions, cures and practices in their heads and they passed it on through the brotherhood. Much was passed in rhymed incantations. This gave form to the knowledge and made remembrance easier; it added an artistic dimension to the science and craft of horsemanship. It gave a Burnsian vitality to the culture of the farm touns.

Horsemen tend to be serious, practical men and most of the knowledge and skills they passed on were practical but they also wished to make their lives more interesting and set their, often isolated, experience in the context of history. Their exultant cultural camaraderie was old long before the Burns' Societies and most Gentlemen's Clubs got going.

The horsemen were very male in their attitudes. They constructed their own Ten Commandments – for their wives to follow! Good humoured

Ploughing match, Strathmiglo, Fife, November 1999. (TN)

commandments – to be taken with a pinch of salt, or snuff, and offered up in good humour.

1) I am thy husband whom thou hast vowed to love, honour and obey – for I have saved thee from all madisons and the terror of all single blessedness.
2) Thou shalt not look upon any man to love or admire apart from your husband. For I am a jealous husband who visits the sin of a wife upon her followers; therefore be truthful to thy marriage vows.
3) Thou shall not backbite thy husband, nor speak harshly to him. Neither shall thou expose his faults to thy neighbour's breast. Should he hear of such goings on, he will punish thee properly – by a deprivation of sundry items such as bonnets, dress and jewellery.
4) Thou shalt purchase cigars for your husband rather than candies for yourself – and that includes tablet if the wife comes from Dundee!
5) Thou shalt not go to evening parties without your husband, neither wilt thou dance too frenziedly with thy husband's friends or thy cousin.
6) Thou shalt not make false representations as to the state of thy pantry, thy house, or thy wardrobe.

7) Thou shalt not listen to any flattery, nor accept any gifts from any man except thy husband.
8) Thou shalt not rifle thy husband's pockets for any money whilst he is asleep. Nor shalt thou read any letters thou mayest find therein, for it is his business to look after his own affairs, thine to let his alone.
9) Thou shalt not conceal nothing from thy husband.
10) Remember to rise early in the morning; not to make him thin porridge; and be prepared, with thy good-wife power; to welcome thy husband at the breakfast table.
11) Look for no jewellery from thy husband on the anniversary of thy wedding day – for it is written – 'Blessed are they who expect nothing, for they shall not be disappointed!'

Those eleven commandments sound very nineteenth-century and must be seen as a ceilidh house addition to the main ceremony of the Horseman's Word. They certainly lack the Druidic authority that underlies the Horseman's Oath and seem to be constructed with spaces for pauses – the kind of pauses after-dinner speakers plant in their speeches – to harvest laughter and self-estimation. In modern times the Society of Horsemen gradually became a kind of working men's club that did little more than nurture the wellbeing

of its members. But right up till the mid-twentieth century the society continued to be a rural fact of real social and cultural importance. It had quasi-religious and real political force. It engendered brotherhood, a lasting sense of responsibility, and it released in initiates a euphoria, a sense of power and communion that was personal and social, sexual and religious, martial and tribal. It gave men of little or no economic or class power a remarkable personal and social authority engendered by character, knowledge, skills and occupational importance.

On a wider, historical level the events and ceremonial of the Horseman's Word is of considerable cultural interest because they retain, in a very pure form, many of the theatrical elements out of which the whole phenomenon of European drama developed. The formality of the Horseman ceremonial is remarkably similar to that on which the early Greek theatre depended. There is a narrator and oracular leader (the High Horseman); there is a chorus (the Horsemen); and a set-piece ritual in which a hero/victim (the initiate) is brought to a state of new awareness – personal and social. The event is important to the participants (unto death), and part of a vital social reality but it is also recognised as 'play', as an artistic construct, as a controlled ritual. The ceremonial advances according to fiercely guarded tradition, and orchestrated to dramatic effect. Like the best modern theatre, events were conducted according to established forms but remained open to 'the moment', the particular happenings of the particular night. Like the theatre, the rites of the Horsemen have ancient, religious and tribal origins.

Consciously, or unconsciously, all the ceremonial is archetypal. First, there is the passage to an appointed place, then the authority of the High Horseman is established. The Horsemen then act as intermediaries and lead the novice in his responses who might, or might not, have been primed to answer certain questions by the older horsemen during the preceding months. The dynamic of the ceremony thus depends on the tension created between the habitual, known elements of the ceremonial and arbitrary surprises. The dramatic force of the language used in the ceremonies was high and there can be no doubt that the importance of theatrical 'timing' would have been recognised by most senior Horsemen. For example with regard to the moment when the initiate was first stripped, when thrust into the kneeling position, when first surprised by the cloven hand. Everywhere in Scotland the oaths and ceremonies were slightly different.

1) I solemnly vow and swear in the name of the Father and the Son and the Holy Ghost and before three Sworn Horsemen that I shall hide, conceal and never reveal the arts and parts of this Horsemanship ...
3) Furthermore I vow and swear that I will not give it nor see it given to anyone under the sum of one guinea, or jewelry to that amount, and a bottle of spirits and a four pound loaf – to be paid down as I had to do myself.
4) Furthermore, I vow and swear that I will give it or see it given without three sworn brethren being present, nor without trying them and retrying them and proving them to be true sworn Brethren.
5) Furthermore, I vow and swear that I will not give it or see it given to a drunkard, nor to a man in drink, nor in any place where drink is sold ...
7) Furthermore, I vow and swear that I will not give it nor see it given to any tradesman except a blacksmith or a veterinary surgeon only – nor even a farmer nor a farmer's son, except he has been in the habit of working horses for three years and made himself the same as ourselves ...
12) Furthermore, I vow and swear that I will not give it to father or mother, sister nor brother, wife nor winch, nor the nearest nor dearest that's in my bosom or lies by my side.
13) Furthermore I vow and swear that I will not write it nor date it, cut it nor carve it – on moss, wood, snow, brick-tile, nor anything moveable nor unmoveable under the canopy of Heaven; for if I do I shall go under no less punishment than this – that my tongue may be cut from

> the roof of my mouth with a Horseman's gully and my body torn asunder between two wild horses.
>
> Now answer: Do you think this bondage to hard to keep? Say 'yes', or 'no' ... 'No – and may God help me to keep my promise. Amen.

Once initiated, a horseman gained a place on a hierarchical promotional ladder (although that also depended on the farmers who employed them) and access to all the veterinary knowledge available to the brotherhood. By the nineteenth century, book information had begun to be an additional source of information to that traditionally transmitted orally by the Horsemen and, gradually, many Horsemen must have incorporated 'book knowledge' into their codes of horse treatment. In addition, because many Horsemen moved into and out of the British cavalry regiments much of the knowledge used within the army, still hugely dependent on horse power, filtered back to Scotland's farm touns. However, most horse knowledge remained traditional and empirical. What worked in practice, and it is interesting that, psychologically and physically, the 'behavioural' methodology of the Horsemen long predates the Behavioural Studies much later pioneered and codified by Behavioural Psychologists like Pavlov and Skinner.

A FEW NOTES ON BREAKING AND TRAINING

as outlined by Professor Beery and various Scottish horsemen before the First World War

For breaking and training a horse, the rules were very simple and effective: 1) Let the horse know, and feel, you are his master. 2) Let him have confidence and disarm him of fear. 3) Teach him to understand the signs employed in working. 4) By continuous and careful practice confirm these into habits. In education and in horse training – like begets like.

It was understood that the temper manifested by the trainer will be transmitted to the horse he wishes to train. Horsemen have always worked on the principle that viciousness is, essentially, the result of conditioned malpractice or unfortunate circumstance – like ignorant and abusive treatment. The idea that certain horses, like certain people, are naturally vicious was a Victorian fiction and a licence taken by novelists. Aspects of disposition and temperament, it was understood, were transmitted, genetically, in horses but few horsemen would then suggest that vice itself was transmitted. The mistake of the novelists was to assume that the horse had reason. But horses do not reason and it is a bad mistake to treat a horse as if it has. A horse must be dealt with through its senses and instincts and the nature of horses must guide the actions of the men who wish to train and use them. First, the instincts and propensities of the horse, as a creature, a wild animal, must be known to the trainer; only then can a trainer use his art intelligently.

Horses are gregarious and sociable, they are herd animals. They like company and dislike being alone. They also have a strong sense of curiosity. This is often prompted by fear or suspicion. For example, if a horse sees a strange or unusual object he will at first snort and shy away – but, if it is not obviously dangerous, he will not rest content until he has got to close quarters and touched it with his nose. The nose has sensibly been described as the horse's forehead. This is not due to any particular acuteness of smell, this sense is the weakest of all the horse's six senses, but due to the extraordinary development of the nerves of feeling and touch in that organ. Having said that, however, horses do have a better sense of smell than a woman and – a much better sense of smell than a man. Women being more like hounds than men – in that respect!

It is natural for a horse, as it is with most creatures, to try to remove anything that annoys it. The horse does this by swishing his tail, kicking with his heels or, if it be to remove something from his back; by rearing and buck-jumping. These actions are instinctive but they can become confirmed and dangerous habits – if encouraged by improper reactions, wrong-treatment or training. In training horses, the senses of touch, sight and hearing are most important. These senses must be educated and this must be done systematically and consistently – beginning with the establishment of good relations with the foal. The eye of the horse must be educated to usual and unusual sights and the ear to loud and startling sounds.

In training it is important to begin with the halter and the head, and to end with the breeching of the hindquarters. Horses cannot breath through their mouths. To catch and halter a colt the old 'Tinker' method was by hallooing and flourishing a stick, then grasping it by the nostrils and stopping the flow of air to the lungs. Thus the horse is compelled to fight for its life until it submits to the strength and will of the man. That is a method that can work but it is the wrong way of breaking a horse in any normal circumstances.

To take an unbroken horse out of a field, go forward together – the horseman behind and two reliable loons, one on each side of a trained and quiet horse – all should proceed slowly without noise or disturbance. If the horse turns and looks suspicious, halt but make no noise or gesture. Should he attempt to break back, face him and stop him as smartly and quietly as possible. Proceed in this way until you bring him to the entrance of the steading or courtyard whither you mean to lead him. If the place be strange to him he will, most probably, lean his head towards the entrance or the gate and snort. Now the horseman leads the quiet horse forward, inside, then stops – with the hindquarters of the horse just a few feet from the colt. They halt just where the colt can almost touch the backside of the lead horse. The stable lads will have dropped back just a little and as the horseman leads the quiet horse forward, the lads move up behind. In all probability the colt will make a bound

Aberdeen horseman, c.1930 (CHS)

forward into the yard, or whatever enclosure you have. And the gate is closed.

Now the colt will run round the quiet horse, hugging him close and shaking his head up and down. After that the quiet horse will be led away and the colt fed with fresh grass and carrots. After that, at your leisure, go into him with the 'third hand', that is a long gentling pole. Hold it towards the nose of the colt about four feet from the ground. If he exhibits signs of fear, keep quiet and speak in soothing tones. By and by he will come and put his nose on the third hand. Now pass it quietly over his head, rubbing gently, and avoiding striking or hurting him. Then gradually bring the third hand along his withers, his back, the hindquarters, rubbing all the while till you get to his hocks. The great thing is to take time, to exercise patience. The object is to beget confidence not to instil fear.

It will be found to be an improvement to tie a bag or cloth around the third hand. When you can touch him and gentle rub him, all over without him showing any resentment, you should move on to the next stage. Holding the third hand in your right-hand, approach the colt with a plain rope halter in your left – with the shank, ten feet long, trailing over your shoulder. Whilst continuing to rub his neck with the third hand gradually bring your left hand forward so as to encourage him to put his nose on your hand. Move the halter up and down very slowly a few times until you feel the moment right to quickly and quietly slip it over the colt's head and ears. As soon as the poll piece is over and the shank is under the jaw, you can pull it through by degrees and quietly adjust the throat lash. As soon as the halter is on you must take your third hand away. Now, pull the colt's head smartly and strongly to the near side, place your right hand on his quarters and give him a push round, all at the same time. Repeat this several times. Then, get hold of his tail in your right and, with a short hold on the halter shank give him a few turns round. After that put on the hair rope – this will form a kind of primitive crupper and the colt will be as good as yours.

If the colt is refractory there is a second procedure which may be employed. It will work best if the enclosing fence or walls are so high as to exclude all sight of the external world. Gentle the colt as before – with the third hand rubbing nose, neck and back. Rig the lower loop of a rope halter to the end of a pole, by passing two turns of the rope round the pole. Now raise this halter gently above the colt's head and gently let the poll piece drop

softly behind his ears. Be careful to be sure that the noseband is brought in front of the ears, then, with a sudden swing, bring the pole down smartly in front of the animals nose – and in behind his lower jaw. Release the pole and your horse is haltered. The utmost caution and temper must be exercised. The operator must not hurry, must not panic or get in a flurry and above all he must show no fear of the horse. There will be no danger of the horse charging the handler if he keeps the third hand above the horse's face – this will deter the horse but also allow the handler to administer a sharp tap on the muzzle if it be necessary.

If a horse is loose and running wild, two men should advance towards him with a rope, a long line, between them. Advance this line and drive the horse into a corner from which it cannot escape. An experienced horseman should then go forward, take hold of the horse and fix two shackle belts, one on each foreleg. A long line should then be put through the nearest shackle belt and firmly held. The horse can now be let go and be allowed to circle. If he offers resistance he can easily be brought down on to one, or both knees – simply by pulling on the line.

In the case of a very timid or vicious horse the most effective plan is the following. Make a noose to form a 'lasso', two to three feet in diameter. Place it on the ground, giving the free end to a competent assistant. Move the horse forwards and backwards until the horse puts a forefoot in the noose. The noose should be pulled up and back to secure the foreleg by the pastern. It is then best to throw the rope over the horse's back for another horseman to work the horse from the far side but, if that is not possible, the leg is pulled back on the near-side and the shackle belt fixed. With such a horse the gentling must then be done with great skill. Sometimes the horse will need to be blindfolded by throwing a rug, blanket or bag over his head.

In lifting the near foreleg by the hand, do not seize the pastern first (as many do) but grip the muscles of the knee repeatedly – to predispose it to bend by reflex action – whilst, at the same time, pressing your elbow into the muscle of the horse's upper foreleg and leaning as much weight as you can muster against the horse. This throws the weight of the horse on to the off foreleg. All the time the left hand keeps a steady pull on the halter. The horse will then gradually raise his near foot and your hand should slide down the leg to grab the foot. Once this is done press the thumb firmly against the sole of the foot. This makes it very painful for the animal to put down his foot – and the operation is complete. The secret of this method of control lies in the use of pressure on various muscles and nerves and these induce the limbs first to bend and then remain bent. In the case of a heavy cart horse, seize the hair of the fetlock and pull up.

To control a horse, fast going in a plough, procure a rod, not exceeding six inches in length, with a crossbar in the centre and a ring in each end, and a ring at the lower end of the crossbar. Fix this rod to the rings of the bridle. The bar is placed between the horse's jaws. Fix a line to the lower end of the rod. This gives the ploughman great control if the horse pulls ahead too fast or becomes restive.

To train a horse to follow the crack of the whip. Tie a plough line to the ring of the datfin and let him go to the end of it; then crack your whip and give him a jerk. Crack your whip again and this time give the horse a little corn and coax him. Serve him in this way until he follows the crack of the whip without the aid of the plough line. After that you should reward the horse by rubbing his nose with oil of aniseed and oil of rhodium.

To catch a wild horse, put oil of cumin on your hand. Approach him from the windward side. Move in slowly until you're close enough to pat him on the nose. Give him a piece of sugar loaf, with caster oil and rhodium. He'll follow you like a dog, or slave. Another way would be to fast the horse for twenty-four hours – then give the horse a cake made from the following ingredients – half a pound of honey, one pound of oat meal, half a pound of gumaraby, two ounces of oil of roses. Feed fresh-baked but cool.

A way of establishing dominance over a haltered but still fractious horse is to grasp it by the nostrils, then when the horse is desperate to breathe – let the nostrils go, as the horse breathes in you blow into the nostrils whilst at the same time jabbing the horse sharply in the armpit of the foreleg with the point of the blade of a knife held securely as to do no damage. That might sound harsh but it isn't and it's a simple cure for a difficult problem. Life still throws up these things. But now – how to dapple a horse?

To dapple a horse
Feed ash buds for one week every morning

To blacken a horse
Take half a pound of bees-wax
Two ounces of ivory black
One ounce of indigo blue
Take one ounce of isim glass
And mix to paste with half a penny's worth of rosin
Or of turpentine.

Spirit of nature
To make a horse fast

Quicksilver to derange a horse
Laudanum to make him slow

Eleven drops of Spanish fly
For a mare and for the kae
Will bring them in season – with a sigh.

Above and overleaf: The rural grandeur of the mid twentieth century, teams of Scottish Clydesdales harvesting corn with binders. (CHS)

To test a horse when buying? This was in the old days. Hide your spurs and your whip. When you're bargaining with someone you know, ask permission to ride the horse for an hour. If your request is refused you may suspect a fault. No further negotiations will be needed. When you ride, mount easily and go off gently with a loose rein, which will make the horse careless and show up any faults he may have. If he is a stumbler you will discover it presently, especially if the road is rough; however, remember even the best

horse can stumble. A young horse of spirit, if not properly broken, will frequently stumble, and yet if he moves nimbly, dividing his legs, he may become a very good saddle horse. But – if a horse springs out when he stumbles, if he is afraid of the whip and spurs – depend upon it – the horse will be an old offender. But good horse, or bad horse, never strike a horse for stumbling or starting. If, after your hour in the saddle, you still like the horse – check wind, his teeth, his eyes, and his legs. These things should be looked at before any purchase is completed.

To stop a runaway horse a man must be determined. He must get, and keep, a firm hand on the reins and grasp the horse by the nostrils – then hold on till the animal is pacified.

If a horse sleeps standing up – give him a good comfortable bed, tie a weight of between seven and fourteen pounds to his tail (making sure the weight doesn't hang below the hock) – or force the horse to lie down as described above.

If a horse is hidebounnd, mix the following: half an ounce of barbadoes aloe with one pound of butter. Make into four balls, roll in as much powdered galap as will lie on a sixpence. Give these to the horse washed down with a lukewarm pint of strong beer. Fast him for three or four hours and then give him a mash of bruised oats in warm water and continue this for three of four days. This will lay his coat and make him thrive. Steady exercise will make him thrive even better.

How to make a horse love or hate you. This is a botanical secret. It depends on a small native orchid (mascala). It is found in woods and marshy places in early summer. Under the ground the plant produces twin bulbs, commonly known as 'bull-bags'. They are of oval shape and about the size of common field beans (not nearly as large as a bull's testicles but the association is clear). When dried and placed in water, one of these bulbs sinks and the other floats. The former embodies hate, the latter love. If you wish to make a horse hate or love you, or another person, the bulbs should be grated down and mixed along with some food and the predicted effects achieved. These witchlike potions are known to be very ancient. They were used by the Assyrians thousands of years ago and news of this was brought back to Britain by the famous anthropologist Layard. As you will realise much knowledge of horsemanship in Scotland is very old.

Another means by which you can make a horse depend on you, love you, become your slave, is as follows. Put some caster oil and oil of cumin in two small airtight bottles. Grate down a little of the wart off the foreleg of the horse, mix this with some oil of rhodemena and store in another small airtight bottle. With the three bottles in your hand, gently rub the nose of the horse – letting him smell and taste the oil traces. Now give him a piece of sugar loaf, or cooked potatoes, with a little caster oil well-soaked in; then put eight drops of the rhodemena oil into a lady's thimble, open the mouth of the horse and tip the thimble over his tongue. After that the horse will follow you like a pet.

Every horseman must think first of his horses and over the years he should think a little like a horse, become one with his horse. There is a rhyme we call the NSPK:

Going up the hill whip me not
Coming down the hill hurry me not
On the level spur me not
In the stable forget me not with clean water
Strike me not if sick or cold
Chide me not with bit or rein
When you are angry – strike me not.

The horsemen worked with an dictionary of codified rules of behaviour. To make a horse stand fast for selling we had the EPD. That consisted of a tincture of opium or laudanum – the quantity depending on the size and state of the horse, or a quarter of henbane (twenty-five to forty drops). Or you could try oil of aron, oil of redgin, or tincture of myrrh or bist on the bit. Seeds of nettles (dried in the sun) make an excellent addition to the diet of a horse. They will improve the condition of a horse and boost your chances of a good sale. The best way to judge the age of a horse you don't know is to look at the teeth. Every horse has six teeth in both its upper and lower jaw until it reaches the age of about two-and-a-half years. These teeth are uniform and smooth across the biting surface. At the age of two-and-a-half the middle teeth are shed, due to eruption of new teeth, these new teeth are hollow. At three-and-a-half years the two teeth each side of the new teeth are shed, these are also hollow. At four-and-a-half the corner teeth are shed and at five years their replacements appear. These are also hollow, with grooves clearly marked on the insides of each tooth. These grooves slowly fill up and disappear by the time the horse is six years old – as do the hollows in the other teeth. By the time the horse is eight years old, all these teeth will have become smooth and full. Separate to these teeth, the sharp single teeth begin to come at four-and-a-half to five years.

There is a small secret sign that will tell you whether a mare is in foal or not – a small swirl of hair appears on her flank after four months have passed. If it's a colt foal the swirl of hair rises, if it's a filly, the swirl remains flat. Of course, four months is a long time to wait and any good horseman will know what's going on by then. One earlier method of testing is to put a small quantity of water into the mare's ear. If she's in young she'll shake her head, if she's not she'll shake her whole body.

In working and feeding horses, the horseman should bear one very important fact in mind. No animal, in proportion, has so small a stomach as a horse. The stomach of an ordinary sized man is capable of holding three quarts of water – a horse, in proportion, is as ten to one to a man – yet the stomach of a horse will scarcely hold three gallons, which is just four times the capacity of a man. From this fact we deduce that a horse needs to be fed limited quantities at regular intervals. The great frame and body bulk of a horse demands a great deal of feeding – but not all at once. The proper way to feed a horse is, as we do with pickles, little and often. In the wild the horse was a grazing animal, nibbling, nibbling day and night.

Today, through the day, no horse should go for more than six hours without food. If the animal is over fasted, its health will suffer and its capacity for labour be impaired. Food should be of quality and water made available. A sound horse will work a full day with the labourers in the fields, nine or ten hours, resting and eating with them, but if the horse is working some way from the farm, nosebags should be taken and four pounds of oats mixed with chaff fed to him during one short stoppage. Oats should be bruised and mixed with water. With food a horse will return from a long day in good spirits but trudge home very weary if unfed for eight or ten hours.

In some parts of the north, horses were fed on cooled potatoes and neeps, in a sloppy state without chaff. This can give the horse a sleek and glossy coat but such feeding must be done with care because a great quantity of water in the system puts a strain on the organs of the body. Too much cut chaff-corn can also be a problem causing spasmodic colic, or girshes – the result of the retention of food in the stomach and constipation. Inflammation of the intestines proved fatal to many cart horses. A quart of yeast and a glass of salt water and small quantity of lard was the remedy we used. But the best thing to prevent colic is the free use of bran in the food. One pound of linseed cake eaten each day – will keep a good horse out in the hay!

Although work on the farms was hard, the day of retirement was a sad day for many of the old horsemen. Some had few comforts to look forward to. Work, the land, the horses were all one thing thegether with us and loathe were we to see any one of them going. The death of a horse was always a sad day with us like – like the death of a man.

Noo whinsday is drawin neer
And I mun sun leave ye.
I worked ye baith for mony a yea
– Tae pairt wi ye does grieve me.

Admired by a' when in the yoke
Twa beauties side by side.
There's nane I ken can equall you
In a' the kintryside.

Wi' glossy skin and harness clean
And brasses like the starn!
Not laike some that I ha'e seen
– Bespattered o'er wi' clay.

But noo I'm weary doon the brae
My limbs are stiff and bent.
I've got my leave, I've pu'd my dae
– And I ha'e naithin tae repent.

Jim Aitkin

of PHESDO, KINCARDINESHIRE

It was a crime to leave the marks of your harness on a horse in my day. They were things the horsemen saw – no one else. We groomed our horses three times a day. Everybody did that then – first thing in the morning – then at dinnertime – then again coming home in the evening. You had to put off the wet or the dust, you had to groom out the marks, you had to give them their hay and oats. Dinnertime we always came back to the stable: that ensured the horses got their rest and the men had time to go home to their wives. We had no bothies on our farms, every man had his cottage and most had a family. Every man looked after his own horses, except at the weekends when we did turn about. An acre a day was the average we did with the plough. Six fifteen was start time. You'd feed and water the horses, then come back in for your breakfast. Then you'd groom the horses and go out to the fields and work till twelve thirty. Then it was back again from two o'clock till half past five. You'd be home for your tea at six. About eight o'clock you'd go out to feed and bed the horses down. That was our day, that was our life. Hard days but good days they were.

Every farm had a couple of pigs and one would be killed each year – hung up, salted, put away into barrels. The women would see to the scouring, the washing, the blood and the sausages. We never had food-poisoning in those days – but regulations have put an end to all that, now the E coli's come in, especially up towards Aberdeen. They say they don't cook their carrots long enough, they've become used to convenience foods! Money has turned them to plastic up there, it's all cellophane wrappings and the little fellows

Jim Aitkin of Phesdo with a foal, and with his breeding stallion, Noble Scot, 2000. (TN)

The young Jim Aitkin and his wife, Marjorie Brooks, and a splendid yard of ricks, Tollytoghills farm, Kincardineshire, c.1950. (JA)

thrive like maggots! Things were natural in the old days and a balance established. Now we have the single reality – men and women in white coats! Instructions come, in black and white, through the post. We had the last of the natural order.

Feeding the calves and pigs was women's work, and so were the eggs and the hens; only in busy times would the women go out into the fields – for the hay, the corn harvest, the tatties. The children just joined in – as soon as they could. They liked to work. Milking, too, was women's work. It was just house cows we had – three or four cows with calves and a heifer coming on. It was all hand-milking. It's a beautiful thing to hear the children bringing home the cows. The lowing of the cows, the women's voices; then you'd hear things go quiet as they went into the byre and the milking began – whilst the men worked on, or stabled the horses. My wife Madge was a farmer's daughter and she always had a soft spot for the kye.

Three years was the age at which we broke horses. Spring was the time for the breaking-in. If you knew what you were doing – it didn't take long. We'd often enough be working them the day we broke them. Starting out there'd always be the two of us, one each side of the head. Our first step was to put the unbroken horse into a sleeper, a railway sleeper, or log. Give any good Clydesdale half an hour pulling a weight like that – and he's away for life. The younger horses would have seen the older horses working – they knew the smell and sound of harness, they knew the ropes. Breaking and working horses was natural for us and natural for the horses – they joined the herd by going out to work The secret was in the bringing up of the foals. First they were handled – then they were used. They knew us as they knew their own mothers. No animal responds more to kindness than horses. We'd work them just the morning for the first week; after that they were content to work stride for stride, hour for hour, with the others all their lives.

For generations the Clydesdale has been bred for temperament. You get very few difficult horses these days. The wicked horses, if there ever were such things, have been bred out of the system. In the old days on some farms, if a particular mare was a bad worker, they used to put her aside for breeding. That could lead to large numbers of bad workers. Poor horses would be sold on – and resold – so certain problems were perpetuated. Then, as now, too many people wanted to make money. When a man found he'd been sold a pup he had a problem. Nobody likes to kill a horse. We've never eaten horses in this country – so what do you do with a useless horse? The best horsemen will retrain but retraining is never easy and that's when human cruelty tends to show itself. However, it's my theory, you don't get bad horses, you only get bad horsemen. Kindness is the thing and the good horseman will work with any horse – at least any heavy horse like the Clydesdale.

The thing is – horses can acquire bad habits, like people, and it's very hard to get rid of them once they've been acquired. The way forward is to breed well and teach them young. Any breeder likes to keep a close personal eye on the ancestry of all the horses they breed. I carry all the family trees in my head – I don't need written records. I don't even need to try to remember things; they just plant themselves in my head – it's what I'm interested in, it's the years of experience. Of course, today, there are official computerised records and these are handled by the Clydesdale Society. I've been a member most of my life and I served many years on the committee. It was founded in Glasgow on the last Tuesday of February 1877. Since that day it's the Clydesdale Society that's set the standard for the breed. They keep records of all the main bloodlines, all over the world. They've overseen the development of what we see as the best characteristics of the breed and the standards by which judges, at all the big shows, make their judgements. Nowadays they work with blood groups and DNA analysis – and they need to because there's been a fair bit of jiggery-pokery being attempted. The names and pedigrees of certain horses have been changed just recently and we have had some very acrimonious discussions in the society. The committee consists of three representatives from each of fourteen geographical areas spread across Britain and Ireland – so, as in a parliament, things can get heated. I've stood down from the committee

but stand by the principles of the society, for more than a hundred years it's served a very useful purpose and the Clydesdale, today, is just as honoured in Canada, the United States and Australia as here in Scotland.

All Clydesdales should look 'handsome, weighty and powerful' but you don't want grossness or bulk. What you want is nobility, a certain gaiety of carriage and outlook, quality not quantity. 'No feet, no horse!' That's an old saying about horses and it applies with particular truth to a working horse like the Clydesdale. We expect to see feet 'open and round like a mason's mallet' and 'feathers' on the lower legs are considered a beauty point. We like a silky coat, a white blaze or markings on the face, and four, flour white feet. The pasterns should be long and set at an angle of forty-five degrees from the hoof head to the fetlock joint. The forelegs must be planted well under the shoulders, plumb, and hang straight from the shoulder to the fetlock joint. There should be no openness at the knees nor any tendency for the knees to knock. The hind legs, too, should be planted close together with the points of the hocks turned slightly inwards. The thighs must come well down the hocks and the shanks must be plumb and straight. A good Clydesdale must be 'a close-goer', the gait straight and close – not like a frog, not like a squirrel – but neat and straight through under the horse. For all their weight a good Clydesdale should appear light-stepping.

The head should be noble, broad rather than narrow, with a good space between the eyes. The profile is flat, the muzzle wide, the nostrils large. The eye should be bright and intelligent, the ears big, the neck long and arched, springing obliquely out of the shoulders, and the withers should be high. The back is short and strong – you don't want a dip, a sag or twist. Although the back of a pregnant mare is bound to go down with the weight of the foal. The chest should be strong, the ribs long – sprung like the hoops of a barrel! And you want a good broad britchin, that's the hips. The hindquarters should be long, strong and well muscled. At rest, the horse should look at ease and be naturally well balanced. Before the judges, all horses must both walk and trot. A good horse should move like a ballet dancer. Viewed from behind, at every step, all feet must be lifted clear of the ground: the action must be close and true. Of colours we have the black, the brown, the bay, the roan and the grey. Though, I don't think, there is a grey Clydesdale in Scotland today. When the Clydesdale was finished as a working horse, all the greys went away for export. Now the brown and the bay are the two main colours, the bay being brown with grey hairs coming through. Colour is something that has always been prey to fashion: some people will say a horse has a 'wrong' colour but, in my opinion, if you've got a good horse he's not a wrong colour – whatever colour he is! And, often, something unusual in the colour or placement of colour can be the thing that catches the eye of the judge. There's something of the peacock in both judges and horses.

Jim Aitkin, a champion ploughman from an early age, showing the youngsters how it should be done, 8th January 1949. Grey Clydesdales are now a very rare sight. (JA/People's Journal)

With regard to a stallion – you want him to look like a male. If you have a daughter you wouldn't want her to look like a man. That's what we want with a horse – truth to nature. You look for the difference. In the male you want a good long arched neck. You want power. You want size. You can get females as big as stallions but what you want in the stallion is muscle and bone. They should look like what they are. They like to dominate and their handler needs to know that. In the ring nobody can really judge their fertility but they should look as if they'd enjoy doing the business.

Some of what I've said about judging might sound a bit vague but the Clydesdale Society likes to encourage its judges not to finalise their decisions by any narrow counting up of points but – by a general asssessment of the whole animal as presented that day in the ring. I agree with that. A horse judge needs knowledge and experience but he also needs to trust his instinct, his sense of 'rightness'. Man and horse must work thegither. Judge and horse must come thegither. You know it when you see it – and you mustn't be taken in by false-show or any foreknowledge you might have about a horse's pedigree or owner.

Good presentation will not make a poor horse good but every horse needs a knowledgeable person on the halter if it is to be shown to its full potential. The good judge must have experience and be both a scientist and an artist. He must have knowledge but even more important he must have a natural way with horses. Wisdom is something beyond knowledge but I have no truck with any talk about supernatural power over horses. There's an old wife's tale that the milt from a foal's mouth will give you power over horses. There is such a thing as milt but I've never seen it in a foal's mouth. It's like a wee fat penny of clotted blood and it's hard. It's there in the afterbirth but I just leave it. It must have some role in the life of the foal in the womb but, afterwards, I see it as useless. At one time it was used as a kind of talisman, to attract a horse to the man who carried it, but no modern horseman should need such a thing.

Size in a horse is more important to the North Americans than it is to us over here. I never measure a horse hand over hand. That's not necessary – I know my own height. I'm seventeen hands, so estimation of height is easy for me. I was made to measure – a Clydesdale man. We measure straight up the front leg to the shoulder – that's 'the height of a horse'. The average height of the British Clydesdale has been 17.2 hands for many years but the big driving horses are all now 18 hands. In Canada and the United States they won't take them unless they are 18 hands. You get Clydesdales up to 19 hands but after that, in our opinion, they won't be Clydesdales. The Americans like big horses as they like big everything else, but horses do seem to grow that wee bit bigger over there. Whether that's due to feeding, to weather, to trace elements in the soil and water, or some genetic adaptation to a spacious new

Rolling and planting neeps, Kincardineshire, 1930s. (PP)

environment – I don't know. But, the same thing seems to happen to the people – Africans, Europeans and Asians all seem to grow bigger in America, and fatter. Thinking about that, I can see that, on a smaller scale, something of the same phenomenon happening here. Aberdeenshire was always a great place for breeding horses and in the days when horses were bred to work, people used to go up there from Angus and Perthshire to take them back. And, very often, we used to hear that, after going south, they got bigger; perhaps it was the extra warmth, the richer ground, the lower altitude. Anyway, those farmers used to get bargains, good horses suddenly became good big horses. In a similar way, Aberdeenshire's long been a great place for seed potatoes – there are less aphids and diseases up there, so they breed small, hard, disease-free potatoes and send them away to be grown as food crops further south.

And another thing about size, it doesn't always work north small, south large. Look at the mammoth and the elephant. Of course the mammoth went extinct but the Chillingham Wild White Cattle, down in Northumberland, prove the point well. They are the direct descendants of the wild cattle from prehistoric times and they're known to have been preserved, untouched, within a walled 300-acre park for over 700 years. They're small for a cattle beast but absolutely wild and very fierce. They used to be hunted as sport. That's how they came to be preserved. There's always a king bull, who sires all the calves during his reign and the herd is usually about fifty strong. They're, genetically, rarer than the giant panda. So, after 1967, when foot and mouth disease got within a few miles of the herd and they might all have been destroyed by the law of the land – it was decided that a reserve herd should be founded – in Scotland. Very few people know about this. A cow and calf, some heifers and a young bull were taken away up to Morayshire and they got themselves a new estate at a secret location. Lo and behold the cattle in the new herd started to grow bigger!

What would be the reason for this? It can't be an end to inbreeding because the cattle have been inbreeding for 700 years and the new herd will be at least as inbred as the old. If it's not genetic it must be environmental. Naturally, these cattle were migratory. In Britain they would probably have wandered, summer and winter, between forest pastures in the wetter west and drier east. They might have followed the same routes for thousands of years but they would have been consistently cropping fresh pastures full of the crucial minerals and trace elements on which all animals depend. Permanently enclosed in their Chillingham park, on ground shared with deer, sheep and rabbits, some depletion of those nutrients must have occurred – but the new herd in Scotland graze on virgin land and the animals have prospered in response to the stimulus of their new environment.

Modern science tells us that the blood grouping of the Chillingham cattle is unique in Western Europe. It also confirms what Darwin thought 140 years ago – that these cattle are related to giant European Aurochs painted on the caves walls in Altamira and Lascaux. The shape of the skull and the manner

Fifty years on! Jim Aitkin still ploughing, still guided by his horses, the geldings Sammy and Danny, Blairgowrie, 1999. (JA)

Thatched farm worker's cottage, Kincardineshire, c.1920. (JA)

in which the horns come out from the head is very different to all other domestic cattle in Europe. All other British cattle seem to be descended from the cattle brought in by the Romans. The Auroch breed is known as *bos primogenius* and the Roman cattle as *bos longifrons*. In a letter to the sixth Lord Tankerville, owner of the herd, Darwin wrote:

> The cow's skull is not yet clean enough for final examination but Professor Rutimeyer feels pretty sure that it will prove to belong to the *giagantis primogenis* race (now reduced in size) which was described by Caesar in the forests of Germany and which is now extinct. It is, however, an abundantly found fossil in northern Europe. I think that his lordship will be pleased to hear that you and your ancestors have preserved alive this grand ruminant.

Breeding is an endlessly fascinating subject. The last Aurochs are believed to have died out in the forests of Poland in the sixteenth century and because of that the Wild Cattle here mean something special to the people of Poland. I was hearing about a Polish woman who went to Chillingham, and when she saw these beautiful wild cattle gathered in a clearing surrounded by

Two Wild White British Bulls from the herd at Chillingham, Northumberland. The breed has now been reintroduced to Scotland, 1999. (FN)

birches, oaks and old pine trees – she burst into tears. Here was Poland as it was. Here was the living symbol of Poland seen at the very moment freedom returned to the Polish people after centuries of division and oppression. That herd meant the world to her and you can see why she cried.

I grew up on a farm understanding that life and work with horses was normal. They measured the pace we lived at. They were an integral part of the reality of the life lived, and life for us was work. Horses influenced the character of all people brought up in the country. The horse gave you patience, confidence, knowledge; a horse forces you to think beyond the moment, beyond your own immediate needs. And that has consequences not just with regard to goings on in the stable and the field but in your home and in the village. Give and it shall be given unto you. If you're good to your horse he'll repay you a thousand fold. And, the needs of horses maintained thousands of jobs in the community, in manufacturing and craftsmanship. I would say that horses even stimulated thinking and ideas – poetry, science and technology. Horses bring things out in people. Horse equipment has to be strong and well made. You have to think big and get things right with a horse. People say that a horse is a creature of very limited intelligence but that is not my experience.

A horse can be smart, very smart. We had a mare in foal. Then she got grass sickness. That's a disease that's been endemic in this country since the First World War. We took her down to the Bush, the Veterinary Hospital in Edinburgh. She wouldn't eat and they couldn't get her to eat. Then she foaled and after four days they asked us to bring her home, here, to die. Madge drove the Land Rover. I was in the float, looking after the foal and keeping an eye on the mare – she just sat there in the corner looking very woebegone all the way home. But as soon as Madge turned down into second and hit the rough ground of the Phesdo drive – her lugs went up and she started nicking away. And, she got to her feet. She knew she was home. Whether such behaviour should be described as intelligence or conditioning doesn't matter – it seems to me, that mare showed a remarkable awareness to external circumstances that, in humans, we would describe as intelligence.

It's very easy for a horse to get homesick. We had another mare that we sent away to a stallion and it was decided she should stay over till we were sure the foal had taken. Well she didn't thrive, she didn't eat, she was close to death – and we were asked to go over and we brought her back. As soon as that mare was home again – she throve! All horses have this instinct for home. And the bulk of them are what we call 'home draughted' – out on a journey they know, exactly, the moment you turn for home, the moment when your outward journey has been completed. They prick up their ears, pick up their gait and step out for home. New life comes into them and their responses lifts their master's spirit, too. That response is not conditional on your turning the horse and heading back the way you've come – it happens on circuits that the horse doesn't know. In similar fashion, back in the working days, in the field a horse would always know when 'lousing time' was nigh. They'd be waiting for some distant bell to sound, or watching for the ploughman to take out his watch, or eyeing the knapsack in which they knew your 'piece' was packed.

Yoking and lousing – the two ends of the day. And a good horse was just as keen to be yoked in the morning as she was to be loosed from harness when the day was done. Man and horse would work as one – be as one – like a good husband and wife. Our horses knew Saturday was a half day and Sunday a rest day and, today, if my horses see the back of the float come down, they know at least one of them's going out for a hurl. They like to get out. If they know one of them's set for a day out – they come up to the gate, asking to be caught – no calling needed. I suppose they have easy lives today compared to the old days. You'll know that little poem, 'The Plooman's Week'.

Soor Monday
Cauld Tysday
Cruel Wednesday
Everlasting Thursday
On Friday – will ye n'e get duin!
Sweet Setterday, and the efternoon
Glorious Sunday – rest forever.

I did more than twenty years ploughing with horses and I was in and out of ploughing matches for fifty years. I won a lot of prizes and that of course was down to the horse as well as the man. Every good ploughman will respect the instincts and eyes of his horse. I tell you this, many a horse I had would remember rocks in a field that I'd forgotten. They always ca' canny on hard ground, they have a memory and they seem to have this sixth sense about what lies ahead. They'd never stand on a nest – a peewit or partridge. Whenever they saw a nest with eggs up ahead, they'd stop and wait till the ploughman came up and moved the eggs over a yard. It's speed and machines that have done away with the field birds – as much as monoculture and high intensity planting.

With the demise of the working horse the whole countryside changed. Most of the smiths went to the wall. Some farms had been big enough to employ their own blacksmith fulltime – he'd keep, maybe, eight pairs shod and then be working at the ploughs, implements and tools, making gates, fences, latches. All that saved time and money, a blacksmith could keep a farm mechanically self-sufficient for years, but he went – as did ninety per cent of the farmworkers, the wheelwrights and cart makers. Every parish had its harness maker, they'd make things as you needed them. We've got a very good collection of harnesses and horse brasses here at Phesdo. The boss, Mr Thomson's very keen on all that as well as the horses.

In the day of the horse, men were indispensable – large numbers of men; single men – so a whole way of life grew up around the bothies. The bothy life was the single life, and for many it was a roving life. Men would be fee-ed for six months, then they'd move on. By agreement they might stay, but most chose to move. 'Six months on a farm and a year in a parish', that became the rule for the young men here. It was a kind of apprenticeship – new farms, new bosses, new workmates, new maids, new songs, new pubs, new places – it was a way of life for the single loons and it toughened you up. They were the young males sent away from the herd – to await opportunity. Many didn't go far; they circled around. Gradually most of them would get married and settle down. Some of them would try a spell in the army or go down into the towns but most stuck it out till retirement and they sometimes found it hard to retire.

The bothy life was a way of life that coincided with the great Age of the Horse. It lasted about 130 years, from 1820 to 1950, but its origins must go way back. And with both horses and the bothy life you get a natural boundary at Stonehaven. There were different traditions to the north and to the south. North of Stonehaven, the men lived in the bothy but they ate in the farmhouse. South of Stonehaven the men lived in the bothy and looked after themselves. That was a product of custom and farm organisation. On the smaller farms to the north, the bothies would be close to the farmhouse and the numbers of men small enough to fit into any good farmhouse kitchen. On the bigger farms to the south the number of bothymen was too high to accommodate in any one sitting in a farmer's kitchen and the bothies were usually placed some way away. So, the life of the men north and south was subtly different and many things flowed from the difference.

Of course, the men eating in the farmhouse didn't necessarily eat any better than those looking after themselves in the bothies. Oh no! Very often the opposite was the case. Some of the bothy men looked after themselves very well and some of the men in the north had a gey lean time because even though they ate in the kitchen, they didn't eat at the farmer's table. In many houses there would be three tables – for the farmworkers, the housekeepers, and the farmer's family. There's a story about a man up on Deeside:

> H'd got gey fed up wi' the fud he was gettin. One day he noticed his soup was sae thin he thotch it micht hae bin watter – but for a few bits of fat floating by. He sat fir a moment, then he went across and looket at the housekeeper's soup. He put his nose down close and spied a few peas swimmin aboot – but he said naethin. Then he went over to the fairmers table where he stoppet and looket down at a great big chicken sitting there on a fine big ashette! 'Ah! Here it is!' he said. 'That chicken must must hae just walket through my plate on the way into yours – and come feeing day – Ay'sl be doin just the same – gettin' oot!'

In the south bothies, each man cooked his own. It was oatmeal and tatties – no meat as a rule, that was it. It was the job of the young loon to stop early, get home and light the fire – for the men coming back. In some places, it was the farm wives who did that. And about most things there was a ritual way of doing it. The loon would never dare to wash his face before the foreman. It all came down the line, top to bottom – pecking order. Very important. In those days the lives of the farmers and the men revolved around their work and order made the work easier. It was still quite feudal here. The maids would sleep in the farmhouse and a close eye would be kept on them. The men were kept at a distance. They'd play cards, they'd have their bothy songs and music – accordians and mouth organs. Some had puzzles brought round by the tinkers. The fairs and Highland Games meant a great deal to the men out on the farms – and they liked to take part. They'd go straight from the farms to the Games – throwing the sheaf, putting the shot, throwing the hammer, lifting weights – that was all home from home to them. Some of the bothymen had bikes but through the winter months many would never leave the farm. The bothy was a world unto itself, half barracks, half workhouse, half youth hostel.

Today they're all gone but there are still about 100 registered Clydesdale stallions in Scotland and about 700 mares. These days we bring the mares to the stallion, by float or lorry, but in the old days it was stallions that travelled the road. Stallion-man was a fulltime job. Every district had a local society that organised things and hired a stallion for a season. Each stallion-man would have his circuit and the farmers and horsemen knew when and where he would be. Your mares stay in season for a week, so if you didn't get to the stallion that week, you had to wait another month – then you'd want to make dead sure, or the summer would be past. The stallion-men walked miles and miles. At the start of the seasons the stallions would be fed up and in prime condition. They stabled overnight in traditional places – on the big farms mostly. Up till the time of the Second World War, all this was very well organised all over Scotland, and they were always premium registered stallions – each with a number issued by the Clydesdale Society. The sight of the stallion-man was a sign of the spring. A good stallion needs good feeding but that's not true of the breeding mares – feed to show but not to breed, that's always been my motto.

It takes eleven months for the mare to foal – so you get an annual crop, and a good mare will go on foaling well into her twenties. The speed of delivery is remarkable. It must be to do with evolutionary need; the force of the contractions is exceptional so that neither mare, nor foal, was exposed to predators, like wolves, for longer than necessary. The birth can be over in seconds. What usually happens is this. The mare will lie down for a couple of minutes, get up, turn round and lie down again and – there's the foal! Now, the foal can't stand, immediately, but the mare can and she'll defend it – defend it to the death. Every horseman knows he must be very careful with a mare on

Right and over page: Jim Patterson of Fettercairn prepares to take a mare to Jim Aitkin's stallion, Noble Scot, at Phesdo, 1999. (TN)

the day she foals. First, she comes in with her teeth, then it's up with her front feet – front feet and bared teeth. Ferocious. She's in there between the threat and the foal ready to fight to the death. It's great. But – if the foal is disabled or very sickly – she stands aside to let you treat it, or carry it away. It makes you feel reverential.

On the farms the horses, normally, foaled in April and went away in October. That's when we speient them – weaned them off their mothers – in October. We gave them six months. In nature they'd feed on till their mother's foaled again but in the old days the mares would be needed for the harvest time – so we used to speient in August or September. And, you could see those mares were glad to be back in harness.

Harvest time was the best time of the year. The farms were like villages in those days – everybody was there, from the very old down to the newborn babes, everybody there for the gathering-in. When your piece was brought out to the harvest field everybody stopped and you ate together. There was plenty of food, good crack and, unless the weather was about to turn nasty, there always seemed to be plenty of time. The days were long but they had shape and rhythm – and it was the horses that provided the measure. They aren't machines that batter on regardless, they needed their rest and they needed their food. Because the horses had to be treated right, the people got treated right, and the children learned by what they saw and heard in the fields. They wanted to fit in. The first thing for us, coming home from school, was always feeding the cows. My wife Madge, she was brought up on the next door farm, used to love taking the cows out in the morning – with the larkies singing, the peewits, the curlews. And she liked coming home to see them again. We had a long happy life together – two horses in the one harness from the very beginning. Her people were all good with horses.

My own father was John Aitkin, my mother was Euphemia Davidson. They had eight children, four boys and four girls. The eldest was a girl and I was the second. We had 103 acres, about fifty beef cattle and just a few sheep. We planted oats and a little barley, plus neeps and tatties. We did all our own threshing and took the grain up to the mill at Glenbervie. A bag of oats was a hundredweight and a half. A bag of barley was two hundredweight and a bag of wheat was two and a quarter hundred weight. Why there were those precise weights and the barley and wheat so heavy, I don't know. But farmers wanted the work done and the men were very competitive as well as fit. Nobody liked to be seen not to be carrying their weight. At the mill I've seen men racing up those narrow stairs – as though their lives depended on it. And it wasn't just the weight – those sacks were railway sacks, very strong but very rough. Your hands were hard and used to work but those bags would leave your nails broken and your knuckles sore for days.

After Madge and I got married we went into Tullytoghills farm, to work for Mr Milne, and we stayed there for thirty-nine years. When he died, I worked for his widow and when she died the farm was bought by Mr Thomson who remains my boss today. He had Phesdo House in those days. It was with him that I moved sidewards into horses – fulltime. I started work with horses long after most farms had gone over to tractors, and I continued to work with horses. I did, finally, move over to tractors in 1962 but I still kept one or two horses on – out of loyalty and for the ploughing matches. Since I can mind, I've always been daft about horses. They've always been my chief interest in life. I was still showing horses and going in for ploughing matches in 1979, when Mr Thomson asked me to look after his Clydesdales and become a breeder. That was the kind of offer I couldn't refuse and I was highly delighted to come over here to Phesdo. That was more than twenty years ago. Old horsemen never die – they just keep working away!

My grandfather went into the Mains of Inchbreck in 1912. He

was ploughing champion at Aboyne, for eight years I think it was. He was not the biggest but he was strong and he was well-coordinated. In 1934 my father took a farm by the side of Inverurie. I was seven and I went to the Braes School and I left on 28 May 1940. That was the day of the feeing fair. Our farmworker went away into the army and I came home from school to start the same day. At the age of thirteen I slipped into the job of fulltime horseman and ploughman like a duck into water. Grooming a horse and cleaning harness, even ploughing often enough, never seemed like work to me. You knew the grooming did the horses good. You knew the harness – shining and jingling – gave them pride in themselves. If they saw you taking down their show harness, up their ears would go! They could hardly wait to get out on the road. We took a pride in them and we had a saying, 'a good grooming's as good as a feed'. A horse in a Scotch collar and a man in a Scotch bonnet following the plough – I know few finer sights. Any big gathering of horses, at a sale or at a show, takes me straight back to my father's day, and despite the floats, the loudspeakers, the concrete stances – the feeling of excitement is the same.

The north east corner of Scotland is real horse country. There's nowhere in Britain more like the Russian Steppe. That's where the horse evolved and horsemanship with bridle and stirrup, probably, first developed. Buchan is flat, slow rolling country with a bracing climate that suits horses. When I was young, each October, there was a three-day horse sale in Aberdeen. In fact there were horse sales every fortnight through the year but the big one was October – Katey Brewster Mart. And there were plenty of others. We went to Auchenblae and Porter Fair at Turriff – that's where you got a free glass of

Mares and foals at Phesdo, 2000. (JA)

port for turning up – but the biggest and the best was Aikey Brae, up at Deer. In my father's day there'd be maybe a thousand horses gathered – Clydesdales, Highland Garrons, Traveller ponies and every kind of ware and entertainment. Aikey Fair was centred round the third Wednesday of July – after the hay and the hoeing and before the corn harvest got started. My father bought many a horse at Aikey Brae. When the horses went from the land in the 1960s, Aikey Fair got cancelled but only for a few years, and when it started up again, I was the first Clydesdale judge invited back. Now, I think, it'll go on forever. It's a lovely sloping site and people say the origins of that fair go back to Druid times. Aikey Brae means the hill of the oakwood, and the oak was one of the trees sacred to the earlier peoples and their priests. You can still see a Stone Circle of huge boulders at Parkhouse and on the fairground itself there are mounds and natural terraces that would have provided vantage points from which to watch the processions and ceremonies – and horse races, if they had them.

Which I think they did. There's a story that Hugh Miller, the geologist, stated that the men who raised the stones at Aikey Brae were 'only bearded children'. By which, I think he meant that the early peoples, being without real buildings, like children, set out circles and squares of stones and imagined them to be something much more – palaces and churches …

After the Druids the early Christians made use of the site. In the sixth century the body of St Drostan was removed from the graveyard in Aberdour and reburied at Old Deer. That event gives rise to another theory as to the origin of the name Aikey Brae because St Drostan was the brother to Achaius, or Yochock, king of the Picts. After that, to commemorate St Drostan and Achaius, an annual holiday was held on the brae. The Picts were good horsemen. Carvings on the Pictish Stones show them used for hunting, for travel and war – but never for work. Later on the Abbey of Deer became a prestigious place and the famous 'Book of Deer' was written there. Then, in 1308, Aikey Brae was the site of the battle in which the Comyns, the Earls of Buchan, were finally defeated by King Robert the Bruce. After that Aikey Brae became a place for annual trysts – until 1601 when the Scots parliament passed an Act in favour of William, Earl Marischall which detailed

Jim Aitkin and Noble Scot show their paces at the Perth Stallion Show, 1999. (TN)

> that there be a frie mercat or fair, holden yearly, within the toon of Auld Deir or a little above the same, where unto all his majesties leidges may resort for buyeing or selling of all sorts of merchant commodities whatsoever as shall be brought thereto, and beginning on the first Tuesday of July and to continue all that week over, with tolls and customs, casualties and other dues used and want.

After that Aikey Brae grew bigger and bigger. They say people measured their lives by their attendance at Aikey Brae. There was a man, Old Cairnadaille, who attended ninety-one fairs. Babies would be suckled at their mother's breast on the brae to get them off to a proper start! In the nineteenth century there might be 6,000 head of cattle passing through Aikey Brae Fair. There'd be cloth, wool, boots and shoes, wooden utensils, hornwork, crockery and every kind of tool sold. The Tinkers would be there in force with their horses, tin and haberdashery, their pipes and songs. Every kind of tent would appear and the fair stretched out for a week. There was money there but not everybody had it. There was a story of a man who bought a horse for eighteen shillings. He tendered a pound. The seller said, 'I've got nae change – but ye can tak anither horse for the difference!' The buyer went down the row and was about to take out a big rangy colt from the middle when the seller shouted out, 'Na – ye can tak ony een but that – he hauds up a' the ithers!'

Drovers took the cattle south. Some would go by Windhill to Auchnagatt and some would go by Maud. The goal would be the Cairn o' Mount by way of Savoch; they'd cross the Ythan at Tanglan Ford, go through Tarves and Old Medrum, then across the Dee at Potarch where the cattle swam, or to Banchory and the bridge. When they reached the Cairn o'Mount, a halt would be called and the beasts have a rest whilst they browsed the hill. Then they'd be divided up before moving south to the Scottish markets or down into England – where they'd be fattened for Christmas. It must have been a grand sight on the Mount with thousands of cattle and the whole of Kincardine and Angus spread out below you.

After 1850, with the introduction of the railway, Aikey Brae began to decline as a cattle mart but not as a horse fair and right into my own day Aikey flourished as the biggest public holiday in the north of Scotland. It was very continental, very unsabbatarian – 10,000 people and 6,000 horses would be normal and the thing about Aikey Brae was its isolation. There are no villages nearby, not even a farmhouse – so the noise of the people, the mass of animals, was a minimal nuisance. Aikey Brae in July was the hub of a great wheel attracting people from far and wide – some made a few pennies giving others a hurl in their carts – but for 'the swack' it was the thought of walking fifteen miles and spending a few nights under canvas or under a wagon that was the attraction. And things didn't change much when the trains came in. The drivers used to

Man and masterpiece; Jim Aitkin salutes Ayton Chietain, a classic example of a good Scottish Clydesdale stallion – the product of two hundred years of selective breeding. Ayton Chieftain, however, never won a major championship. (JA)

make unscheduled stops opposite the market stance and deliver Aberdeen to Aikey Brae on the dot. And that reminds me of a story. There was a man called Francie James, 'the Markie'. He came from a one-cow croft out on the hill at Cook King Edward. He was a piper and an athlete well-known at the Highland Games. He was a man who liked to cut a dash and accept a challenge and, when he first saw 'the iron horse come snorting up the valley' he was delighted to accept a challenge to race her! No shalt could out run the Markie! Why would he not best a train! He stripped his top and lined up in the field, level with the front of the engine – then, with a long whistle from the train the two set off together. Francie started deliberately slowly, matching his stride with the pistons – like a gazelle – then, as he closed on the edge of the field, to a huge roar from the fairground crowd, Francie surged ahead and bounded the fence like a deer. Then, looking over his shoulder, he again surged ahead, but, slowly, the train gathered pace and drew relentlessly abreast of the tiring man – then ahead – then out of sight. Tooting its horn! The Markie gave up and returned – to the cheers of the crowd. One of them called out, 'Bate, Francie?' 'Aye,' he replied, 'but gin I'd had her i' the Moss o' Byth, I'se sweer I'd hae gi' her a gey reid face!' And up there, today, I'd back the man every time. The lines are away but the braes still there and the river where Francie ducked his head in the water after the race and rubbed himself down with a towel.

The Fairs and Games gave the farm folk a rare break from their labour and a lot of the bothy songs tell stories of that. We were always happy to have a laugh at ourselves.

O noo I'm tired o' my farming work,
I'm tired of my labour –
I'm gaeing awa doon to the Games
Tae try an toss the caber!

Wi me do dum de, my diddy dum da,
My diddy dum do, dum diddy O.

I gangs doon tae the Games Park
An' the first thing that I see –
Is twenty kilted Hielan' men
A gathered roond a tree!

Wi me do dum de . . .

There were farmers in their Sunday best,
Babbies in their prams
But me just like a muckle fool –
There in my nicky tams!

Then a lassie, she cries oot;
'O Jake,' she cries to me –
'Come show these kilted Hielan' lads
The way tae toss a tree!'

Noo I've been fed on tattie kail
An' I've been fed on brouse –
But how I'm goin' tae toss this tree
O God – he only knows!

So I took twa steps forward
And my banes they gave a crack
And the very next thing that e'er I kent
I was lying on my back!

George Maxwell, horseman and shepherd, Aberargie, Fife. (TN)

Noo I have courted mony a maid
Aroon the barn door –
But to lie and cuddle a big pine tree
I'd never done before.

Tae mak your fortune at the Games,
That's a thing ye cannae do!
So awa ye go you ploomen lads
– Just bide behind yer ploo!

Iain MacInnes

FOREST HORSEMAN, INVERNESS-SHIRE

For six generations our people have been foresters and horsemen here in Strathspey. We came in after the battle of Waterloo. My son would have been the seventh generation. But in all that time – working with axes, saws, heavy timber, horses, carts, steam-mills – we never had a bad accident – and I've never heard tell of a bad accident in the forests here. Just two accidents stick in my mind, one in my father's time and one in my grandfather's. One concerned a horse, the other a man's hand.

It was wintertime, two of my grandfather's men were coming home through the wood, with a cart full-laden with timber. One was the carter and the other was a woodcutter. There was snow on the ground. It was evening time, the moon was up, it was very very cold, no wind. The horse knew his way so the two men were walking behind together, with the carter just half a pace ahead of the woodcutter – who was walking with his big axe in his hand. The logs would have been sticking off the back-end of the cart. Every woodcutter had a big, seven-pound axe for laying-in, and a small axe of one and three quarter pounds: you could put the small axe away in your belt but the big axe you had to keep in your hand. So, feeling the cold coming up through the haft, the woodcutter swung the big axe round, to wedge it in one of the logs on the back of the cart, just as the carter put out his hand to balance himself – on the very same log. The hand went down and the axe came down: all four fingers went into the snow. There was nothing you could do about that in those days. The woodcutter bound the wound with his handkerchief, helped the man up on the cart, and they carried on home. And that man never held a grudge

Unknown Scottish Lumberjills ready to set off for a day in the Speyside forest during the Second World War. (LM)

Iain MacInnes of Carrbridge, Inverness-shire, one of the last forest horsemen in Scotland, 1999. (TN)

against the woodcutter. He accepted that accident was chance, or fate. And, in a way, he felt himself lucky because he was a carter – because he could work as a carter with six fingers but if he'd been a woodcutter his working days would have gone the way of his fingers.

The second accident, I know more about – because I was there and I know what led up to it. I didn't see it, but I heard it. We were working in Strathconon, just after the war. We had a beautiful chestnut Clydesdale, a gelding; Jock was his name. He was one of the best workers we ever had. What a character he was. He had a style of bringing timber down a steep face like no horse I ever heard of. Most horses would need a man to go up a hill beside them – but coming down, all the horses were happy to stride on, alone, and the man could stay safe, out of the way of the timber. Every horse used to work out his own way of doing things – keeping ahead of the drag coming down. That's what we call a load of timber. Those horses were marvellous.

A normal drag would consist of ten or twelve trees – depending on their size. On flat ground everything was easy but many of the hillsides we worked were steep; so steep you had to set the horse well above the timber you wanted to drag – whilst you sorted the chains – because the horse was slipping all the time, slipping down the hill. If you knew your business, you'd be finished by the time he'd slipped by. All we had in those days was two chains and a swingle-tree. So, as soon as the drag was chained and hitched – you'd throw the lead-rope over the neck of the horse and away he'd go. On a fast path, the logs would soon catch up with the horse – and things could get difficult. Most horses took the pressure out sidewards – let the logs swing round in front of them and then holding steady till they slowed to a stop at the bottom of the slope. But Jock, he was strong and he was fit and he was a very high spirited horse, he used to gallop down, ahead of the logs, and spin round at the bottom, and the chains would break free of their own accord – spraying out the logs like fireworks! We used to say that Jock was the master of the galloping-drag. It might have been dangerous because we'd have a steam-mill somewhere close by to saw up the logs. But Jock always knew what he was doing and he knew to keep a safe distance from the lads working the mill. And he also knew how to handle tree stumps – against which a drag might get stuck – he'd pull to the side, try this, try that. Many a time I saw him turn and pull a drag back up the hill – to start again fresh: all that by himself without a word of command. That horse had a mind. If there was a genius horse, it was Jock.

Jock had a partner, a black cob/Clydesdale gelding. His name was Princey and as he grew older he too developed a trick that was quite all his own. Because he was slow and a wee bit stiff in the back legs when Princey saw the drag catching up behind him he used to spread his feet, let the logs through between his legs, then sit down on the back of the drag and peddle away like a big kid on a bogie! We'd always drag the timber down points first, so Princey looked as though he was riding a rocket! Or if the snow was deep he'd look like a girl tobogganing – his mane in the wind like a scarf or long hair! He enjoyed it. He'd hold his hind legs out – up in the air – and peddle away with forelegs! Princey would sledge his way down any suitable slope – in dust, rain or snow. I've seen all that. It was a pity there was nobody about with a camera in those days. Princey could have become a film star – he was a dare-devil but, as far as I know, he never got more than a bruise or a scratch. That was Princey, but it was his mate, Jock, who had the accident and it's a very strange story as to how he came to it.

My father had bought Jock when he was five year old. He would have come off a farm. My father didn't breed horses, he didn't have time for that, but he always enjoyed buying horses. He had a set circuit of farms he bought from but if he was out on the road and he saw a nice horse he used to go in, ask if he could have a look at it and maybe he'd make an offer. He enjoyed the crack, and many a tenant farmer could pay a year's rent from the sale of a good cross-Clydesdale. The crofters and farm people still worked close to subsistence and money in hand made all the difference. He normally bought in horses full grown, six to eight years, so Jock at five was young for us – but from the start Jock was good, the star of the forest. He came in when I was a boy and when the Newfoundlanders were beginning to go home, after the war. That was 1945/46. The Newfoundland men were good with horses and Jock settled in very well with his new master, a man with a lovely, quiet Canadian voice and that horse took to drag work like a duck to water – galloping down through the trees like a hunter – and we all got very fond of Jock.

Well, we were camping in a bothy, working up at Convechie, when Jock's Newfoundlander heard his passage confirmed and went home to Canada. So, my father took on a new man, Angie Robertson, and he gave him Jock because he was the best young horse we had. But the trouble was, Angie Robertson was a very brusque, loud speaker and Jock didn't like that style of speaking. No horse likes a man shouting, a dog barking, angry bangings and bad temper – in the stable or out on the hill. So, those two didn't get on. Angie Robertson would be in grooming Jock and we'd hear a few kicks thumping the stable planks but it was only when my father saw Jock coming out one morning – wild-eyed, unbrushed and ill-kempt – that he knew something was wrong and he asked Angie what the trouble was. Angie claimed the horse was an ill-tempered brute. He said he could never get round the far side to brush him. Well, my father took a hand and he tried to teach Angie gentler ways and he tried to get the two of them together. A fortnight went by. There was no improvement. In fact things got worse. If Jock was in the yard and he just heard Angie's voice his ears would go back – and you knew trouble was brewing. Nothing could be done, so my father put Jock back with the last of the Newfoundlanders and he moved Angie clear of the horses altogether. And a month or two later, Angie got married and left Carrbridge. He went away with his bride to work, down at the Singer sewing machine factory, at Clydebank. He was there for three years. Then he came back, and again he asked for work in the wood. Right or wrong, my father took him on. But, do you know this, as soon as Jock heard that man's voice in the yard – his ears went back and he was stamping! He remembered. But Angie – he'd forgotten, this is God's own honest truth, Angie didn't recognise Jock! Chestnut is the commonest colour for a Clydesdale, and three years is a long time for a five-year-old horse: Jock had filled out and Angie didn't recognise this massive strong horse as the youngster who'd been his old foe. Maybe that was his problem, he was a man with no perception, no sense of judgement whereas Jock had a mind – and memory like a razor.

Well, my father didn't tell Angie Robertson the big Clydesdale was Jock. Why I don't know – maybe he was thinking that three years might have taught Angie something. Maybe, he was thinking that if Angie approached Jock just like any normal horse – if he didn't come forward either defensive or afeared – everything would be all right. Anyway, he was paying the man to work! So, Angie was assigned to work with what he called 'the big chestnut gelding'. For a second time it was fire and water! That man couldn't help but speak like a bad-tempered dog and, after a fortnight, my father decided to work Jock himself and he put Angie Robertson to work at the mill – well away from the horses. However, by that time Jock had become a threat – not just to Angie but to every man in the camp. I remember my father saying, 'I'll have to get rid of that man or get rid of the horse – or one of them, or one of us, is going to get hurt!'

Sometimes I wonder if Jock heard and understood what my father had said. Well, it was a beautiful morning up there in Strathconon and I remember my father taking Jock away up the zig-zag path to start work; to start dragging down the timber. It was very steep ground, and that would have been another reason why my father decided to work Jock himself. Well, I hadn't long started laying-in a big larch tree, when we heard a great crash, a great crashing coming down through the trees. It was Jock. His forefoot had slipped on a wet flat stone and for some reason he didn't fall up the hill, he fell down the hill, and he pitchforked down, somersaulting down through the birches. That horse weighed well over a ton. He came down two hundred feet. I heard his dying cries coming through the trees. He went over a ravine and came to a stop fifty yards from where I stood. His back was broken, his hips, his legs. He was dead when we got to him. Two six inch birches he snapped like twigs. My father was coming down through the trees and when he came up to us the tears were coming down his face. We buried him, up there in Strathconon. It was a big job but there was a certain satisfaction in having to dig so hard a ground to bury him. It was raining by the time we'd finished and my father sent us back to the bothy, and we got a good fire going. And we talked. That was a great horse, that met the wrong man. I always feel a horse knows more than you think. Some people say a horse has no reason at all but I've seen them think ahead, just like we do. And they remember like we do.

I was born in 1929, in Grantown-on-Spey. There were six youngsters in our family. I was the second eldest but my mother used to always say I was the weakling. I used to get extra milk and every day they'd send me out to my granny at milking time and she'd get me to drink as much as I could – warm milk straight from the cow. Nobody worried about pasteurisation in those days. My granny just had a sieve to take out any hairs and muck floating about and that was it. That was the old way and mother always used to say it was the milk pulled me through. This bungalow is new but it stands on the site of my grandmother's house and MacInnes' have lived in here these six generations since Waterloo. The names of the men were James or John, Hamish or Iain. I've got about eleven acres. It's good sheltered ground with the river Dulnain to the north, the viaduct to the west, the pine forest to the south, and a lot of new houses springing up to the east on the Carrbridge side. It's a sun-trap in summer and a frost-bowl in winter.

I went to school in Duthill, up the road there, and I left at fourteen years of age. That was 1943, it was wartime and they needed to get everybody out working as soon as possible. I went in with my father. Since 1815 there was always at least one of our family worked in the Stathspey forests. First they worked as labourers, but for the last three generations we've all been contractors and we always worked horses. I'm out of the wood now but I still work horses,

Overleaf:
Man power, horse power, and steam power sharing the work in the Strathspey forest, c.1920. (LM)

for the visitors up at the Landmark Visitor Centre, and I have a pony trekking business. Thirteen ponies. My father worked Clydedales right up until 1960, then the tractors took over. When I joined my father, my first job was driving Clydesdales. We weren't taught to drive horses, you just got on with it. We'd been brought up amongst horses and we were always out in the woods with my father. He was a great horseman – but he didn't set out to teach anybody, that was the style of it in those days, you learned on the job and you learned by experience, watching the older men. My father was a man of principle and he worked his horses according to a set of principles but none were ever stated. He believed no horse needed a whip. I've seen my father go over and take a whip from a man driving with a whip. He'd say, 'That's not necessary' and that would sometimes be enough to change a man's ways for a lifetime. He was a very gentle man but he knew where he stood, and his men knew. My own style of horsemanship, my own knowledge of horses, comes direct from him. The horse is a wonderful creature. A good horse will work as though it knows your mind. They do what you want before you ask them. They're creatures of habit, they need to be trained but once well trained they don't need much of a clue to get started.

Originally it was oxen that worked in the forests here – as they did on the farms. Oxen were used until quite recently on the Seafield estate. In the nineteenth century, when bigger horses like the Clydesdale began to come into the north a debate was engendered as to which was best and most economical – the ox or the horse. It seems obvious to us today but one thing in favour of the ox was his flavour! You could eat him when he got old or injured. That was never true of horses, not with us here. Also, oxen were less expensive to feed. But, in the end, the horse took over – just as he was replaced by steam engines, petrol and diesel. The horse had a much longer working life, they could do a much wider variety of tasks, they could work on much rougher and more difficult ground. And a big horse is stronger, stronger than any working animal – bar an elephant. Another thing, most men find a horse more companionable than a beast, though there's a lot of people get bitten by horses but very few get bitten by cows! The horse is, naturally, a noble creature; men and women fall in love with horses and they enjoy the process of looking after horses. They become part of your life. I don't think oxen would inspire you in the same way. So there we were – the horse won out and for a hundred years the Clydesdale was king of all heavy work in the forest – till the Caterpillars came in during the Second World War. It was the Canadians who brought them, then the tractors came and the W.D. four-wheel drives – so, after reigning for a century the Clydesdale went down before a tide of technological and managerial change that proved irresistible.

The Strathspey wood contractors all worked for bigger timber merchants. The big firm here was Frank Sime of Inverness. My grandfather worked as a foreman for them for years and years. He worked all his life from

Strathspey foresters, c1890. (LM)

home. A hundred years ago there was so much timber here that nobody needed to travel far to work and the trees were big. By my father's day we were going out to Strathconon, to Connich and elsewhere and we lived out in bothies for weeks – cooking for ourselves, entertaining ourselves with music and songs, puzzles and books. I used to play the mouth organ and I used to sing, even though I didn't have what you'd call a good voice. That was the life I joined at the age of fourteen – a life in the forest, with a horse, two axes and a saw. It was understood that I would join the army at eighteen but the war ended and I stayed on in the wood business. It was good, healthy work. Sometimes I'd be with my horse and sometimes with the woodcutters. We'd lay-in the trees with the big axes, we'd work the crosscut saws in pairs, we'd trim the timber, and I'd get the horses to drag the wood out to the travelling mills – steam-powered saw mills on ten-inch iron wheels. They were pulled from place to place by horses; two, three or four horses according to the terrain. The boiler burned wood and the steam drove a circular saw. Four men would be felling, two men dragging and, usually, just one man working the mill and one man carting the timber away. All our loading was done by sheer muscle power – man and horse. But we used our heads – we'd tie a big log by a chain to the pole on a wagon and the horse would pull it round up the skid onto the wagon – where the men would sort it. The timber was cut into various set lengths – for pit props, sleepers or whatever and then it was carted away to the railway stations. Eight foot six, ten by fives, that was a size I always remember. Eight foot six, twelve by sixes, that was the crossing size.

The first memory I have is of horses pulling carts laden with timber, up the brae here. I was two or three years old. That was a grand sight for a boy. Some went to the railway station, some went to the water mill we had on the river here. There was a dam. The timber would be rolled off the wagons straight into the dam where they floated until they were ready for sawing. This ensured the logs were clean going into the saws and the water wheel powered the saws. Later on Frank Sime built the most up-to-date sawmill in Scotland out at the back of Carrbridge station. Everything was run by electricity, hydro-electric. I was manager there for twenty-five years.

When I was a boy work in the forest started at seven o'clock but long before that the carters would be up, feeding and grooming and getting ready the horses. We always had an hour's break at dinnertime, that was for the horses more than the men, and we had a short break-off, morning and afternoon. We finished at five, five days a week and twelve o'clock on Saturdays. Sunday, with us, was always free of work. Nobody cut wood on a Sunday. And even today I wouldn't chop sticks on Sunday – and you still wont see a man in the wood working a Sunday. But weekdays, the only things that would stop us was heavy snow, very strong winds or pelting rain. My father was good about that. He was free to make up his mind and he did and if things were really bad he'd send us home or if it was just rain he'd say, 'Right boys, lets get an hour in and then away home'. So, we'd work an hour, not minding getting soaked to the skin, then we'd be home to wash and dry out and we'd be free for the afternoon.

We had a pattern to how we used horses. The strongest of the young horses would be put on the wagons. That was the most strenuous job and it was the young horses that had the energy and liked to use it. The best horses, like Jock and Princey, worked on the heavier drags and the old horses worked on the pit props. That was light work. All the pit props went through Frank Sime and although they could be hard taskmasters they always made sure the horses were treated properly. In fact, many a time, I heard it said that that firm treated their horses better than their men. If your horse needed something you'd get it right away, if you needed something for yourself – you'd most likely be sent away with a flea in your ear! That was the way it was. But we all liked to see the horses well-treated, and my father used to have an arrangement whereby, when our horses got old, or needed to convalesce, they were sent up to good grass and shelter at Beauly – sometimes for a fortnight, sometimes for the rest of their lives.

A man had to be fit in the forest in those days and you got very fit, felling all day. The foresters working the machine saws today still work very hard but I don't think they'll be as fit as we were. Unless it was actually raining or snowing, all we wore was our trousers. That would be eight months of the year. Any kind of boots or shoes did us. Today the boys have to wear all this

A steam traction engine showing its power, over good firm ground, Scottish Highlands, c1910. (LM)

protective gear – steel-caps, visors, helmets, padding. They get hot and sweaty and their bodies can't breathe. But we, we'd be out there in the sunshine, unencumbered, we would sweat but our bodies could breathe and the sweat would dry on the skin. When we came home in the summertime, we'd get changed and play football; today the boys come home exhausted, covered in stour. All they can do is slump down and watch television, or go out for a drink. They get dehydrated. The machine increases the speed of felling, by several times, but forestry's become a lonely business, every man keeping up with his relentless machine. A lot of the joys gone out of it. I'd say that.

Often enough we'd have competitions in the wood – competitions in sawing – two against two. That was when your skill in sharpening the saws came in. My father had that down to a T. Through the war, every evening, he sharpened the saws of the lumberjills – they were the landgirls sent into the forests. He had a knack that we tried to imitate. Great strings of sawdust was what you wanted, the longer the better, not a shower of dust. The long strings were proof your saw was sharp. We would have chopping competitions, lifting competitions, we'd make our own cabers. But sawing was the thing and you got to know the characteristics of the different kinds of trees. Each woodman would carry a small bottle of paraffin to douse and clean the blade and every man carried his own wee metal wedge – for when the tree closed down the saw. In felling a tree the first thing you did was the laying-in, which some people call dobe-ing – that was taking the edge off the bark, all round the tree, and cutting in deeper on one side to set the line of the fall. With a larch you needed to cut in a saucer shape to stop the tree splitting as it fell.

I told you we had few accidents but that was because we took things steady; we knew which way a tree would fall and we knew how to make it fall the way we wanted. And we cut very low. Today, speed is the thing they're after and the power-saw men cut high but, in our day, we cut as low as possible – to get the maximum of the best timber. The timber merchants coming round would tell us, 'Two inches at the bottom is worth three yards at the top. Two inches of clearage is more than enough! See it done ... You can't do anything about the tops but make sure you cut low where it counts!' Fifty years ago we'd push down the heather around every tree. Today, they don't do that. Many a time I've seen the timber merchants coming round, trampling the heather, measuring the distance from cut to ground. Many a day we came home with our knuckles skinned because we cut so low – whipping our hands on the roots of heather. That was the traditional way with us – but the Canadians, they had always stood to saw their trees in Canada and that's what they did when they

Below and opposite: Rare photographs of Scottish log-floaters, at work on the river Druie, Inverness-shire, c 1890. (LM)

came here. That was all right in the rush of war but it's not what you want in the longer term. A forest of stumps makes an ugly forest – for years and years. That was the Canadians, not the Newfoundlanders; Canada and Newfoundland were not one country in those days.

Most of us would have our preferred partners, sawing, but very often you just worked with the man beside you. Some men could saw both left and right and some would be one-sided. We all had our own styles and rhythm. It was pulling, not pushing, that was important. We had a lot of Germans with us, prisoners-of-war. There was a big camp at Nethy Bridge and they came out to work in the forests. Some would go back at night but whole gangs would bothy out for weeks on end, no guards, nothing. It's surprising looking back, and every man was paid the same as us – only their money went to the Government, not to the men, and not to my father. It was up at Dalnahaitnach that we were working then, on contracts to Sir James Calder. Dalnahaitnach is the place where wee Hugh MacAndrew took out the Lochaber men with bow and arrows, back in the cattle reiving days, the seventeenth century – but the Germans – they didn't try a thing with us. The only problem they caused was, when they left, their horses all spoke German! They'd used their own language to command the horses and in a few months the words had stuck. We're planning to take them to European Court for change of use and abuse of power! With us, the commands were very simple. *Hi* was right, *Wheescht* was left, *Go on* was go on, and *Whoa* was stop. That was basically all you needed – but a good man with a good horse could do almost anything.

We found a big difference between the older Germans and the younger men. To a man the older fellows were decent, hardworking and they wanted no truck with Hitler at all – but the younger lads were still, what you might call, Hitler fanatics and very often the two groups would be arguing amongst themselves. That shows you the power of education and propaganda. We become what we've seen, we are what we've been taught. But there was no fighting, no trouble at Dalnahaitnach in my time, and in all those years, 1943–6, my father only sent one man back to camp – saying he didn't want to see him again. He was a blond, bone-idle, lazy youngster, very conceited and a very good footballer. We all said he'd play for Germany. He was very good, he played for the village team, for Nethy Bridge. When he went back we never heard of him again but we imagine he became a professional – he was so good. Another man was a butcher, a monstrous giant of a man. Whoever captured him deserved a medal! He had phenomenal strength, he always sawed one-handed and he always worked the big axe, one-handed – but, with us, he was quiet as a lamb. He was one who spoke against Hitler and he was one of those who wrote to my father on his return to Germany. Many of them did. They liked it here. It was better than the Eastern Front. They liked us as much they hated the Russians.

All that was up at Dalnahaitnach. It's all deserted now but in those days one of the last of the old Gaelic-speaking crofters lived there. His name was Duncan Mackintosh. I remember him trying to buy a horse off my father and getting more and more excited – trying to beat the price down – he was pummelling my father's chest saying, 'Come down, come down, come down man, I can't pay that, come down, come down man!' Then he took his bonnet off and he was striking my father with that! I was watching them. And it went on till at last they struck a deal and shook hands. It was good. No harm done. It was just the old style and the two men meant it and they enjoyed it. Duncan was his name. He was very religious, a very severe Free Presbyterian of the old school, as was his wife. They came to Carrbridge on their bikes every Sunday, to the kirk. He was a good man but a wild and very passionate man and when I think of him I think of that song about the blood feud between the Mackintoshes and the Gordons:

Turn Willie Mackintosh, turn I bid ye!
Gin ye burn Auchendoon, Huntly will heid ye!

Hang me, or heid me – that willnae stay me,
I'll burn Auchendoon, or the life lea' me.

And comin' o'er Cairncroon, an' lookin' down man,
I saw Willie Mackintosh burn Auchendoon, man.

Hard times, rough times, good times we had in the forest; we worked very hard but we had time for a break, we had time for a blether, we had the sense to leave a boggy stance of trees till the frost came – and the ground froze solid to let you in. I've seen us stop to watch the deer, we knew where the lairs of the wild cats were. We had our horses. It was the horses ensured we had a full hour at dinnertime. One of the boys would be detailed to get a fire lighted and the billy-can boiling before we stopped work – so a hot cup of tea would be waiting. During the war it was cocoa, because tea was on ration. In the summertime, most men with a horse would take them off to the shows in Grantown and Muir of Ord. The farm boys would be showing pairs but the forest men would always show a single horse. Great gatherings they were – most people knowing each other. And I'd go up to the Wool Sale in Inverness with my father to buy in new horses. We'd send them home by train in special wagons. Horses and steam-engines give a steady pace to your life. To see them there in the sunlight lifted your heart in the morning – sheer beauty and power.

I say that now but, before the war, there were still a lot of bad horses about. The breeding wasn't systematic in those days. There was need for all kinds of different horses and beggars couldn't be choosers. People made do. If you had a horse that kicked, you didn't stand behind him, if he was a biter you kept clear of his head. Very often a bad horse would be sold round and round – until somebody had the will to put him down or the skill to train him properly. The trouble was imprinting – once a horse gets into bad habits it's very difficult to change him. Like Germans it's necessary to get horses when young and train them well. The origin of the word education is Latin and it means 'to lead on' – that's exactly what you need to do with a horse – gently lead on – and then each stage of learning will build, one on another, by repetition. And you have to be clear and you have to be firm and stick to simple principles. For example, my father would never keep a horse that didn't lie down to sleep. We had heavy work to do, so he wanted his horses fresh in the morning. Now, I don't know if if he was right about that because a horse can sleep perfectly well standing – they have this instinctive process whereby, if they drop off into sleep, their legs lock firm. That response must go back to the time when horses were wild and had to be alert for wolves and predators. And they're the reason why a horse always rises on its front feet – doing that a horse can see what's about whilst he's rising. Cattle rise with their back feet first because they don't depend on speed but their horns. A cow rises ready to fight, a horse rises ready to flee.

One strange thing about horses is that although most horses are much bigger than most humans our bodies are quite similar and we get very similar diseases – cancer, heart attacks, influenza; and horses all have different characters, like humans. I have one here that's very, very nosey, he's always pushing in; he's the one that lets you know what's going on in the herd, he's the watchdog – if ever there's a movement down there by the river, or here

Two more-mature lumberjills at work, showing they, too, can do it! (LM)

amongst the pines – he's on the alert. And all the rest of the herd will be wary till he knows what's what and calms down. When he's calm the whole herd is calm. Like people, horses are the product of both their genetic heritage and their learned experience. And I've come to see that some people are good at recognising the nature and needs of a horse and some are not. You need a certain amount of imagination, you have to know the rules and be prepared to work beyond them, always alert to the unexpected. For example, I recently bought a horse from a dealer, something I very rarely do, and it's turned out that this horse didn't like to be shod. Of course, that's natural enough, but we didn't know this horse was difficult in this particular. He came in shoeless but because we trek over a lot of rough ground all our horses need to be shod, so, straight away we got the farrier in. Dylan was the name of the horse. He was fractious but we had no reason to think him determined. I was stood at his head, holding him whilst the smith set to work. Maybe I wasn't concentrating one hundred per cent but that horse, suddenly, swung his head round – and broke my jaw! We had to stop. And that horse still refuses to wear shoes. I decided to get rid of him as soon as I got home from the hospital. I phoned the dealer and he was good, very reasonable. He said, 'Bring him back over, that's OK. You can choose another horse, or have your money back.' Then something happened, just before I was going to take Dylan back, a big German came into the yard – six feet tall, dressed to the nines, jodhpurs and all, and he called out he wanted a big pony to ride!

Now, maybe, I shouldn't have done this – I gave him the shoeless, jaw-breaking pony! I advised him to stick to soft ground. I told him his name was Dylan. He said, 'I hope he's not got an Irish Temper!' 'No, no,' I said, 'he's fine as long as you don't take him down to the smithy – he doesn't like being shod!' 'Good, good,' he said, 'I like to ride Indian style!' And off he went. Four hours later, back he came – splattered with mud, high as a kite, shouting out in loud voice, 'This horse is the best horse I've ever ridden! He goes like wind, steady as a rock!' And he started to sing that song, 'Blowin in the wind/The answer, my friend, is blowin in the wind, the answer is blowin in the wind . . .' Well, I told him, he could have the horse, I'd sell him on the spot. And he would have bought him – for more than the price I paid – except for the fact that he lived in the centre of Cologne. Well, that German made me think again about that horse. My jaw was now mending and I was becoming very fond of Dylan so I asked the vet whether it would be possible to keep that one pony unshod. All the riding ponies have to be shod by law and we get inspected every year and the law can come down like a ton of bricks . . . Our vet here was very helpful, he said, 'Dylan's a fine strong horse, if he wants to be unshod – why not? Horses ran free for a million years before we put iron on their feet! Let's see how things go. As long as he doesn't suffer, I'm for it.' He gave me some stuff, like surgical spirit, to toughen his hooves. So, Dylan was happy, the vet was happy and I was happy. Now, three years later he's one of the best horses I've got. He carries all the Down's Syndrome girls. He's marvellous. He's not worn a shoe since he broke my jaw and we've had no problems at all with his feet. My only problem is the head behind my mended chin!

We never did shoeing ourselves. In the old days we took horses up to the smithy in Carrbridge. When we were out in Strathconon the smith would come up to us on the hill. About every two months he would come. Nowadays all the farriers go round with a van. The forest shoes were the same as the farm shoes. We had special studs for frosty weather, sharps and blunts, to give the horse a grip. Changing seasons, changing times, we always adjusted. We had a black Clydesdale, named Charlie, when we bought our first new International tractor. It ran on TVO, tractor vehicle oil – it's mostly paraffin. Those Internationals were good but they only did four miles an hour – the same as Charlie. Normally the TVO was stored in ex-army Jerry-cans but one day, someone, for some reason, put TVO in a galvanised bucket just like the one used for taking water into the stable. That night, Charlie came in from the forest very tired and very thirsty and there in the yard was his bucket! He went straight over and drank it dry. TVO! Dear, oh dear, we thought he might die. We gave him water and bedded him down and next day he came out – right as rain. A good deal slimmer but right as rain – with a mountain of dung in the stable behind him! Within a week he was gleaming, solid as bull. That horse put on muscle like nobody's business. What happened was this, the paraffin scoured every worm and parasite out of his body and he came away twice the horse. It was an accident, like the invention of penicillin – a miracle cure. The only thing was, that Charlie never drank from another galvanised bucket till the end of his days.

We fed our horse four times a day – early morning, dinnertime, teatime and night-time. In nature a horse will browse all the time, not like a cow that eats till it's full and then lies down to ruminate. The cow's got four stomachs and re-digests its food but not the horse. It's happy eating a little all the time but, of course, it can't eat whilst it's working, so his nature has to be trained – and the promise of food is one reason why the horse becomes dependent and responsive to his master. A good horse will do anything for his master. Recently I lost a horse called Bob. We used to work together up at the Landmark Centre, showing the visitors how the Clydesdale served the foresters in the olden days. He was a great horse, the best horse I ever had – but he got cancer of the tongue and died at just eleven years old. I still miss him because he'd do whatever I wanted before I asked him. It was uncanny, amazing.

When Bob saw me coming, he'd open the gate for me. When I'd put on his collar and bridle and thrown the lead rope over his neck, he'd set off and stand between his chains ready for work. He was always ahead of me. He was the horse I used for my demonstrations when the school children came. And that horse would listen to my introductory remarks just as keenly as the teacher would and as soon as I'd say, 'Now children, I'd like you to follow me down to the logs ...', Bob would be off. Then we'd all follow Bob down and he'd perform every stage of the job to perfection – unasked. Then when he'd pulled the logs back up to the mill, he would shake himself, stand there, and wait for Question Time. The children would then ask me questions – they might ask about Clydesdales, about the forest, about steam-power but most of all they'd ask me about Bob. Life is in the particular. The children loved him, just as I did. And when I paused to say, 'Right now – no more questions?' – meaning we were finished, Bob would lift his head, pause a moment, and walk off to his hay bag. I've seen the children clap him as he went. Spontaneous. Bob was always ahead of the game. In fact he became a star, in a small way, and I used to encourage the children to write letters to Bob, to send drawings and any stories their teachers got them to write. And every painting, story and drawing they did I pinned up on the walls of the stable. That kind of thing drew the children back – and the teachers – to see Bob, and their drawings all around the walls of the stable. Going into the warmth and the dark, with the smell of the hay and the horse coming out warm to meet us, I used to imagine, sometimes, I was taking the children in to see the Child of Bethlehem. It was just imagination but that was what I used to think. And I would be so happy to see them delighted by the mystery of life in the stable – with Bob looking round over his shoulder. So, you'll understand how upset we were when he was put down at just eleven years of age. A beautiful horse.

The Clydesdale is the noblest of all our heavy horse breeds, in my opinion. The Shire is a heavier horse and, on average, he may be another hand at the shoulder but there's something fine about the Clydesdale. Of course, there are plenty of Clydesdale genes in the Shire and plenty of Shire genes in the Clydesdale. However, they are different breeds and my preference is for the Clydesdale. He's got strength but he's more of an athlete – he's nimbler on his feet and better in the hills. The Shire's intelligent but I can't imagine he's got more intelligence than the Clydesdale. The Suffolk Punch is a massive and a very powerful horse but, for me, they are that wee bit ungainly, too much weight in the hams. They seem to be less well-proportioned than the best of the Clydesdales though I was hearing that Lord Clarke, the man who made the television series on the history of civilisation, liked the Suffolk best of all. He thought his sense of form, in sculpture and architecture, was nurtured by his familiarity with the prize Suffolk stallions his father kept. They kept a stable of Suffolks and his father was so proud of them he used to get all his pairs, eight or ten of them, paraded every week after Sunday lunch, before the house, and the whole family would go out to admire and enjoy them. So, when he looked at sculptures he studied them like Suffolk Punches – that's why he liked Michelangelo, Henry Moore and those strapping nude ladies painted by Rubens.

I'll tell you about my son, he would have been the seventh generation of MacInnes working the Strathspey forests. He loved horses and he was a very

good forester, he learned from my father, the same as I did. But, by the time he was growing up, the horse was away. He knew horses but he went off to work with the power-saws. He was strong and he enjoyed that but he was always wanting to get back to the Clydesdales. He had a plan to set up a new small business – working fulltime with Clydesdales out in mountains, in the inaccessible parts where even the four-by-fours would be struggling. Unfortunately, he died at just twenty-six years of age. He took his own life. We knew he had bouts of depression but we didn't know things were so bad. It was myself that found him, outside in the van. He'd hitched up the exhaust and directed it inside through the window. It was a terrible time for us. Nine months later my wife died. Now I'm here on my own. We didn't know. Neither of us knew how bad things were, nor did his doctor. He'd been off work but we thought he was getting better. On the Friday the doctor told him he could start back to work on the Monday but that very evening he went out and took his life. It was a tragedy for us.

After the war there were a lot of outsiders coming through here and one of them came from Fife. My father took him on and gave him a horse to work – a grey, a big Clydesdale. He was a fine high-stepping horse always wanting to be off, wanting to be there before you. He was a proud horse. He had a sense of style but this Fifer was a cruel man with a short temper – two of the worst traits any horseman could have. Of course, my father didn't know this at the time, so he put the two of them together, the big grey and the loon from Fife. Well, the two of them were out in the forest and that man lost his temper. We knew that horse could be difficult – not standing still, setting off before you were ready – but nothing could excuse what that man did; he crashed that horse across the face with an iron-pin from one of the carts – they're big heavy pieces of metal. Of course nothing could hide the injuries that grey suffered and my father sacked him on the spot, drove him out the camp – before the men could get at him. We never saw him again.

The skull of the horse was badly fractured but, do you know this? That horse recovered and within a week he was out working again. Amazing – he was wanting to work and he worked with us all season, still high-stepping, still full of style. But his face never healed and gradually the stink from the bones rotting in his head became too much for the men to bear, nobody could work him. There was no penicillin in those days. There was nothing we could do. He didn't seem to be suffering in himself but my father decided he'd have to send him down to the knacker's yard. He was kept quiet in his stable till the day came, then we bridled him gently and took him out in the yard and he was so pleased to be there in the sun, in the fresh air. He thought he was going back to work and he set off down the road head up, high-stepping – with all the style in the world. Full of energy, full of courage, full of pride to the last. If men behaved like the best of horses I would be more religious than I am. My father used to go to church, up in Carrbridge. But then he stopped going. And he had good reason.

A man had come into the village who wasn't a good man. Before he came here we heard he'd drowned his own dog in a bath. He was another man with a temper. A man on the run. He had a wife and several daughters but the wife was ill and she died of cancer soon after she came in. After that, we learned that that man interfered with each of his daughters, one by one, as they came of age. It was a scandal. Each of the girls left home as soon as they could or they dared but no stop was put to it. In those days that kind of thing was kept entirely quiet just as, today, things have gone to the other extreme. But this man, he was working for us in the timber yard and we gradually began to suspect more and more what was going on. And, all the time this man was going to church, the same church as my father. There he was – his head down in his hands – every Sunday. And that was it, my father couldn't sit praying in a church across the aisle from a man like that – whilst the minister turned a blind eye. There was silence and inaction. His daughters must have been terrified of him. The thing was, that man had come out of the army and he was disabled. Nobody liked the man, even before they knew what he was doing, but all employers had been strongly advised to take the disabled and war wounded and to look after them. He had this ticket which he showed me, a disablement certificate, so we felt obliged to take him on at the mill. He wasn't a young man then and he's long dead now but – he was a monster and I'm very sorry he crossed our path. Somewhere, during the war, he'd got frostbite – in both his hands and both his feet but nobody could excuse him for what he did. Maybe he'd done something very special in the war and the authorities were protecting him – I don't know – but what I do know is that my father stopped going to church because of that man and his shadow is still with us.

There's plenty of memories bring the tears to my eyes but I do have a story that paints a better picture of what mankind can do and should be. And, again, it shows what a great nature and what a great memory the Clydesdale has. There was a man, William Cameron to name, who lived down in Perthshire at the Yetts o' Muckhart. He came out of Lochaber, when he was seven years; that would be back about 1891. His father took a sixty-acre farm. That boy grew up tall and strong and he was a man very fond of Clydesdale. He went away to be a soldier in the Great War and in France he was very badly injured. He used to tell the story, and it was true, of how he came back alive. There were thirty men, terribly wounded, dragged into a hut, after a big attack, way ahead of the front line. All the hopeful cases had been taken back. There was just one English doctor and two Red Cross stretcher-men left standing, so the doctor had to decide which man to take with them, back to their own lines. He went down the hut, speaking to each man who could hear, he told them he'd be back as soon as he could – with help – though he knew all but one of them would die. When he came to Willie Cameron, he asked him how he was. He saw that he was a big strong lad and he nodded to the Red Cross men – this was the man. A bullet had just grazed his forehead but a machine gun burst had gone through his hips. His eyes were a very clear blue and he was the one put onto the stretcher and carried back to our lines. After more than a year in various hospitals he finally got home to Muckhart. Two years passed before he could stand but then, on Hogmanay 1921, he was leaning against a door watching the dancers when, quite suddenly, the urge came on him to dance and he went forward and he danced with a girl called Margaret. Everybody there stopped to watch and when the music stopped they clapped and cheered Willie Cameron to the echo. And then he knew that he'd come through. That was the happiest moment of his life. He bowed to Margaret and he went back to lie down on his bed.

Well, he slowly recovered and went back to work on the farm, on the land where the golf club now is. And that girl went away to Canada but he was writing letters to her and she returned to marry him but the strange thing is, that after just four days, they parted and went their separate ways. Something was wrong. She went back to Canada. He stayed there on the farm in Muckhart. His father died, his brothers went away, here and there over the world, one went to work in Edinburgh, one took a croft in Argyll. First he lived alone with his mother, then he lived alone by himself. The same best suit he bought for his twenty-first birthday he wore to church till he died. He liked the children to come by and speak with him. He went to the kirk and he became an elder; and of course he still had a bullet wound on his forehead and the women in that church spoke against him – about his suit, about how he might wash the soot from his forehead, about how he shouldn't be talking with the children! He was too proud to say that the soot on his forehead was carbide from a German bullet.

All his life his best friends were his horses and he won many prizes at the Kinross Show and once a year he would take the train to Edinburgh to see the big pantomime. He was a man with a very kind heart and when he was finished with a horse on his ground he would send it out to Argyll to his brother – where the soil and work was lighter. He would never sell a horse to the knacker's yard, he'd put it on a train to Argyll. And those horses would work out their last days there in the west. Well, one horse was a special favourite. She was a mare he'd delivered himself as a foal. For fourteen years they worked together, then, when she got to seventeen, she began to find the Muckhart work too hard – so, Willie took her down to Rumbling Bridge and put her away on a train to Argyll and for ten years she worked out there on his brother's croft. Then, when she was no longer worth her keep, this brother wrote to Willie saying what a great servant she had been to them both – but the time had come

to put her down. He was just letting him know. But, when William heard that, he couldn't bear to think of that dear old horse being put down – so, by return of post he wrote to his brother, enclosing a five pound note – to pay for the mare's rail fare home to Rumbling Bridge station. It's long gone now.

Two weeks passed. Then, one evening, there was a message from the stationmaster informing William, the horse had arrived. Willie went down and there she was, peering over the side of a big horse wagon, in a pitiful condition – thin, exhausted, trembling from head to foot. William almost wished he'd never ordered her home but he fed her and watered her. She seemed to know him but maybe she didn't. She came down the slide and the two of them, very slowly, set off up the hill. When they got in sight of the smithy on the brow of the hill, Willie noticed that the mare had quickened her pace and when the Ochils came into view through the trees she stopped – there, where her old farm was laid out before her. She stood and she pricked up her ears, and she gave a little neigh – recognising the fields she had ploughed and harvested so many times. And then she stepped out again – lifting her feet, and her head went up high, her nostrils wide, looking round her. Well, after that, she settled down and she lived on another six years! She lived on till she was thirty-three years of age. That, Willie used to say, was the best thing he ever did – bringing that old horse home.

Left: The observation tower (built with assistance from Iain MacInnes and Paddy) rises above the forest canopy at the Landmark Visitor Centre, Carrbridge, 1990. (LM)

Right: Iain MacInnes feeding two of his favourite trekking ponies, beneath the railway viaduct over the river Dulnain, Carrbridge, 2000. (TN)

Overleaf:
Over two hundred and fifty horses gathered for the 'Cryin' o' the Fair' at the Castle Craigs, Langholm, Dumfries-shire, 1980. (TN)

Part Three

Bordermen

Jock Anderson

of TEVIOTDALEHEAD, HORSE BREAKER
and SHEEP FARMER

I've been breaking horses for forty years but I always think there's one book worth looking at again. It's called *Prof. Beery's Illustrated Course in Horse Training*. What I know, what I've learned, and what he taught me have, over the years, merged into one. To train a horse, properly, you need to work with the horse before it becomes aware of the great strength it has. A horse that knows its strength will use it against you. What you want is a young horse, an unspoilt horse, with no bad habits. It's always best to write on a clean sheet because, as Beery points out, however intelligent a horse is or may seem – no horse has the power of reason. Horses react according to instinct. This instinct is modified and controlled by training. It is up to man to use *his* reason and experience to nurture and control 'the pure instinct of the horse'.

It might seem obvious that all teaching should start with the basics and with repetition but – the obvious is, too often, forgotten. A horse, like all animals, is composed of bone, muscle and nerves. The bones are the framework of the body, the muscles are the motor power. The nerves, with the brain at the centre, are the controlling power. The horse has an unusually superior development of the nervous system; this gives it great control over its bones and muscles. For example, if you strike a horse lightly with a whip you get an immediate response whereas, an elephant, for all his intelligence and massive strength, might not notice anything at all. It's this nervous system that makes the horse special – not size, or strength, or mental capacity. The brain of a horse is extremely small in proportion to the size of its body if compared to the brain-body proportions of a man. Also the convolutions which attest to the brain's development in the higher mammals are almost completely lacking in a horse and the various 'activity centres' within the brain seem to be strangely unconnected. For instance a horse may fear an object seen from a certain angle but be indifferent to it from another angle. An untrained horse can be totally incapable of seeing two different 'impressions' of one object as being one and the same object. This phenomenon springs from the fact that the horse has evolved to see and respond differently with its two eyes. This means that each eye (and both sides of a horse) needs to be separately and individually trained. All lessons and programmes of training must take account of this fact.

The sense of touch is the prime sense used in training horses. Thus – association by touch should precede new knowledge learned by sight or sound. For example, to begin with, the touch of a whip will be the sign for 'go on' but soon the mere motion of the whip will suffice and, finally, a voice command, 'get up', will be all that is required.

The eyes and ears are of fundamental importance in training and understanding a horse. They feed the horse information and, just as important, they feed information to the horseman. Every horseman will watch the eyes and ears of his horse. They invariably show you what the horse intends to do. The ears forward and not stiff indicate content. The ears forward and stiff indicate danger ahead. The ears slightly back but not stiff indicate that the attention of the horse has been drawn to something behind him. If they are back and stiff the horse senses danger behind. The ears turned backward, close to the head and stiff indicate a fighting mood. If events are occurring to the side of the horse, the horse's two ears act independently. The eyes and the muscles of the horse react in essentially similar ways. Hard tense muscles always denote unease, soft pliable muscle show that the horse is relaxed and in your control. No horse is able to 'lie', or dissemble, about these kinds of reactions. With knowledge and control a man can do almost anything with a horse, without such knowledge a horse is an unpredictable and very dangerous animal. In training a horse, absolute attention and concentration is needed. The trainer must be alert to take advantage of all signs of wilfulness and submission – immediately they are indicated. In starting any lesson it is crucial to know what you want to do and how you plan to do it. Go straight to your point without deviation and do one thing at a time.

Because the horse cannot reason, every action by the trainer fixes impressions into the nervous system of his horse. By constant repetition, responses become conditioned habits and normal reactions. This means that if any impression you do not want is repeated – you will be imprinting bad habits. These will be difficult to eradicate. Never affirm or imprint bad habits. The phenomenon of imprinting is hugely important in all animal behaviour but of especial importance to the horse. And it is apparent that the greater the initial

Limeyclough farm, Teviotdalehead, home of Jock Anderson for many years, now farmed by his son. (TN)

resistance you get from a horse, the greater will be the impression made when you gain your point. The new habit being more strongly fixed into the horse's behavioural response by the preceding 'battle'. Because of the resistance offered, once the breakthrough comes, it is overwhelming; like a membrane punctured or a dam breaking. A consequence of this fact is that it is never a good idea to start training a horse under eighteen months of age because its natural resistance is just not great enough – the colt's brain being so pliable that a good habit learned can, at that age, still be modified, or lost, or become a bad habit by lack of subsequent reinforcement. But from any age – never let a colt know that he is as strong as you are. And, never lose your temper with a horse because in losing your reason you place yourself on the same level as the horse – and, strength for strength, most horses will have the advantage over you. And nobody should want to throw a pony about!

We know that my family for five generations have been shepherds and farmers. My great-great-grandfather was John Anderson. He did some droving and he did very well. He was buying cattle at Falkirk Tryst and bringing them south. That would be in the middle of the nineteenth century. Some he might sell in the Borders here but most he would take down into England. In two years he made himself a lot of money and he bought Brodker Hill, that's a big farm of 2,000 acres at the top of the Ettrick valley. He got the farm, 800 sheep – everything, lock, stock and barrel for six hundred pounds, though that was a lot of money in those days. Things went very well for him till his bank collapsed, in Glasgow. Many of the Ettrick men banked over the hill, in Moffat, with this big Glasgow bank and when it went down they went down. Times were hard and my great-grandfather went out onto the hill, as a shepherd. He always wore his plaid, the shepherd's tartan, grey and black check, and he always wore the Eskdalemuir bonnet – that's the wide flat hat we all used to wear. And, I remember his dogs – he always had brown and white dogs, he wouldn't work with the black and white. My grandfather was the same – he was a hill shepherd – a man with a plaid and a dog at his heel. All the old men around us wore the plaid, when I was young. There was man up the valley from us, Dickson was his name, who I never saw wear anything else but his plaid.

I remember my grandfather very well. He was born up at St Mary's Loch but came down to Ettrick in 1909. As a boy he watched the last big droves coming down through the valley, that was before the railways made the drovers redundant. And that's were I was brought up, at Hind, in the Ettrick valley. I stayed there till 1946 when my father got a job at Shuancleuch. That was a good farm in those days but now it's all under water – the reservoir flooded it in the fifties. My first job was by the Leithen Water. I was one of eight shepherds but now that's all away too – under trees, afforestation. My first spring up there by the Leithan Water was very hard, 1947. Snow on the ground from 24 January till 11 April. Later on I worked for MacFarlane at Selkirk, breeding the Blackface rams. It was all sheep with me in those days, not horses. Then I moved on to the Lammermuirs and got married to a shepherd's daughter.

We moved up to Haresnip, in Ettrick, where I was manager for sixteen years. After that I had my twenty-one years at Limeycleuch, working for Sir William Strang Steel. That's when I got into the horses. I got involved in research and development! I found horses a very handy tool for shepherding sheep. I think it's fair to say that I introduced mounted shepherds in the Borders. At least in modern times. I had worked horses on the farms of my boyhood and I'd had a pony, myself, when I was a boy. I can remember my grandfather saying, very clearly, 'Keep that pony away from the sheep!' That was the conventional idea here – keep horses well away from the sheep but, with the numbers of shepherds going down, I began to realise how useful they could be for working the sheep in open country and after I took over at Limeycleuch I started shepherding with ponies, in a serious way. It was an 'advance' that worked very well for thirty years – till the motorised four-wheeled bikes put a dead stop to it. They were a great invention for us and we few 'sheepboys' went the way of the cowboys.

At Limeycleuch I had three shepherds on 5,000 acres, each with a hirsel – that's a certain number of sheep on a certain amount of ground. Each shepherd has his own territory, his own hirsel, and he's responsible for everything that goes on. Our shepherds would, normally, be married men with a family. Each would have a house and a small steading, out on his hirsel. The normal thing was for the shepherd to check his sheep twice a day on the hill. Inspection by horseback took a lot of weight off the shepherd's legs. Of course, any good shepherd would be very fit and the younger ones, at least, would enjoy their rounds on foot but the horses could save time, effort, money – and they brought a special satisfaction all of their own. And for me, working with the hill ponies became not just part of a way of life but also a small business. What I used to do was this – go down into England and buy feral Fell ponies cheap, straight off the hill. You had the markets at Appleby and Wigton, or you could buy privately. Thirty years ago you could buy the best of them for £30 a piece. Fell ponies. That would be October time. They were wild, they'd never been touched. What I looked for was a good strong horse, a well-formed horse. You didn't need to worry about hardihood. They were all tough – it was always a question of the survival of the fittest on the Fells and, even today, there will be two or three hundred of them running wild on the Howgills and round about.

I like the idea of there still being wild horses here in Britain. Of course, there's cruelty and maybe they'll have to be banned, like hunting – but we like to think of them as a reserve pool of unspoiled nature, ready for use if all the clever breeding programmes go wrong. It's nature that always puts the house back in order – and only man is vile! I always enjoy going down to those sales. The Cumberland men and the Westmoreland men had been overseeing those ponies for generations. They let them run wild – because they know how evolution works and they know how to handle those horses. It was a way of life for them – and I became part of it. For many people culture is education and art galleries but for us, culture is what we do with our hands, what we do, make and experience every day of our lives. Don't get me started on the ban on fox hunting or I might become what a good horseman never is – a man whose reason is clouded by passion! But it's difficult for us to understand why what we do should be banned by those who don't. Should bullfighting be banned – and the paintings of Goya and Picasso and Stubbs! It's a nonsense. Hitler banned fox hunting just as he banned the art he didn't like! We fought him for six years.

Still, to get back to Fell ponies – I'd go down to Westmoreland with a lorry and bring back three or four, or maybe a half a dozen. Then I'd break them and train them and send them out to the shepherds. They then each worked one for a year and I kept a pool of spares at the farm. After that, I'd sell them all on as trained riding ponies, and they were excellent. It was a hobby that became a small business with me. I'd buy them for £30, get a year's work out of them and, without being greedy, sell them on for about £130. My children enjoyed them, the shepherds enjoyed them and across the country I had a demand I couldn't satisfy. Horses, of course, are hard work – with feeding,

Jock Anderson riding two of the many wild Fell Ponies he broke to use for shepherding and hunting, c.1980. (Jock)

grooming, saddling and cleaning but, just as the cowboys were sad to see the Old West go, so I was sad when the Fell ponies went from Limeycleuch and the skyline horse was replaced by the bikes.

Our ponies went away to be used by children and the disabled, some went for hunting, some for the Common Ridings, and some got retrained for carriage driving. That's become a big sport. Two of my best black Fell ponies were bought by Prince Philip, Duke of Edinburgh, for his carriage racing team. Sir John Millar came to see me. He's keeper of the Queen's horses at Buckingham Palace. He stayed the whole afternoon and we spent a long evening talking. He was a grand old gentleman – couldn't have been nicer. And before the morning came, we did a deal and those horses have done very well all over the country. In fact I'd say my horses have helped revive interest in the breed – they're very adaptable and just the right size for modern recreational riding.

Most of my ponies stayed here in the Borders but the word, like water gets around, and I got another call from London. A lady, Rosemary Allan, wrote to me from the Diamond Riding Centre for the Disabled, asking me if I could supply a big gentle pony that could carry a bit of weight. You see many of the Down's Syndrome children can be very heavy. So I wrote back to say I'd send down a mare, that I thought would do well, on the understanding that if she didn't come up to scratch, I should be happy for her to come back home. Well, a lorry came up and away went the pony. Within a week she wrote to say the horse was a marvel and would I send down another! Horses give children pleasure and they give children confidence – just as hunting gives adults pleasure, and courage, and – that's why the new puritans want to kill it. The simple, physical lives of horses compliment the physically simplified lives of disabled people. Water finds its level. Over time I sent down two more fine geldings and that whole project throve.

Left: Jock Anderson and Wattie Robinson, two stalwarts of Borders' hunting, await the arrival of the pack, Limeyclough, 1999. (TN)

Below: The sound of the horn! Who says horses don't like hunting? (TN)

The idea of breaking in horses makes some people shudder – some people would like to pass a law banning the breaking of horses – they think life grows on trees! Like an ostrich they think if they put their head into a book of law the world will come out like they want it to be! We're beginning to live in a world cocooned from reality and it's going to get worse. But if you want to work or ride horses – you have to break them and I enjoyed the breaking of horses. I don't apologise and I'm not cruel. Once you know what you're doing the process becomes a fascinating challenge. Everything must proceed one step at a time. I follow Beery very closely but you also learn from experience, you can't help it. You learn to read a horse, to know what's going on in its mind. I've always found sheepdogs difficult to train because I can't read them in the way I can read a horse. Collies have got their own minds, very quick minds and, often enough, they'll decide to do something before you realise they've decided to do it! But – with a horse, I know what it's going to do, or wants to do, before it does it. And the good horseman, knowing what he wants, will always anticipate the situation in hand and counter any inclination a horse has – to go its own way. Some people have a way with dogs, I have a way with horses. A horse will always respond – if you act appropriately, but even the best trained of dogs will, sometimes, think for themselves! Now, whilst I like an independent spirit in a man – and in a good woman – I don't like independently minded dogs going out on the town, or an independently minded horse testing its hooves on the stable door.

Life is too short for flannel here. To make a living in these hills you have to keep your eye on the ball and, as I said before, the eye is a crucial tool in horsemanship. With a young horse for example it is very important that you keep your eye on his eye. It's a strange thing and it must have very ancient evolutionary origins but two engaged lines of sight seem to take on substance – it's as though the two lines of sight are braided together in an invisible rope and, whilst you keep your eye locked on his, that horse will follow you. Even if he's untrained and wild, he'll do that. And doing that you can train the eye of that horse into absolute subordination but – if you go round to the other side of the horse, to the other eye – unless it too has been trained – that eye and that horse does not know you and will be in no way subordinate. You have to train both eyes, both sides of a horse, separately and independently. That seems so simple when you know it! But imagine the mastery the first man who consciously realised that fact must have had! No wonder the first horsemen have been honoured across time and no wonder the horsemen kept such secrets to themselves. I've heard it said that many of the world's great lovers, like Don Juan, Aristotle Onassis and Cleopatra used and controlled similar powers.

So, there I was up at Limeycleuch running a sheep ranch – we were living the life of Texas cowboys in the Roxburgh and Dumfriesshire hills – in the mid-twentieth century. In fact, we've just made things easier and more

Wild Fell ponies with new born foals, on the north Pennine hills above Kirkby Stephen, 2002. The young are protected at the centre of the herd. (TN)

pleasurable, at least, for the likes of me who likes riding horses. And I liked to think we were going back to the old ways: horses have been shaping life here for thousands of years. It's a prehistoric landscape we have in the Borders and I like it. You'll know the poem of Hugh MacDiarmid

> I had the good fortune to live as a boy
> In a world a' columbe and colourde-roy
> As gin I'd had Mars for the land o' mu birth
> Instead o' the earth.
>
> Nae maitter hoo faur I've travelled sinsyne
> The cast o' Dumfriesshire's aye in me like wine;
> And my sangs are gleids o' the candent spirit
> Its sons inherit.

We had 2,000 breeding ewes and about 500 replacements on 5,000 acres. And that number has hardly changed in hundreds of years. Why should it? When Gallahaugh Estates bought Limeycleuch in 1903 the farm carried the same number of sheep that my son carries up there today. Some farms have pushed and pushed up their numbers but we never believed in that.

My principle was 'sustainability'. And as regards the money – in farming, it's not so much how much you spend or put through the bank, it's what you've got left at the end of the day! We did well up at Limeycleuch. It's a place that costs very little to run. We killed our own meat. We let things run. I was paid a salary and I got a commission on the profit that I made. Sir William Strang Steel was my boss but he just let me get on with the business. Now it's his son, Sir Michael, who's the boss but he leaves all the decisions to the men on the ground. All the shepherds were local men in my day, except for one 'quiet yin' who came down from Ayr. He didn't fit into our way of work at all. He was a low countryman and it's my experience that a low countryman doesn't thrive in the hills. You need to be bred to it and to be part of the place. I had two single men but, otherwise, all my shepherds were married men with families. They were Bordermen with Border wives and the children kept the glens alive. The schools laid on a bus service. It was long days they had. In wintertime they never saw their homes in daylight through the week, and it would be rare for them to see their fathers but by the light of lamps or the fireside.

Sheep shearing was still a social event in our time. Everybody went. Now it's a business, a race, with teams shipped in, moving round. That saves the hill men a lot of work but you lose one of the highlights of the year on the farm. Life needs a measure, we liked a marked pattern to the seasons. A hundred sheep a day each and you were happy in the old days. Today, they get through 300. One hundred sheep was work but we had good crack and we finished just the same. You could look across the sheds and see what you had done. You could choose the day – plan with weather you saw coming on. Now everything's booked in a year in advance. But there you are – the population's away from the glens – things change. In the Ettrick valley, from Ettrick brig to the head of the valley, that's eighteen miles, there used to be seventy-four single people when I was a young man. Now there's five and they're well spread in years. You could have a good dance with seventy-four people – and you had the married yins! Some of them could still lift a leg on a Saturday night! With the five up there today – you could hardly make a square, or hold up a bar.

Whilst the school teach all about the Highland Clearances the hills here are being laid bare of people now – my own grandchildren are away, or going. They've done very well at school and, of course, every kind of farming's up against the wall. You'd think the world doesn't eat any more! And farming's full of paperwork. The money's not there and the old satisfactions that made hardship a pleasure are being whittled away. People have their cars but the social life of the glens is a pale imitation of what it was. The television's done its bit. I was never a tele-fan. That flickering black and white screen is a mean little snipe when compared to human companionship. I deliberately keep a very small set so that I don't get seduced too often. I'm retired here in Hawick and my life is quiet. I go out to the accordian clubs and dances, I go to the shows and the Ridings in the summer. My wife died a long time ago now. I've got a girlfriend and we've had a few holidays abroad – I'm catching up on the holidays I never had when we worked year round to keep the nation fed. I still go hunting, I help out at the lambing, I judge sheep.

After my wife died, my son took over Limeycleuch and I moved into the town. I don't want to be a nuisance to anyone. It's a good place I have but Hawick is a town very much in decline. You wouldn't think it would be – an ancient burgh set in a beautiful landscape but the streets are empty – nothing in them but the traffic wardens. All the main industries have been hit by change and recession – farming, weaving, tourism. House prices, I hear, are the lowest in Scotland. We have high unemployment but the Social Work Department is shipping in outsiders to bury the dead! They're very considerate. Not long since they moved a woman down here from Glasgow – an unmarried mother with a bairn, her house was furnished, her lawn was cut, her bushes pruned. They looked after her very properly and that was nice and I wish her well but, in the old days people here looked sideways at what we called a kept woman – nowadays the state keeps an army of women and employs a battalion of social workers to look after them! But as they say, 'things can only get better'. Certainly food is very cheap – the supermarkets here are discounting everything. But down Hawick High Street the shops are dying like flies and, on the hills, the farmers are being cut down like corn. And these supermarkets see to it that most of their workers do less than twenty-two hours a week – so they retain control over their wages and behaviour. Twenty-two hours a week – whilst out on the farms men are doing 120 hours, just to stay solvent. Solvent abuse!

Still, I'm not a grumbler. It's not in my nature. We've had a good life and it's mostly good yet. I was lucky, in my time we still had things under our own independent control. We were self-sufficient. We grew a few oats, potatoes, vegetables and we always had a pig and few cattle beasts. We could go out to the horse fairs or follow the hunt without asking anyone's permission or fear of imprisonment. Ours was the last generation had it both ways – ancient and modern. I've been up to see Dolly the sheep, but the first thing I remember was watching my grandfather setting out with a big flock of sheep for Hawick, all on foot, sixteen miles. That would be 1930 or 1931. It was a two-day drive, sixteen miles; then it was sale day, then he had a fourth day – walking home. We looked forward to sales in those days, it wasn't just a big rush with an Ivor Williams trailer. You'd set out early morning, take your time through the day, pen the sheep for a night at a farm and stay over. Have a talk, have a dram. That was life in the old style; when something was done you did it with style – there was no other way, not for us. Then the lorries came in through the thirties, but the war put a stop to all that and for five years we went back to the old ways – no petrol, no lorries! When I was a lad of twelve or thirteen, many was the time I drove sheep, in the old style, and many was the time I

Overleaf:
A convivial dram as dawn breaks at Limeycleugh. Half an hour later the hunt is ready for the off. (TN)

went down from Hindup to Hawick station and Selkirk station – to drive cattle home. You felt like a king, at one with creation.

The big farms used to employ what they called a droving shepherd – that was his job – to move the flocks from pasture to pasture and to take them away to the trysts. Early in the year he'd be down at the farm for the lambing, the clipping, the marking, the shearing – then he'd be away droving all summer and autumn, taking the flocks to Hawick, Ruthbury, Wooller, all the big marts, even well down into England. He drove from the back, and he'd have just the one dog. No goats to lead the way as they have in Spain and the Alps. They'd wander along at a good natural pace, the sheep browsing then scurrying on. It was always a great sight to me and it's no wonder that so many of the old shepherds here were strong for poetry and song. We used to have the Herds' Suppers. Every valley had one up till the time of the war. That would be wintertime, or early in the New Year, ahead of the Burns Suppers. Speakers and singers would come in. Somebody would propose 'the Farmers', somebody propose 'the Town and Trade', and somebody propose 'the Shepherds'. They were great nights. Now there's only one Herds' Supper still on the go, up at Lauder. The one at Benty dropped away about nine years ago. But even up at Lauder, with shepherds free to come in from all over, it's mostly lorry drivers and council workers these days! Some of them are very good singers but it's not the same if you don't have a big base of working shepherds. The shepherds are a cast all of their own. Arthur Elliott, he's a carpenter from Langholm, he's a very good man for a Shepherd's Supper – he knows James Hogg and all the Border poets. I like Hogg myself. My favourite is, 'When the Kye come Hame'. It's a beautiful song with a beautiful tune but you very rarely hear it these days.

> Come all ye jolly shepherds that whistle through the glen
> I'll tell ye a secret that coachers dinnae ken.
> What is the greatest bliss that any man can name?
> It's tae meet a bonnie lassie when the kye come hame ...

We also had the Shepherds' Meets at the back end of the year. All the shepherds would meet up to exchange any stray sheep they had acquired. There was one on Ben Cheviot and one on the Lammermuirs, there was one between Ettrick and Moffat. There's one that still goes on in Galloway and another up at Barr in Ayrshire. They were big events up till the First World War. I've heard that at many a Meet certain shepherds forgot to take their new-found strays home! They were big gatherings whose origins must go back hundreds of years – like the handfasting. It was a chance for the herds to get together after their months alone on the hill: folk would bring a bottle and something to eat, sort of style.

You see, most of the marches were open in the old days. The practice was that twice a day the shepherds would walk their boundary. Our

Scots Lowland shepherds gather for a big shearing, c. 1900. (From a postcard, TN)

sheep know their own ground, it's a natural instinct for them to stay where they were reared. And the sheep were so well shepherded in those days that, even when they mingled at the tops, they'd come apart at the sight of the shepherd and go down onto their own ground. One whistle and the two flocks would separate. Isn't that a beautiful thing? A beautiful thought. Now – with fences, less shepherding, more other dogs, more strangers on the hill – if the sheep see anybody they scatter in a dozen directions. Sheep might seem stupid but they know enough to sometimes wander back to the Ettrick valley – from Cumberland! I've seen that happen, weeks after a sale.

Another place where they still have a Shepherds' Meet is at Marsdale in the Lake District. First there's the sheep business, then there's the hounds. It's a grand day out and I still go down. It's a party for the countrymen. At night they have a 'tattiepot' and a celebration in one of the hotels. There are some great singers amongst the Cumberland men. A song I always liked was the 'Kielder Hunt', Willie Scott used to sing it. I worked with Willie for many years and I knew his brothers. It was Willie who became the most famous shepherd singer, of his time, in the Borders but there were plenty more. Willie went onto the circuit, but I'd say that each of his brothers was a better singer than he was! Tom was a beautiful singer, and Sandy and Jock were both very good. It just happened that they didn't get taken up on the folk scene. They let their brother go. It's nice to keep a good thing to yourself! And I'll tell you this, one of Willie's well-known songs, 'The lads who were reared amang heather' was a song he got from me. That was a song my mother sang and it was from me Willie heard it first. Then he learned it. I like the old ballads and I like a song to tell a story.

Willie Scott's mother, she was a character! She was the old style, writ large as life. Wife to a shepherd living way out in the wilds, she was tough as old boots. For weeks she had a sore foot. It got so bad, she walked into Hawick to see the doctor. When she took off her shoe the doctor said, 'Mrs Scott, I'm sure that's the blackest foot in Hawick!' 'Och weill doctor,' she said 'you're wrang about that! The other's much blacker! I washed this ane this morning- fir thy e'en alane!' Like her, as a boy, we had no modern conveniences but – we had most that goes to make a good life. At Limeycleuch, the burn always ran beautifully clear and it was full of fish. Now, with so much afforestation on the high ground there's too much nitrogen and not enough oxygen and that pushes the numbers of fish right down. The water still runs very clear but it can't be as pure as it was. It was great for the children to play in. Here in Hawick I still always wash in cold water. It's a habit you get into – it's only when visitors come that I switch on the heat. Gets the blood circulating in the morning. Colonel H. Jones VC – he always took a cold shower in the mornings! Argentine machine-gunners took him out, but here it's not guns that are the problem but bureaucratic hassle – good farming men have been forced to suicide by relentless hassle. 'There's a muckle slippery stain outside every yins door!' I heard my grandfather say that. And I think this new parliament's got a lot to answer for. Its interference in the countryside is driving good men to despair.

My grandfather had poems that used to terrify me as a boy: he got them from a man called Sandy Glendinning. I can't remember any of them now, but for bits of this one:

> Sic a sicht that Samuel saw
> Between the house and Trushie Law –
> A great big dog wi starin' een
> Towin' a coffin on a chain ...

I heard him recite that often enough and it used to make my hair stand on end. He was the friend of the poet, Dalglish, from Potburn farm, Ettrick. Dalglish wrote a good poem about the lambing.

It's four o'clock, the wind blows shrill,
Snaw on the hechts is lyin'.
The muirland shepherds, aff tae to the hills
Wi' crooks and plaids are hi'in'

At ocht oclock they a' return
From amang the bent and heather,
Tired, wet, weary and worn –
'A' things wrang thegither!'

If ony question ye should ask
They look as fierce as Satan!
But soon sad faces they unmask
For they are fond of bacon . . .

Reivers, huntsmen, shepherds, all had their songs. There was plenty of Burns in our house – and we still had what he found in his day. I always enjoyed the 'Twa Dugs' and 'The Jolly Beggars', and my heart still leaps at the sight of the hounds streaming across a hillside. So, whatever happens, I stand with Burns – and I wish the huntsmen well. May no last trump ever sound in these hills.

A fig for those by law protected
        Liberty's a glorious fest
Courts for cowards were erected
        Churches built to please the priest.

What is title, what is treasure,
        What is reputations care?
If we lead a life of pleasure,
        'Tis no matter how or where.

Walter Robinson

LANGHOLM CORNET

Watt, or Wattie, is what they call me, Wattie Robinson. I was born in Langholm in the county of Dumfriesshire, in 1916. I was Cornet of the Langholm Common Riding in 1937 and now, in the year 2000, I'm senior ex-Cornet by a good number of years. My wife, Madge, was Bra' Lass at Galashiels in the same year, 1937. Neither of us was born to wealth but we have both always ridden horses, fished for salmon – loved poetry and song. Since I retired we've lived here, just above the new Borders General Hospital, four miles outside Galashiels. Madge says, if she dies in this house, she knows she'll die in Paradise – she believing that the Scottish Borders are Paradise, the best and most beautiful place on earth, and I wouldn't disagree with her – would I?

I was brought up poor. My father was a sheep-skinner, three days a week. That was all the work he could get for years, in the twenties, but those three days gave us time – for fishing, for shooting, for hunting with hounds. As a boy my first job was looking after the pony Dr Calder had bought for his son, Noel, and looking after the horse I also got the chance to ride. That was me hooked for life. It was 'lend-lease' that first gave me the opportunity of riding the marches around Langholm and it became a habit I couldn't break for seventy years. In fact I rode – till I couldn't mount – except by a hoist! Three years ago I celebrated my diamond jubilee as Langhom Cornet – that's the thing of which I am most proud – to have been Langholm Cornet and upheld the honour of Cornet for sixty-three years. Certain things stick in your memory for ever. I remember accepting the flag, the standard, as though it were yesterday.

Wattie Robertson where, for sixty years he liked to be – on horse, in the open air, amidst his beloved Border hills – on the watch for foxes. (WR)

My father came home on leave in 1917, from France. I was just one year old but I remember his rifle standing there in the hall, in the umbrella stand and I can still see that rifle as clear as I did then. It was a surprise – seeing a gun in the hall and having a man in the house! Before the war my father had served his apprenticeship as a butcher, up in Fife. Coming back to Langholm the only work he could get was in the skin works. Sheepskins. His job was to pull the wool off the skins and class it in the different boxes – wool from the forelegs, tails, shanks – the fine wool off the tummies and the rough wool off the backs – everything was boxed and sent down to the mills. Things were tight. My mother died when I was fourteen year old, just leaving school but I had aunties on my mother's side and on my father's side and I was well looked after. Certainly as far as meat was concerned. I could have eaten any number of skins!

My father was not a horseman. He couldn't afford to be – but he was a fisher. You couldn't take a horse in his day. The day of the reiver was over. So he never got a horse but – you could still take a salmon and he did. The economy was poor in the twenties but the rivers were good. It was eighteen bob for a fishing ticket in those days. That was a lot of money – but it served the whole season. My father took me with him – till I learned the trade. That was the Esk, the Ewes and the Wauchope. Latterly it has been the Tweed that

Wattie Robinson with his proud mum, Langholm, 1925. (WR)

I've fished and looked after. No fisherman can ask for more than a beat on the Tweed. I was custodian of some of the finest salmon waters in the world and, all my life I've hunted – in Paradise! So, I've had a good life.

Leaving school, with my mother dead and having to earn my living – I went into a wee foundry in Langholm as an apprentice engineer and fitter. We did everything, tool-making, welding, fitting, blacksmithing. It was steam provided the power. Then, when I was out of my time, I got a job with Cairds of Langholm. I was engineer to the mill – it was my job to keep everything working. I was there for four years. Then I went up to Burns of Galashiels, where the foreman was a Langholm man, Andy Morrison. They say that God himself was a Langholm man! That's a fact that comes in handy for the Langholm folk but for me, having a Langholm-man as foreman was quite enough! We got on very well and when Andy decided to start up on his own I went with him. For ten years, I was his foreman – all through the Second World War. We travelled the Borders keeping every kind of mechanical and electrical machine in good order. Selkirk, Gala, Earlston – six plants in Galashiels alone. In particular we oversaw all the machine tools. We enjoyed that because it was mostly girls on the lathes. Both the army and the navy asked that we be called up – but we were working seven days a week and in the end it was decided we couldn't be spared from the Home Front.

I remember the war years very clearly – the bailiffs were off! Madge remembers the First War – she's older than I am! From 1914 until 1921 she lived up at Dalnaspittle, on the heights of the Drumochter Pass, on the Perthshire and Inverness-shire border. Her father worked on the railway. There was just her mother, father, two grandparents and herself. And the wind. The first snow of winter fell in September and it was there on the hills till April. Dalwhinnie was the nearest place of human habitation, that was seven miles. No wonder she's put up with me all these years. If they wanted some messages they just stopped the train and climbed into the cab at the summit. There'd be two engines pushing and one pulling. It was never a pound of sugar they bought, Madge says they always came back with a stone. It was never a loaf of bread but six loaves and a bole of meal. No wonder they have to hoist me onto my horse – she's always fed me like Henry the Eighth! For weeks they'd see hardly a soul and the deer would come right down into their garden. They had a deer hound. All they had to do was to let that hound out of a night-time and there'd be a carcass by the wall in the morning. Like a lion that hound would take his prey by the throat, take it down, strangle it and drag it home. Roy was his name. Madge loved that hound. He was much taller than she was and when the family moved down to Springburn in Glasgow the two of them became a famous sight. So much so that they invited taunts and one day Roy thought Madge was about to be attacked by two boys and he went for them. The police were called and there was a big discussion – there was demand

that the hound be put down – and he might have been but for good sense prevailing – and Roy was allowed to live out his natural life. That's what I like to see – nature and common sense having their course. Of course I never saw him but I've heard great stories about Roy – he crossed the ground – and I can see Roy as he was in his prime! A little bit of imagination is all you need, a little pride in the other, a little bit of sensibility – that dog kept the family for years!

A few years back there was an article in *The Sun* about the wild goats of Drumochter. There's a big flock of them up there and Madge wrote in to tell them they were her goats! And that was true. They kept three goats up there by the line – two nannies and a billy. They were their only source of milk and when they left, in 1921, the goats got left behind. They weren't supposed to be left! The whole family went out by buggy, down the line – one of those hand pump-action buggies you see in the black and white comedy films! Well off they set, the buggy heaped up with household goods and Madge sat at the back – with the three goats on tethers behind. That was her job, to trot the goats to Dalwhinnie station. Well, as her father pumped and the buggy began to pick up speed downhill – the goats held back and, after a short battle, Madge lost the war! The goats scarpered off into the sunset and they've been breeding away happily from that day to this. So, when *The Sun* got Madge's letter they sent a reporter up to Dalwhinnie to check out her story – but nobody there remembered the incident! Which was not surprising because Madge is older than the last of their locals! But they just thought she was a silly old woman making things up and they didn't bother to run the story. If only Roy was still here – he'd sort *The Sun* out, no bother!

In 1948 a new job came up at Galafoot and I went for it, Sewerage Works manager. I got the job and it suited me down to the ground. Like machine maintenance, sewerage is a seven-day-a-week job; unlike machines sewerage systems very rarely go wrong. Things turned out very well. I was responsible, year in year out, for Gala sewerage for twenty years – till regionalisation, when I took early retirement. I had three or four men under me and I soon got them gey well trained up! I knew the job and I enjoyed the job. The men knew me and knew when to call me. As manager I had the freedom to choose my free time – and I took it! Why not? I took it when it suited me. I knew the men who had the Gala fishings and I became responsible for the beat. I went shooting, I went hunting and, of course, I've never missed a Common Riding in Langholm – not since the day that I was born.

My mother was a Watson and her mother was an Elliot and it was the Elliots, with the Scotts, who kept the Common Riding tradition going in those days. And there are plenty of Scotts in my ancestry too – so I was brought up to the Common Riding – it's as natural to me as eating and drinking. In Langholm – and I'd say this is also true of Hawick, Selkirk and Gala – the

Wattie Robinson, salmon fisher, coming home from a day on the Tweed, 1940s. (WR)

Common Riding is the heart and soul of the town. It's coloured my life as it colours the town. It is the past and the present and I've no doubt it'll go on when I am dead. I remember my first ride. I was stood at the square pump watching the riders coming by, and I must have been gey dejected looking as Dr Calder came by leading Noel on his pony. And he leaned out and took me by the hand and he said, 'Come on Wattie, you take the reins, I'm not walking another step!' I was nine or ten years old and I walked on. Soon enough, Noel got down and gave me a shot – and I never looked back. Noel could ride but he didn't love horses as I loved horses and he didn't feel the Common Riding as I felt it. He was away at school in Melrose. So that was it, we two went round together – and I was hooked for life. We didn't ride two-back. That's the thing the Tinkers do; if you see two people riding together, especially bareback, you'll know they're Tinkers. Two people on the one horse looks like something from way back – but that's not the way we ride in Langholm. So, either I rode, or Noel rode and I led till we'd crossed the Ewes onto the Castleholm.

Later on, when I started work, I used to plan well ahead. We used to hire horses for the month before Common Riding day because we were getting more and more ride-outs. You needed to be fit and the horse needs to be fit. It was me that proposed the Castle Craigs Club and I was a founder member. Last year there were only two of us left, Kenneth Neill and myself. Now he's gone and I'm the only one left. He was living over at Annan and I would have liked to go to his funeral but he was dead and buried before I knew anything about it. Gala's some distance from Annan but I was disappointed that somebody somewhere didn't let me know. Maybe the youngsters thought he was the last! Maybe the Annan people think me dead or past standing at a

Wattie Robinson, Cornet of the Langholm Common Riding with his Right and Lefthandman and other Common Riding stalwarts, 1937. (WR)

graveside but I was very sorry to miss that last farewell. I went out every year to the Castle Craigs, until ten years ago. It was the mounting that stopped me. The spirit was willing but the legs rebelled. I used to have to get the horse into a hole, or up against a wall or gate – and these things aren't always handy out on the hill.

The Castle Craigs is one of the main stopping points on the riding of the marches. It's a rocky place on the other side of Whita Hill. We 'Cry the Fair' out there as well as in the Market Square and the Castle Craigs Club organises a 'rehearsal' ride out to the rock and organises various other events through the year. And it's great to be able to pay back the town for the good things it's done for me. Every year since I was golden Jubilee Cornet I've filled a greybeard for the Castle Craigs. What I originally did was to send down six bottles of Famous Grouse from Gala. And four bottles went into the greybeard and two went into the pockets of the attendants. That was all right, that's what I intended but then the committee suggested it was best I sent down a cheque. First of all it was fifty pounds they asked then, last year, the request leapt up to one hundred pounds! No wonder God's a Langholm man! He's got it made! It's not the money, it's the principle of the thing – I like the bottles, I like the greybeard, I like to feel things in my hand and between my legs – I don't want a Common Riding of cheques and virtual realities – I like the thing itself! A dram's a dram for a' that!

You'll know the Cryin' o' the Fair? It's John Elliot cries it – standing on the back of a horse in the Market Square:

> Seelance! This is the proclamation of the Langholm Fair and Common Riding – held the day after the Simmer or Lamb Fair in July annually.
>
> Gentlemen – the first thing I'm gain' tae acquaint you wi' are the names of the Portioners Grounds of Langholm, and from whence there services are from –
>
> Now Gentlemen – we'll gang frae the Toun
> An first of a' – the Kil-green we gan roun.
> It's an ancient place where clay is got
> An' it belangs tae us by right an lot.
> Then frae there the Lang-wood we gang throu',
> Where everyane may breckons cut an pu'.
> An last o' a' we tae the moss do steer,
> Tae see gif a' oor marches, they be clear;
> An' when unto the Castle Craigs we come –
> I'll cry the Langholm Fair and then we'll beat the drum.
>
> Now gentlemen – what you've heard this day concerning gaing roond oor marches – it is expected that everyone who has occasion for peats,

> breckons, flacks, stanes or clay, will go out in defence of their property, and they shall hear the Proclamation of the Langholm Fair upon the Castle Craigs.

Later on, when the horsemen have been out to the Castle Craigs, and the parades have been through the town, everyone gathers for the Fair to be cried for a third time:

> Now Gentlemen! We hae gane roun oor hill,
> Sae now I think it right we have oor fill
> O' guid strang punch t'would mak' us a' tae sing –
> Because this day – we hae done a guid thing!
> For gangin' roun oor hill we think nae shame –
> Because frae it oor peats and flacks come hame!
>
> Sae now I will conclude – and sae nae mair
> And gin ye're pleased – I'll cry the Langholm Fair!
>
> Hoys Yes! That's ae time!
> Hoys Yes! That's twae times!!
> Hoys Yes! That's the third and the last time!!!
>
> This is tae gie notice – That there's a Muckle Fair tae be hadden – in the Muckle Toon o' the Langholm, on 15 July, auld style, upon his Grace the Duke of Beuleuch's Merk Land, for the space of eight days an' upwards; an a' land-loupers, an' dub-scoupers, an' gae-by-the-gate swingers that come here to breed hurdums or durdums, huliments or buliments, hagglements or bragglements, or tae molest this Public Fair

– they – shall be taken by order o' the Bailie and Toun Council, an' their lugs be nailed tae the Tron wi' a twelve penny nail! And they shall sit doun on their bare knees an pray – seven times for the King an' thrice for the muckle Laird o' Ralton – an' pay a groat tae me, Jamie Fergusson, Bailie o' the aforesaid Manor – an' I'll away hame an' hae a bannock an' saut herrin' tae me denner by way o' auld style!

Huzza! Huzza! Huzza!

I suppose there are people who won't know what the Langholm Common Riding is, and some of them would like to know. Well, it's simple. Most of the towns of the Scottish Borders have Common Ridings – and Langholm's is the best! The riding of the marches goes back to the days of the border reivers, to the wars with England, and to the assertion of territorial rights by the clans and townspeople. Some of the ridings have always been attached to annual markets or other celebrations. All of them involve horses and riding the marches. They're public events for the whole community. They're not pageants, they're real events, solid historical events. The fair in Langholm dates back to a Royal Charter of 1621 but this official fair was preceded by earlier markets which provided an annual holiday for the local people. Some of those markets seem to have combined the sale of sheep and exchange of women! In Eskdale the annual market was also Handfasting Day, which was a traditional form of marriage. As far as we know couples would meet at the confluence of the White Esk and the Black Esk, that's up to the north of Langholm. They joined hands and married themselves – pledged themselves to each other for a year – renewable. Very modern! Then down they'd come to the Langholm Fair to enjoy themselves. Handfasting must be the remnant of a very ancient custom. The hills to the north of Langholm are claimed be the last abode of Merlin – the wizard responsible for the education of King Arthur. Well, be that as it was – every year on Common Riding Day the people of Langholm re-gather and affirm their loyalty to their native place for another year. People come home from all over, from Canada, Australia, New Zealand, America, Hawick! Once the Common Riding gets into your blood you're finished! The central man is the Cornet. For most of the Cornets – Common Riding Day will be the greatest day of their lives. The Cornet is a young man chosen to represent the town – and it's a big responsibility that no Cornet in Langholm has ever abused. He leads the town out for the riding of the marches.

Assertion of Scottish rights on the border and the assertion of the rights of local people to their common grounds goes back many centuries but the actual statute, recognising Langholm's rights to 'the land that belonged inalienably to the community', only goes back to 1759 when a law was passed by the Court of Session in Edinburgh. That was the time when a great deal of land all over Britain was being enclosed and it became necessary for the town's people to stand against further encroachment by various landlords. After that the people were asked to annually inspect and mark the boundaries of the recognised 'common lands'. The first man to organise and lead the marchers here was the town drummer and fair-crier, Archibald Beattie, and – he did it for fifty years. Even I only just beat him! He dug the sods, rebuilt the cairns, drank from the wells. In those days very few ordinary people would have had a horse – so the marches were beaten on foot.

It was after the end of the Napoleonic Wars that the horses began to play a big part. The Scots Greys had camped out on the Kiln Green, Langholm, on their way north after the battle of Waterloo. It happened to be the night before the Summer Fair – and I think that famous event helped revive the horse-riding traditions of Langholm. Nowadays there will often be more than 300 horses in the town. That's a lot of horses. You get the clatter and thunder of hooves, you get dust, steam, the flash of flints; there's no grander sight for me than the Cornet coming forward with the standard and all the colours stacked up behind him. Cornet was the name given to the lowest rank of commissioned officer in the British Cavalry regiments. The ceremonial colours in Langholm are changed every year – according to the colours of the horse that wins the Epsom Derby – that's because the first Derby was run in 1759, the year Langholm got its rights. Many things about the Common Riding have got some arbitrary origin but in Langholm one thing is certain – everything is very democratic. The Cornet is chosen by popular vote and all events organised by the Common Riding Committee – which is responsible to the people of the town – you have to take account of popular feeling but always we keep a watch. It's very easy for a clique to form and I was thinking, just last year, that some members of that committee would be better out of it – some of them have become anti-democratic, mischief makers. They speak when they shouldn't and they don't speak when they should. So I spoke up against them. They had been trying to get things hammered out behind closed doors – before the committee met. That's not democracy and that's not Langholm. I'm glad to say I was listened to. That was for the second time, I spoke. The first time was a few years back – when a man born in England was elected Cornet – by a large majority of the town's people – afterwards, certain members of the committee came out against him, calling him all kinds of names. They had no damned right to do that! He made a damn good job of it – and as senior ex-Cornet I had a job to do – holding up tradition and the democratic rights of the Langholm people. I spoke up about cliques – and I spoke up about my greybeard – Whisky and Liberty gang thegither!

Betty Chambers (Mrs W. Robinson), Braw Lass at Galashiels 1936, with the Braw Lad, Sydney Goodsir. (WR)

Sometimes there may be five candidates for Cornet, sometimes just one – if people know one young man is likely to be the overwhelming choice. I was defeated on my first attempt in 1936 and I was elected at the

Sydney
Yours Sincerely
Betty Chambe

second. I was twenty-one years old and that, I would suggest, is about the right age. The Cornet is always a youngster and he's always virgin to the task in hand. He has a Righthand Man and a Lefthand Man – them being the Cornets from the previous two years – it's them that guide him, show the new man the ropes. The Cornet is bound to be a good horseman and a local man of good character. Once he's elected, that's early in June, the Cornet will have a full programme of duties. He'll respond to invitations to events in Langholm and abroad – he'll attend Hawick Common Riding, the Selkirk Common Riding, The Bra' lads, Lauder, Jedburgh, in fact cover the whole of the Border country.

In the old days the Cornet was one of the prime fundraisers for the Common Riding – he'd have to go around the pubs with 'a book' collecting money. There will be dances he must attend, his place of work will put on a show, there will be speechifying, singing and dancing. He'll go to the church for the Kirking of the Cornet and he'll lay a wreath at the War Memorial – a wreath of heather he himself has picked, with his Right and Lefthand Man on Whita Hill. The bottom of the hill is the place because it's sheltered but still catches the morning sun. The parents of the Cornet will set up the Banna' Tastin' with barley bannocks set out on a table and whisky provided, old style. It used to be a small affair but the Banna' Tastin' became so popular that it's now become almost a public event. It's held in the British Legion and you expect 300 people. In my day you'd be lucky if the Cornet's house had a piano – today, musicians are queuing up with their instruments and people coming in with speeches written out on sheets of paper! In our day there was nothing like that – it was all from the heart and all for the moment. As far as we know the Banna' Tastin' originated in William Street: there was a woman there whose name was Lieb Ha'. She used to make bannocks and invite the Cornet and his men up for a tasting. Whisky would appear and a good old fashioned jollification ensue. She was an old lady who took this duty onto herself; maybe it was part of an old family tradition that she extended to the Cornet – I don't know, but whatever it was, old Lieb Ha' started something. Elizabeth Hall was her full name. In my day it was Mrs Dunbar of George Street who cooked the bannocks and a great night we had.

The ex-Cornet's Association meets in the Eskdale Hotel on the Summer Fair's Night – the night before the Common Riding. And the tradition was that, at nine o'clock, everyone followed the flute band down the street to the station – to meet the last train and welcome the exiles home. Now there's no train and no station but the tradition continues. Everybody knows what to do. We don't need a master of ceremonies. Out on the hill we have a marshal, that was Alec MacVitie for years, but even he has little to do. Next day, things kick off at five in morning, when the flute band sets out to waken the town and lead everyone out for the Hound Trail. That's a ten-mile hound race and it starts the day. It's a grand sight.

By nine o'clock the horsemen are assembled in the town square. It's the Provost who hands out the standard. 'Hail Shining Morn ...', those are the words I like to hear. The Cornet is instructed to carry the standard – 'aloft aroun' oor marches and, at close of day, to return it to me – unstained and unsullied'. The Cornet and his Right and Lefthand Men all wear a black bowler hat, formal riding clothes, a sash and rosette of the Derby winner and a spray of lily-of-the-valley. The bass drum then sounds three times – slow – the beat is very slow – they copied it for *Mastermind* on television! Then the Langholm Brass and Silver Band leads the procession off for the first of the many parades round the town. The Cornet follows the band and 'the Barley Banna' follows the Cornet. That's the first of the four emblems that play a very important part in the day's events. The Barley Banna is a circular wooden disc on a wooden pole; on the disc is placed a good round barley bannock and a large salt herring – both transfixed by a twelvepenny nail. On the bannock, on each side of the herring, is a letter B. The Barley Banna bounces along at the head of the procession as a symbol of the feudal dues the town paid the baron who first established the annual fair. Later on the Barley Banna is joined by a crown of red and white roses and the giant Langholm Thistle. Finally, they are joined by the spade that digs the boundary sods.

Back in the square, John Elliot 'Cries the Fair' and the Cornet leads the charge up the Kirkwynd, up Mount Hooley and out onto the hills. That for me is the heart of the Common Riding – the horsemen out on the hill. Back in the town the band will be playing 'The Bonnie Wood o' Craigie

Cornet Robinson, toasted with barley bannock, salt herrin' and barley bree, at the well on Whita Hill, 1937. (WR)

The privilege of old age – Senior ex-Cornet Watt Robinson rides ahead of the Cornet on the Castleholm, 1999. (TN)

Lea' and the children will be carrying their heather besoms through the streets to welcome the riders home.

Drums i' the Walligate, pipes i' the air
Come and hear the cryin' o' the Fair

A' as it used to be when I was a loon
On Common Riding day in the Muckle Toon.

The bearer twirls the Bannock and Saut herrin',
The Croon o' Roses through the lift is farin',

The ocht foot thistle wallops on high
In heather besoms all the hills gang by.

Beauty and love that are bobbin there
Syne the breengin' growth that alane I bear

An Scotland following on ahint
For threepenny bits spleet-new from the mint.

Drums i' the Walligate, pipes i' the air
The Wallapin Thistle is ill to bear.

But I'll dance the nicht wi' the stars o'Heaven
In the Mairket place as shairs I'm livin'.

Easy to carry roses or herrin'
And the lave may weel their threepenny bits earn.

D'il the star! It's Jean I'll ha'e
Again as she was on her wedding day.

That's Hugh MacDiarmid, my father knew him. I'm not such a fan myself but MacDiarmid describes the Common Riding very well – except for one thing – he misses out on the horses. And for me the whole ceremony depends on the horses!

My own day as Cornet was a glorious day. The sun shone from morn till night. 1937. That was the last good day before the war. In fact, my year was followed by five wet years. I carried the standard again during the war years because, with so many young men being away and all the restrictions, things got curtailed. But the Ridings went on. Nothing will stop the Langholm Common Riding! It breeds a great comradeship. When I was Cornet it was Dave Bell who used to transport me and my horse out to the other Ridings, at Hawick, Selkirk and Gala. He had a contractor's business and he employed a groom, Robbie Wilson, and we used to ride together. That same year he lost his leg in a motorcycle accident, up on the Galaside but, next year at Hawick, there he was! I can see him now, riding up to the back door of the Crown with his pin-leg sticking out like a sore thumb, his back straight as a die! He saw a boy and called him over. 'Gie us a han' w' the horse,' he said. As Robbie dismounted he spied a tanner, a sixpence, on the step of the back door of the Crown. He picked it up and said, 'My God, this is goin' to be my lucky day!' Well, he rode the marches and afterwards we went away to the races. He had ten pounds in his pocket and he put every penny on the Hawick Cornet to win the big race – at ten to one. Well, that horse came in first and Robbie came up to me with one hundred and ten pounds in his pocket – that was a lot of money in those days; 'Watt,' he said reaching behind him, 'here's ten pounds. And it's not for the book, it's for your own pocket.' All the Cornets kept a book of income and expenses and in my day the Cornet got ten pounds for the year and there was Robbie giving me ten pounds for myself! Then he was away back to Hawick to give the boy who held the horse his share as well.

Most Cornets will tell you that being Cornet is the greatest day of their life. Alex McVitie returned from service in France to be Cornet, in 1919. He used to say, 'to be Cornet gives you an inexplicable feeling, it's very emotional; the handing in of the flag brings tears to your eyes'. All the old timers have their own spot where they stand every year to sing *Auld Lang Syne*. If you turn round – you know they'll be standing there. And if they're not there – you know they're dead. That is always a very moving occasion. In the afternoon there's horse racing, sports, Cumberland wrestling, the fair. In the evening the Cornet leads the dancing with a polka. That's on the Castleholm. Then he rides back at the head of a great procession – for the handing in of the Standard and the last singing of *Auld Lang Syne.*

After the Common Riding, hunting was always the big thing to me. I started when I was a boy. We used to go out on bikes to follow the hunt. It was a way of life for us, the Border way of life. Up before the dawn, out to a meeting place – horses, hounds, the sound of the horn – we were learning the hills, getting to know every earth, every river, every glen. Getting to know our country, the land of our ancestors. We'd meet, have a dram and a very strenuous day. That was our life and now – they're set to ban it. It's a question of liberty to me. A question of tradition and history and culture. We've been hunting these hills for thousands of years. It's not for educated, city people – who our hands have fed and defended for generations – to now tell us, 'stop it, it's cruel!' I'm an old man – passed fighting but not past caring and I hope those who propose to break us will have a fight on their hands.

Foxes here need to be controlled. He who thinks poisons, or gunshot, a more civilised way of controlling foxes, than the beauty, the form, the order of a hunt, must have had their minds and sensibilities crippled by years of poor company and impoverished experience. What happened to Johnny Armstrong may well happen to us – but it won't be right. Before going out to meet his king, Johnny paraded his men on the castleholm in Langholm:

They ran their horses on the Castleholm
They brak their speirs with muckle main,
Ladies lukit frae their loft windows –
God bring oor men weil back again.

That's Walter Scott – a distant relation of mine and what he describes sounds very much like the Common Riding. After that they went up to Carlinrig and thirty of them were hanged. That was James V. He came down to the Borders to impose his order. Johnny was executed but his spirit lives on and his death sparked one of the great ballads of the Borders. And I prophesy this – it'll take more than a few thugs from the anti-hunting brigade and their lily-livered apologists to knock the spirit out of the Border men. They'll want to ban rugger next! We'll take them on. Little do they know. One thing – if they ban fox hunting – the farmers will get rid of all the foxes in their vicinity. The few foxes left will move into the cities and live on the dumps. Is that what the city folk want – miserable, arthritic, disease-ridden foxes scouring their rubbish tips! 'One Law for the Ox and the Ass is Oppression.' That's William Blake – he didn't like it and we won't have it. We'll live free or foxless! We know every earth – we can fill them, destroy them. We don't want to do it but we will. We kept a controlled fox population alive – for the hunt. No hunting, no foxes, it's as simple as that. They can keep them in zoos, and stuff them in museums – but we don't want them here in the country if we can't

Come rain or shine! A proud father and daughter are greeted by enthusiastic supporters in the streets of Langholm, 1962. (WR)

W. MURRAY
BAKERS
ETHERINGTON & MURRA

control them and enjoy them in our way. We've always worked at the balance of nature, we control numbers but we've never sought to exterminate. There's a poetry in hunting of which the callow educated man knows little or nothing. I remember, we once raised a fox at the top of the Cheviots and we ran that fox down a mile and a half. It was getting sore whippet when it came to a field with a chicken shed in it and it leapt up on that roof and lay as still as a stone. Well the hounds came up and they went round that chicken shed and round again and they had no idea where that fox had gone! We had a grandstand view and we enjoyed that scene so much that when we came down I said, 'That's a fox we'll leave for another day! Brains have beaten braun this time.' So we drew the hounds off and went away home. Aye. We still had freedom to choose our actions in those days. Hunting – you usually know how your day will start but rare is the man who knows how it would end. That's where the poetry comes in. Hunting as a process is an imitation of existence – and we would ban it!

I remember an earth up at Borthwick, on what was Tom Scott's ground, where we never went and failed to find a fox. We never dug it. We had a hole at the back of the earth, which we covered with a stone. All we had to do was roll back the stone and put in a terrier and out the fox would come at the front. We had some marvellous runs with those foxes; strong, big, healthy foxes, and many of them would end up in an old badger set at Milcinton Bank – undiggable – with a drystane dyke on top and a steep fall away to the river. It was a great place for a chase and more than once, up there, it was my horse that saved my life – digging in his heels as we came to a wall – he seeing a fall ahead that I – in the heat of the chase – had forgotten. A good horse acts as his rider's brain in the chase.

Three or four days a year I still watch the hunt from my window here. There's a big badger set up in the nick of that field. I watch the hounds come down and the fox bolt out at the bottom. They usually follow just the same track – across the flat field, then into the Asylum glen, then away out to the Eildon Hills. It's not brute force and ignorance. It's not cruelty – it's like a game of chess – with the huntsman and the hounds engaged in a game of wits with the fox. You play your hand and he plays his. There's knowledge in it, there's art in it and there's a certain level of science. Weather and terrain have a big influence on the scent left by the fox. On a good scenting day, a fox will rarely outrun hounds for more than two miles but on a poor scenting day a strong fox will run on for five or ten miles – the hounds losing and finding the scent, retracking and running on. A hard wind will lift a scent. In the hollows the hounds will run well where the scent stays down. On the tops they'll just throw up their noses and gasp for scent – like drowning men gasping for air. Then, it's the huntsman's job to draw them back and cast them forward – to find the line. It's the right cold days you get the hard wind. A dampness is good for a scent and, if you're on soft ground, frost is the best of all. Frost holds the scent at nose height for the hounds and a good frost gives the horses that firmness they need. A hard frost is almost perfect for hunting – but frost is a killer if you're caught on the sidlings – if you suddenly find yourself crossing a steep scree-covered slope – because on the sidlings man and horse can find themselves going down very hard – you must either stop and climb up or go down. For any rider to go on – sidling across a mountainside – is foolhardy madness. But I've seen it.

There's a long history and an etiquette to hunting. In hunting, everything is done with the horn. You must learn to recognise the notes of the horn – just as the hounds do. There's the gathering of the hounds, the going away, the death. All that's there on the horn. There's not much speaking goes on. Hunting's not a matter of talking, shouting and holla-ing. The hounds will be 'whooped' over a wall, the huntsman will toot to encourage them. If a fox gets up in the open, the whips may holla to get everyone going but all in all hunting has decorum. The style is the man. The rules are few but important and there is a hierarchy; there's the master of hounds, the huntsman, the whips and a field marshal to control the riders and followers. That's where the name Field Marshal comes from. It's understood that all followers keep back behind the pack – you also keep off young grass – moving up by the head-rig, up against the wall or the hedge ... The master of hounds is the supreme commander but it's the huntsman who is in charge of the hounds and all the

Tired but deeply content – Watt Robinson and Joe Donaldson, listen to the singing of Auld Lang Syne in the market square, Langholm, midday, 1980. (TN)

particulars of any day's hunting. The whips will usually be kennelmen. Whoever they are, they will be men who know the hounds, individually; they'll also know the country and all the processes of hunting. With a big ancient hunt, like the Buccleuchs, everything is well organised and professional but there are also plenty of small packs, farm packs. We set up our own pack, the Borthwick Water. People like to make out that hunting's a sport for toffs alone but, in reality, hunting touches and interests many people of different kinds.

It was Alec Baldry who was our huntsman at the Borthwick Water. He was contractor, he was digging drains all over the Borders and – he liked hunting. He knew the hills like the back of his hand. He worked for the farmers – but he found it the devil's own job to ever get any money out of them! So to ease his frustrations he took up hunting. To start with he had a bit of luck, he won a sweepstake which allowed him, and his friend Desperate Dan, to buy horses. We soon discovered he was very, very good – and we set up our own pack. It was like a cooperative. Because I was both a horseman and a blacksmith I used to break and shoe the horses we used. The farmers round about used to give us hay and corn at cheap prices. I don't think anybody, ever, paid a subscription at the Borthwick, certainly I didn't. Meat for the hounds would come in from all over. We raised money at dances, we had sweepstakes – and many a great day we had with that pack. The farmers became very keen to invite us – they knew we killed foxes. And they liked to come out with us – they began to hope Alec would forget about the money they owed. Some neck! But Alec was a terrier and very right he was! I'm a good judge of huntsmen and I would say that Alec Baldry was a great huntsman, one of the very best. The only mystery was – where he came from. His mother's husband was a herd, but the whisper was – it was the farmer, not the herd, who saw Alec into the world. When a herd's out with his flock on the hill, nobody can be certain what's going on in the stable! Some people even suggested Alec's father was an angel! He even had a good laugh about it himself! No huntsman is afeared of the truth – but, whatever his origin, Alec Baldry was a great man of the Borders – he was our John Peel – and with Alec we hunted from the top of Borthwick right across Eskdale and up to the top of Ettrick Penn. The other side – we left to the Liddesdale Hunt. We never went out on to their ground – unless, of course, a fox took us on. Each pack has its own country but nobody stops if your fox crosses the border! However, if the fox goes to ground, abroad, you don't dig on another hunt's turf. You can put a terrier down but don't dig. Draw the hounds off, go back to your own. Etiquette and tradition are full of respect for your neighbour.

The Borthwick was a great wee pack – and I stayed with Alec Baldry until the day he was killed. He was killed by one of his own caterpillars – a caterpillar tractor. He was in wellington boots, greasing underneath. It must have come off its blocks and it crushed him to death. He had been our huntsman

Walter Robinson at Carlanrigg beside the memorial to the Border's hero, Johnny Armstrong of Gilnockie, 2000. (TN)

for years. He'd never asked or expected to be paid. He did it for love of the hunting life but when he went there was nobody to replace him – nobody would take the job on unpaid. He had this dedicated spirit and there was no one with the time, or will, or the money to carry on what he had started – so the Borthwick Water pack was disbanded and that was that. Now we're down to the traditional packs – the Buccleuch and the Liddesdale but I'm very keen that the sound of the hunting horn will echo here long after my bones are dust.

O Scotia! My dear, my native soil!
  For whom my warmest wish to Heaven is sent!
Long may thy hardy sons of rustic toil
  Be blest with health, and peace, and sweet content!
From luxury's contagion, weak and vile!
  Then, howe'er crowns and coronets be rent,
A virtuous population may rise the while,
  And stand a wall of fire around their much-lov'd Isle.

That's Robert Burns. He cared for the partridge and the man, the fox and the hounds.

Arthur Elliot and Adam Murray, the Blind Bard

My father stood on a horse for forty years. When I tell folk that, they don't believe me, or they think I'm up the pole – like Simon Stilities! But it's true, my father stood on a horse, every year, for forty years – and his father before him. Walter Elliot. And my brother, John, he's now done it thirty years. When he steps down, it'll be his son who takes over. That'll be, as we say, one small step for him but one enormous step for mankind!

You'll know that Neil Armstrong, the first man on the moon, was a Langholm man – at least a man of Langholm descent:

Armstrongs and Elliots you know where they were bred
Above the dancing mountain burns among the misty scaurs
And in their veins, the Border lads, the reiving blood runs strong
The blood that's up before the dawn and home behind the stars!

Few people would call me a horseman but I've ridden plenty and so did my ancestors. Riding and standing on horses is a heritable right with us! Almost I should say! Because Langholm is a very democratic place and we Elliots could be voted down off that horse any time. Clan Elliot have been in the thick of Border life for centuries and now we 'Cry the Langholm Fair'. By tradition that's done from the back of a horse. I used to hold the head, or sit in the saddle with my father behind. Now it's my brother – he's got a voice would waken the dead! That's what you need as a Fair Cryer.

I'm a carpenter and joiner to trade, just retired, and twice the age my greatest predecessor was when he was crucified. Christ the carpenter, Christ the Palestinian Jew from Nazareth. I don't compare myself to Him,

The Langholm Cornet thunders up the Castle Wynd, 1999. (TN)

Dawn, 1980, Arthur Elliot sets out with the flute band, to rouse the sleeping citizens of Langholm, Common Riding Day 1980. (TN)

otherwise than by occupation, but I think religion's got a lot to answer for – here and all over the world. I've hung a thousand doors and put the roofs on hundreds of houses but – having reached retirement, I'm going to enjoy myself. Despite my arthritis. Poetry, fishing, shooting these are the things that I really enjoy – and hunting too, though you have to look over your shoulder to say something like that these days. Some people love money and the power it brings, some people love comfort and woolly socks, some people thrill to the rise of their stocks and shares and the escape this provides from themselves: I love the cold of a good Borders morning and the thought of being all day in the hills, going down to a dark pool to fish, with the half light filtering in through the trees. Guddling trout I've felt very close to God, but war – in the name of religion, or ethics, that's beyond me.

Who is God? What is civilisation? I don't think those people who would ban hunting are any more civilised than we are? We don't want hunting introduced to the suburbs of Edinburgh, nor do we seek to ban the Theatre of Cruelty, or Body Artists and self-mutilators! No, but we do think that hunting, down here in the hills, is acceptable. Hundreds of thousands of abortions each year are perfectly legal but for chasing a stinking fox – we'll be locked up in prison. Man's inhumanity to man knows no bounds but hunting foxes will be ended! We don't declare war on the 'uncivilised' things that go on in the towns – why should the townsfolk terminate what we've done for thousands of years! I hope they'll find they've bitten off more than they can chew! We'll send them homeward – to think again!

Our Elliots come from Copshawholm, that's right on the English border. The place has been called Newcastleton since Cromwellian times but the older name is Copshawholm and we Elliots still call it Copshawholm. Might this too become an imprisonable offence? It was my great grandfather who moved north to Langholm, to work in the textile mills and by my father's time we were dyed-in-the-wool Langholmites. He started out as a textile worker but went into journalism. Our family is related to the Grieves, who produced the poet, Hugh MacDiarmid. His real name was Christopher Murray Grieve. My father knew him well. Neither man would have any truck with sentimental tosh or social pretension. They were for the rights of the common man. They would challenge God himself let alone established law! MacDiarmid wrote a poem about meeting God – on the Copshaw road!

He said that he was God.
'We are well met,' I cried,
'I've always hoped I should
Meet God before I died.'

I slew him then and cast
His corpse into a pool,
– But how I wish he had
Indeed been God, the fool!

I think that's great. It's a real meeting, between a modern mind and an ancient, archetypal myth – the idea of God as being a man. The very

The Langholm flute band leads the way up to Whitaside for the Hound Trail at 6.00 am, 1980. (TN)

idea! How feeble can God get! He didn't create us – we created him! He is the summation of our best hopes, no more.

Dumfriess-shire is a strange and chivalrous place. Cornwall claims King Arthur, as does Wales, Somerset and Carlisle but – we have a good claim here in Dumfriess-shire, a pre-eminent claim. At least Arthur, whoever he was, was flesh and blood and it's not chance that I was named Arthur. Merlin was, certainly, a Dumfriess-shire man. Our family is full of Arthurs. John and Christopher are the other names that keep reappearing. We follow King Arthur. We've fought for king and country across the generations and – we like hunting. We can't help it! My middle name is Nicol; that name comes like an intrusion in our family history but it's a name I'm proud to carry. It came to me from a dead uncle. A Langholm man who went out to South Africa after the Great War. He joined, then left, the South African police and was murdered.

What'll happen to me is still not clear, but what happened to Nicol seems clear enough. He was a soldier of the Great War, in France. When he came back to Langholm there was no work – and most of the good hunting land had already been taken by the Duke of Buccleuch! So Nicol emigrated. He spent some years in the South African police, then decided to branch out as a cattle dealer. He went out onto the veldt, with a lot of money on him – ready to start dealing – and he never returned. The story came back that he accidentally shot himself with his own gun! We have no doubt that all talk of an accident was part of some wider ploy and cover up. Nicol was a crack-shot with a gun, he'd spent years in France as an infantryman. He'd cleaned his rifle, in the mud of Flanders, hundreds of times and they told us he'd left his gun against a door, ajar! The wind blew, the gun slipped and he was shot through the head! I don't believe it, though Nicol could be cantankerous. He sometimes invited trouble. He was a brilliant horseman but he could be cocky. He stood for Langholm Cornet and lost the vote – because he was over-confident and went off to play golf when the vote was there to be taken. Out in the bush a proud man might well make enemies but Nicol would never have left a loaded gun against a swinging door. Our family was deeply hurt by Nicol's death and when his wife, my Aunty Chrissie, came back here, she remained very close to us. I suppose South Africa was still pretty much like the Wild West in the twenties and the Boers might well have been happy to repay a few scores. Anyway, I was given his name and later on I was proud to name my own eldest daughter, Nicole.

The Langholm Common Riding's always meant a lot to us Elliots. I rode my first Common Riding in 1947. There's a photograph of me at the horse's head, listening to my father 'Cryin' the Fair'. Growing up in Langholm, you, naturally, become an enthusiast and once you ride you're hooked for life. I've never owned a horse, I've always hired, or borrowed horses but every year I used to feel – this is something I must do! If you're away, you still have this

Above: Crossing the Lambhill for the Langholm Hound Trail, 1980. (TN)

Overleaf: Hounds and owners await the start of the ten-mile Langholm Trail, 1980. (TN)

need – to be home for the Common Riding. And if you're here – you're in the grip of Common Riding fever all summer long. Hammering wood, on the rooftops of Carlisle or Newcastle, I'd be hearing the beat of the drums and the Langholm songs. It's the human condition to get accustomed to this or that, to become conditioned to what you know but some things are better and richer than others. We are all the products of our time and situation, yet we can choose and, one thing I know, if I was young today – I wouldn't choose to become a joiner. Fifty years ago we didn't have much choice, and very few got the government support that youngsters, today, take for granted.

I served an apprenticeship – I did the lot, undertaking, carpentry, roofing. I played rugger. I did my National Service and stayed in another year. I was out in Singapore and Malaya. So I got a medal but I spent most of my time down around Plymouth. I like Devon and I like Cornwall. They used to stand up for themselves but, unfortunately, no longer. Cornwall looks set to go the way of the hounds. They, like us, must stand up for themselves. I used to love hearing the Cornishmen sing, 'And shall Trelawney die?'

... And they fixed the where and when
And shall Trelawney die?
Then twenty thousand Cornish me
Will know the reason why!

We'll cross the Tamar, land to land,
The Severn is no stay,
With 'One and All', and hand in hand,
And who shall bid us nay?

Trelawney he's in keep and hold,
Trelawney he may die;

But twenty thousand Cornish bold
Will know the reason why!'

Plymouth, in my day, was a smart new place, courtesy of Adolf Hitler! He bombed the city as much as the docks – so the whole centre had to be rebuilt. It's windswept but it emerged as one of the first New Towns of postwar Europe. I liked it. So, when I left the army I stayed on to help build the Tamar Bridge. A great time I had but, of course, I was back for the Common Riding! And I told the Cornet, Andy Morgan, what great times there were to be had down in Plymouth and, once the Day was over, we went away down to Devon for a week on the spree. I took him into all the navy pubs in Union Street. I remember one where a man called Bob played the piano for sing-songs. Navy songs, Blues, whore songs, folksongs, but – Andy's head was still full of the Common Riding. Those songs get in your head and you can't get them out for weeks. So there was Andy enjoying his beer – but wishing he was back on his horse in Langholm! And, he was soon calling out 'Bob, Bob! – Play us "Jeannie's Black Ee"!' Bob looked at him. 'Whistle it,' he said. Andy was a good whistler. Bob listened for a moment then he too started to whistle – then, away he went on the piano, beating out 'Jeanie's Black Ee'. It was great and we had another Common Riding night – down there in Devonport! 'The Bonnie Woods o' Craigie Lea', 'The Girl I left Behind', 'A' the Airts', 'Will Ye No Come Back Again', 'The Rowan Tree', 'The Old Folks at Home'. Army, navy, the locals, everybody enjoyed themselves and especially Andy Morgan. He gave Plymouth a Common Riding concert – for free.

Union Street was the only place I ever saw a working boxing booth. What I saw was no fake. I saw man after man going hammer and tongs. And, do you know this, around the ring – all the talk seemed always to be – about Tommy Farr, 'The Iron Jaw'! It was just like Langholm! Everybody remembered the Tommy Farr/Joe Lewis fight. They'd heard it on the wireless. And, I have to say, I've been guilty of Tommy Farr talk, myself. Not so long ago I was recounting the story about Tommy Farr and the Langholm men when Edwin Morgan, the Glasgow Poet Laureate, came in. He listened for a bit, then went white as a sheet – and he had to be helped out. That was in the Crown Inn. During the war, two Langholm men, who'd gone into the army, were sent to Brighton – where Tommy Farr ran a pub – in his 'retirement'. They went in for a dram and a chat. They drank too much and one of them started baiting Tommy Farr. He wouldn't stop. He challenged him to fight. At last, Tommy Farr went for him and with one punch, broke his jaw! End of story – that was it! It was that that drove Edwin Morgan from the Crown Inn – forty years after the incident happened! That shows how sensitive a poet can be to things. 'Negative capability' is what John Keats called it: the ability to feel yourself in other shoes, other situations; to become one with the sparrows pecking about

Langholm Common Riding, 1999. (TN)

the gravel. And the Langholm man? Once he'd recovered he was ne'er so proud as when he spoke of his 'battle with Tommy Farr'!

Later on, my wife to be, Sheena, came down to Plymouth to see the sights. I took her up onto the new bridge and she was the first person, other than us builders, to cross the Tamar Road Bridge. Just as Isambard Kingdom Brunel had been the first to cross the Tamar Railway Bridge he designed, one hundred years before, so Sheena crossed the Road Bridge. It was me that had the designs that time! She's the finest thing I ever saw. The Tamar Rail Bridge was Brunel's last great project and he asked that the workmen trundled him across, just once, before he died. And Sheena, she was a farmer's daughter from Bonnie Galloway. I sought her out – like Rabbie Burns. Each time I came home I used to borrow a horse and ride over to see her. It seems a very old-fashioned thing to do now, looking back. But I enjoyed it and one of the by-products of rides was that I got to know all the blacksmiths round about. The man himself was Jim Millar of Waterbeck, by Crowdieknowe. It was he who made the 'twelvepenny nail' that my father used to hold up when he was 'Cryin' the Fair'. Jim Millar was a man who had no chest. His chest had come out through his back, so to speak, with all the years of bending over the hooves, holding the weight of so many horses on his shoulder. I've seen the same thing amongst many smiths – their chest goes in pigeon, and their backs bulge up like a tractor tyre.

John James Beattie was the great Langholm blacksmith. He was a Common Riding enthusiast – if ever there was one. It used to bring him work but that wasn't it; he loved the tradition, the history; the sight and sound and smell of the horses. All his life he had his own spot where he stood for the handing-in of the flag at the end of the day: for the old-timers, that being the most emotional moment. Beattie's spot was a dangerous spot, right by the flank of the horse of the Righthand Man. But John James knew horses, he could control horses like nobody else but, of course, as the years went by, the police began to take responsibility for order and safety – and they took exception to this man who stood in the middle of the square by the horses. They decided to move him – they tried to move him! Every year they tried to move him, for 'his own safety'! Every year they tried and every year he stood his ground – until he died. He wouldn't shift and why should he? He had shoed and carried the weight of thousands of Common Riding horses – till they had forced his chest out through his back! And he wanted to be by the Cornet at the handing in of the Flag! Why should such a man bend before the will of a young constable, endeavouring to make his mark? Long may the smith stand by the horse of the Cornet.

Standing on horseback, John Elliot cries the Langholm Fair, 1999. (TN)

Well, I'm glad to say, John James won his battle – staying resolute till the end. Common sense and circumstance must have a place in implementation of the law. Unfortunately that's more and more going out of the window. If John James had stuck to his spot today, he might well have ended up with a custodial sentence, an endless custodial sentence – like that man down in England who refused to wear a crash helmet when riding his motorbike and got sent to prison – forever! As soon as he'd finish one sentence he'd celebrate by going out for a ride – without a helmet! And, of course, every time the police would be waiting and every time he was re-arrested. He did sixty consecutive prison sentences – till he died of a heart attack! Was that a victory for law and order? Is that what civilisation brings us to? Is that why millions gave their lives to contain Kaiser Bill and Adolf Hitler? Surely there was some way out of that cleft stick – other than endless imprisonment. Couldn't they have forced the fellow to take out some form of insurance policy – making him responsible for all and every accident or injury he caused – because of his lack of a helmet! A stubborn man, who won't wear a crash helmet, is imprisoned for life – whereas IRA murderers do a few years before turning to journalism! And it strikes me, that if John James Beattie had been a solicitor, or a police inspector, I very much doubt if he'd have had the trouble he did. There's still a strong prejudice against the man who works with his hands.

My father was not a terrorist but he did move into journalism and, over the years, he wrote some good poetry. And I've always had a big interest in poetry ... I have a gift for remembering poetry, it never takes me long. I'm a Burns enthusiast and I enjoy every kind of meet where poetry and song are part of the proceedings and over the years I've discovered some very good, unknown, poetry in Langholm and Eskdale. It was Sheena who really made the discovery. She used to work up in the Old People's Home, at Greenbank, and it was there that she heard this old man, Adam Murray, speaking his poems. He was blind and ninety-four years of age. It was Christmas time and the nurses were asking the old folks to sing and recite and entertain each other. Everybody was asked to contribute. Various songs came out, 'Knees up Mother Brown', 'Daisy', 'The Mull of Kintyre', that sort of thing, until they came to Adam Murray who sat with his stick in a corner seat. Although he was blind, his eyes were always open; they never shut. They were red raw, like fresh wounds, and his hands were huge from years of work outdoors in the cold. He had been a shepherd. He'd never married and always lived on his own until he was taken in to Greenbank at the age of ninety-two. Well, he, who had been almost silent through all his months in the home, was asked if he would sing. At first he refused but then, when he was asked a second time, he cleared his throat and like a bard, he began:

I do remember, I long shall remember,
A dark misty day at the end of November,
A shepherd was going his rounds –
When he found such a scene (one is apt to remember!),
A dead body all covered in wounds ...

It was stretched in full view with its face to the sky,
As if making appeal to the All-Seeing-Eye!
The right arm, which failed on that last evil day
The assassins rude hand to arrest,
Was lifted above – as if pointing a way –
To the land where the weary shall rest ...

Then he stopped and apologised to say he'd made a mistake – and started in the middle of the poem. He started again, at the beginning, and out came this marvellous long ballad that lasted twenty minutes. It told the story of a packman murder, up in Eskdale, sometime around 1820. These two packmen had met up and begun trading together – till one killed the other. A great hue and cry ensued; finally the murderer was recognised in Nairn and brought back to Dumfries where he was tried, convicted and hanged by the neck. The poem ends with these two verses:

At that moment a crash and a loud peel of thunder
Strikes the hearts of the gazers with terror and wonder –
Another bright flash and another loud crash
– the rain falls in torrents and the huge living mass
Is off helter-skelter to the houses for shelter –

And the murderer left all alone in the helter.

What became of the body I never have heard,
The doctors would hack it to bits I suppose.
When brought into the booth it was stretched on a board
And a galvanic battery applied to its nose
– when it instantly started to kick and make faces!
Weill, weill, those doctors are pretty hard cases!

Adam Murray reduced that Christmas room to silence. It was a classic, unknown Border ballad and it proved to be just one of an armory of poems old Adam kept in his head. He had come down out of the hills – like a bard, like a Border balladeer of the olden days – and the strange thing was these unknown poems weren't his own poems, nor were they anonymous – they were all written by a Canadian called Alexander Glendinning. A man who had emigrated from Upper Cassock, the uppermost farm on the Esk above Langholm. And, Glendinning was the boy-shepherd who found the body with which Adam had, mistakenly, started his poem.

Alexander Glendinning came from one of the very old Eskdale families but times were hard and personal circumstances forced him to emigrate, sometime in the early nineteenth century, to Canada. Out there he did well – logging and farming and sending his poems home to people here, as letters. He asked that his poems be read out in public and they were. As an old man, having made money in Canada, Glendinning got a selection of his poems published and six books were printed. Where those books are today, I don't know; they certainly don't have a copy in the National Library of Scotland but, what we do know is, one copy of the book was given to a minister of the Kirk up in Ewesdale and, when Adam Murray was a young man, that minister lent Adam the book. And, before giving the book back, that young boy learned every one of those poems. Then he kept them in his head for eighty years. He used to recite them, to himself, most evenings of his life. Occasionally, he would recite for others to hear. The poems became like friends, they embodied what he knew of life in the hills and much of what he thought about life beyond. He met them like friends, every evening. He had his work, he had the Kirk and he had this bank of poems.

Glendinning's poems seem to have represented to Adam what life was about; they were more vivid than his own experience. They formalised and eulogised the world he had known as a boy, and, at the end, blind and alone in Greenbank, Glendinning's poems meant everything to him. He wasn't a singer but he recited all his verse in a deep, sonorous, bardic voice that was a kind of prose-song. He knew he carried something special and he gave himself to his poems with gravitas and style. I got one of my friends to go down and record all the poems he remembered: it was lucky I did – because within a month of the poems being recorded, old Adam was dead. It was as though, knowing his poems were preserved and passed on, he had no further reason to live – and he died. The story of Adam Murray reminds me of the story of the first known English poet, Caedmon. He was shy of his gift and for a long time refused to sing when the harp came round but, at last, when he did – all around were amazed. There is something sacred about both the making of art and the passing down of treasured possessions. There's a lovely poem by Thomas Hardy about his mother singing all her oldest songs, one last time, before she died.

'I am playing my oldest tunes,' declared she,
 'All the old tunes I know, –
Those I learned ever so long ago.'
– Why she should think just then she'd play them
 Silence cloaks like snow.

When I returned from the town at nightfall
 Notes continued to pour
As when I had left two hours before:
'It's the very last time,' she said in closing;
 'From now I play no more.'

The Cornet and his horsemen inspect the Langholm marches, 1980. (TN)

A few morns onward found her fading,
And, as her life outflew,
I thought of her playing her tunes right through;
And I felt she had known of what was coming,
And wondered how she knew.

That was written in 1912. That would be about fifteen years after Adam learned the poems of Alexander Glendinning … Art, like life, is collaboration. I don't think Adam ever made up a poem of his own but he carried Glendinning's poetry like nobody else. Various people in the Border counties know bits of some of Glendinning's poems but Adam Murray was the only person who carried his master's work, like a book. Maybe some of the poems got changed a bit over the years but that doesn't matter: that was always true of the ballad tradition and Adam Murray's 'selective' adaptation of Glendinning's poems mimics, in our time, the handing down of ballads down across the centuries.

The Glendinning poems tell us what kind of a place Eskdale was 170 years ago and they are of continuing importance. For example, it seems highly likely that Hugh MacDiarmid was influenced by Glendinning and the tradition Adam Murray was part of. MacDiarmid was to become a highly intellectual and revolutionary poet but there's no doubt he owes much to his Borders inheritance. It is quite possible that MacDiarmid either saw Glendinning's book or heard Adam Murray reciting (they were distant relations).

Of course, MacDiarmid wanted much more of his poetry than either Glendinning or Murray but – all three belong to the same tradition, the same family and in his *Second Hymn to Lenin*, MacDiarmid asserts his commitment to the Borders, to Scotland and mankind:

> Black in the pit the miner is,
> The shepherd reid on the hill,
> And I'm wi' them baith until
> The end of mankind, I wis.
>
> Whatever their jobs a'men are ane ...

It seems clear to me that local poetry here, carried by men like Adam Murray, shaped MacDiarmid's poetry – just as the song tradition of Ayrshire shaped the poetry of Burns. One of the big ballads Adam Murray recited was *A Letter Home from Canada* and it contains numerous similarities with themes and forms to be found in MacDiarmid's most famous poem, *A Drunk Man looks at the Thistle.* Both poems present particular experience as a vehicle for a poetic dissertation upon life. Glendinning views Eskdale and the world as an émigré in Canada; MacDiarmid views the world from Langholm on Common Riding Day. Glendinning asked that his poem be read out, as a public letter, to all his old friends still living where he once lived: MacDiarmid challenges the universe.

There lived lang syne in Es'dale Penn
A shepherd lad called Sandy Glenn;
If some auld comrade wants to ken new word o him,
The laird can easily tak him ben –
And read this poem.

But leuch eneuch naebody kens and naebody cares
How Sandy fens, or how he fares,
Whether he lives (withoot oor tears)
Sitting secure in his own log-built hut
Or catchin' bears!

Poor fellow – his was a sad case!
Hard fortune buffed him back and face
And sent him from his native place as poor as Job
To scrackle on a wild goose chase –
Half roon the globe.

O woe at heel and weil I ween
To mony a strange land he's been
And mony an uncu' face he's seen
Since that wey day – from Eskdale's bonnie hills o' green
He turned away.

Ye who are in parlour, warm and snug,
With tea spread on your own hearth rug
And at your hand a sauncy jug –
Sit chatterin' by the chimney lug,
At home and happy –

Here's tae yer Health – an Joy be wi ye!
Ye little dream what they must dae,
Wha leave their hames and put to sea!
But gentlemen – 'tis just as weill,
Tween me an you, ye dinnae ken!

Just think noo o' they puir luckless wretches
In a ship's hold under hatches,
Among two or three hundred lousy bitches,
Bluid o' blue ruin!
– These, as the vessel rolls and pitches, cursin' and spewin'!

Lang in the Atlantic sea we splashed,
Now up we clomb, now doon we dashed
But oor auld ship those servants thrashed,
Still strugglin' through!
An a' the white foam boiled and splashed beneath her prow.

Still to the West oor bowsprit stood
And still we banged the blistering flood –
Till at last the sailors roon sound, 'Land Ahoy!'
We started up at news sae guid
And danced for joy.

All hail Columbus' forest green!
All hail New York's own city screen!
All hail to Jonathan – oor frien! But low wiell me,
What curious coons!
How lank, how lean, them Yankees be!

Barefaced, din, thin cadaverous sichts!
They look as if they've lain for nichts
Deep underneath a celary kist or Baltic wash –
Then bolted up frae mortal fricht –
Tae scare the craws!

These are the Free Men! These the fellows
That boast – they can buy and sell us!
They whipped John Bull – and John they tell us
Whips every nation!
So – lets get in some retaliation!

They whipped the British! They're the knaves!
The maist they whipped is three million slaves!
'Two thirds Black Nigger!' The lave shout out!
– Bred up and driven to fairs, fine sirs,
Like sheep and nout!

Hullo! The steamers off full skimmer –
We're splashing up the Hudson river! Damned Yankees!
Yes, the coons are clever – for a' their ta'k –
The Maker got one, 'Now or Never!'
And that's a fact!

What if the old boiler, now and then,
Burst its pan-wheel! 'Fetch water, men!'
And before you cry 'How, where or when!'
They're fixed up clever, blawn up the steam
And off again as fast as ever.

Still steaming on a northern tack
We passed the Catskill mountain track
And thence to Albany – where back our steamer turned:
While up the vale of the Mohawk
– Westward we journed.

But should I mention every stage
We passed on this great pilgrimage,
Instead of one small lettered-page or single column,
The very titles I engage
Would fill 'em all.

We passed ... No matter where we passed!
We crossed Ontario's lake at last
To Scarborough – where our lot was cast for several years;
Which place we found, you know the rest,
A place of tears.

But now ... on the Axle river's bluff
Here sits my bad ship – sure enough!
My toil's too hard, my coats too rough to dream of wealth!
And yet – I really think I'll thrive
If I keep health.

When I cam in – fa' was the year,
The licht o day scarce glimmered here:
A dark lookout! But never fear, we started choppin'!
We've now a dozen acres clear
And a wee bit croppin'.

I, awhiles, look doon my clooted breeches!
The crutch, juist noo, wants two or three stitches!
But what care I for fortune's freaks – they need nae jaicket
Who ha' nought else to do for weeks
But trees tae worket!

This clearin' land's a rough concern
For me – puir feckless body's bairn!
Where each back's bent wi' steel or iron
And loggin' wark till Friday e'en
And mony a starn.

You moorland blades would laugh tae see
A band o loggers at a bee!
Smart chiels wi' handspikes warkin' free, in shirt and breeches,
And teamsters loud wi' 'high' and 'gee'
– Twirlin' blue beeches!

Spade-carrier Willie Erskine leads Arthur Elliot and the Cornet across the Ewes, Langholm 1980. (TN)

Still – Canada, say what you wilt on't,
For my pairt I can say no ill o't!
There's mony a good gangin' busy mill frae morn till dark
And every man gets bread and yellint
That likes tae wark!

A stout young chap that can begin
An' drive ahead through thick and thin,
May safe enough leave kith and kin and cross the water.
Wi' common sense it's ten tae yin
He'll mend the matter.

But for your pingin' half-bucks,
That cannae wield the woodman's axe
And have nae sense tae drive an ox – this much is clear:
They'd better stay among their ain folk
– they're useless here!

Gi'e my respects to yin an a'
Between Black Esk's mouth and Budbeckslaw.
I would like wiell tae get across on Monday nicht
And crack tae you aboot Canada –
An tell ye richt.

Belike – there's still a few that I would ken;
Boys, since I left, hae grown tae men
And doughty lads well figured then, in manhood's prime –
I think I see their half wits wane
And beard's o rime!

El croon has got a wee bit bare on't!
I'm certain yours has little hair on't!
I'm thinkin' – there was little spare on't – when I came oot
And seven years hae shaven more off't
– There's little doot!

Not yin in fifty mourn for aye
Though dinae say I'm doon the brae!
Although my beard is not quite grey, my cheeks are thinner
And my complexion, truth to say,
Is a trifle dinner.

I cannae run frae dawn till dark;
I'm stiffer – in the way o' wark!
But set me doon wi' knife and fork – I'll fail ye never!
And I can talk aboot church and state
As fast as ever.

Mind me tae Violet, Tom your brother,
John Bell o' Fingland, John's kind mother
And sandy Welsh – an every other auld friend aboot!
That Heaven may bless ye all the gither –
Is my prayer devote.

The Cassock folk (of course, that's hame) ...
Jim never writes me – that's a shame!
He'd raither mend some grand kirk scheme or toot a trumpet
Denouncing that redoubted dame –
The Roman Strumpet!

He's found out through some calculation
When every empire, state and nation
Arose and fell!
Things far beyond my numeration –
What he wants, I cannae tell.

He ken's the horns of Daniel's cattle!
The field o' words they call 'the Battle'
And he's found the date that's fatal to Papal Rome –
When little bairns will rattle doon
St Peter's Dome!

What serves this lamming?
Just think o' coofs, like you and me,
Wha scarce can count to two or three
– Mak six or seven!
Whilst he, to philosophy is dreeven!

Tell Midler, I'm well pleased to hear
His tups are still famous far and near!
I noticed in the prints last year – an orra lot
Brought fourteen hundred sovereigns clear,
Right on the spot!

I clapped my hands for half an 'oor
And shouted 'Well dune Es'dalemuir!'
Ten pund a piece for seven score o' clippet hoggs
Beats all I ever heard before,
'Mong herds an' dogs!

Good sheep they are, well fed, well fleshed!
Tell him one thing, at my beheist,
He shouldnae geld a single beast but keep and sell them
Twe stones heavier at the least!
Don't mind and tell him!

But I must stop and say goodbye –
To you and yours – Health, Peace and Joy,
And good upon your sheep and kai, croft and kailyard.
I am yours most respectfully –
Your friend the Bard.

P. S. I lift my pen again to say –
You'll mind and write me somewhat day?
I look not for a lengthy lay, like this o' mine –
THE NEWS, in just a hamely way –
Will please me fine.

And Wattie Elliot – here's to you!
Lang may ye climb the Midhill Brew,
Lang drive a guid fat ewe – fan-der-winnae!
As every year ye older grow
Still makin' money!

Top: Cumberland Wrestling on the Castleholm, Langholm, 1980. The Fair Crier, John Elliot, sends another fellow back over the border! (TN)

Bottom: Having done his duty, inspecting the marches, Arthur Elliot relaxes with two of his daughters in the noonday sun, Langholm, 1980. (TN)

Adam Murray started his working life up on the Ewes, then moved over to West Dumfriesshire where he worked five or ten years as a horseman before, finally, coming back to work the rest of his life as a shepherd here. Adam never travelled very far from home. This is one reason why he admired Glendinning so much – but he did know the Gallowayside and one of his favourite poems tells a story about bodysnatchers from that part of the world. It's called, *In Dumfriesshire, Scotland.*

In Dumfriesshire, Scotland, some forty years back
There was no little stir and a great deal of ta'k
Aboot a clash, then arisin', wi' Resurrection Men,
Wha poached oor kirkyards to supply – the Dissection Men!

At the time I have stated our story is dated
And I give it to you as I heard it related
One winter, 'fore supper, by one Robert Farish,
Quite a respectable man and clark o' the parish.

A person had died, so our story begins,
In the Galloway district, somewhere in the Rinns.
A person of note, by the name of MacDonald,
Whom they'd buried deep, deep in the lee o' Kirkconnell.

And, the body to save from the men digging thieves,
Two men were engaged to watch nightly the graves,
With guns loaded up to make sure of a Clearance
When the first Resurrection Man made his appearance!

Kirkconnell, long famous, the wide world o'er,
For the grave of Fair Ellen and Flamey her lover,
Lies low on the link o' the Kirtle's left bank
Surrounded by shady trees, leafy and dank.

In the midst o' that lang, lonely place o' the deid
Stands an auld mouldy vault wi' small room overheid!
To this room then oor watchmen marched up every nicht
And there mounted guard till return of the licht.

Like trusty good fellows they stood to their posts
Midst the hootin' hoolets and the sighin' o'ghosts!

In a clachan hard by lived an odd sort o' fellow,
Andrew Irvine by name, and a souter to trade.
The neighbours said, 'Andrews apt to get mellow –
But naebody ever saw Andrew afraid!'

One day he went doon tae the auld borough toon,
Told his wife he'd be hame aboot mid aifternoon;
Got through his business, bought leather and bristles,
The merchant and he – merely whetting their whistles!

But, as ill-luck would hae it, when near Kirtle Brig,
He met in wi' Bill Thomson and Jock o' the Rigg!
They couldnae be thirsty! It wasnae their nature!
Sae the three went in – for a drap o' the creater!

The glasses got clinkin',
Oor worthies got drinkin'
Till twelve o' the clock!
When douse folk should be winkin'!

Andrew bolted upricht – bade his comrades goodnicht!
From Boniface he borrowed a bower for licht
And put through the woods – by a footpath and style
Which led richt by Kirkconnell. 'Twould save him a mile!

Away he went singing, '*March, march in good order!*
For all the blue bonnets are o'er the Border!'
When outside Kirkconnell, he now made a halt
To run-off the first rush of an o'erdose o' malt –

When a volley was fired o' powder and lead
That wakened the characters aroon Kirtlehead!
The herons and hoolets got sic a fricht,
They flew up and hardly could tell where to alicht!

Andrew snudged away hame but his dander was up.
The thing was absurd! The thing was abrucht!
What business had they, under any pretence,
To make fun for themselves at their neighbour's expense!

They micht laugh if they will,
Let them laugh at their leisure!
They must fen blast the bits
The souter can measure!

Next day, Andrew went up to the manse o' Springkell
(The servants and he were acquainted quite well),
Got the keys o' the vault from the footman, Bill Dobbie,
And an auld bugle horn that hung in the lobby.

That nicht, when oor watchmen repaired to their post,
Andrew Irvine was already playing 'mine host'!
(In sapping and mining, those atop are at fault!),
Andrew Irvine was watching, deep doon in the vault!

All was silent as death. Andrew's throat whispered 'now'
And a low moaning note on the bugle he blew!
Our watchmen started up – and stood still!
But they spoke not at all, not a word – good or ill.

The next sullen boom – rose a full octave higher.
They bolted! Who'd blame them! And then ran like fire!
A third dreadful blast sounded louder than ever.
A parting salute – as they splashed through the river.

Andrew, who found his wait had gained him the outpost,
Now turned to the citadel.
But stepping upstairs he took prudent care –
Lest the enemy should fall on his flank, unaware.

'Twas a beating it's true, but he did not pursue.
They might return, who could tell, and the conflict renew!
But they returned not at all, they had gone far away!
Ta'en the road like Lamp Lighters, near to New Galloway.

Andrew got the spoils – a good shepherd's spread,
Some cheese, and bread too and a bottle o' brandy!
The last didnae get very far, I'm afraid –
The place was sae damp! Sic things come in handy!

The plaid he took home and for mony a year
At Kirk and at market he constantly wore it,
Told it's tale and said, should 'an owner appear',
He was ready and willing at once to restore it!

But naebody, ever, appeared as a claimant,
So Andrew fell heir to that fine piece o' raiment.
It was a black and white plaid –
With P.B. for a name on't.

Our story is ended – and now for the moral:
He who would get peaceably through this ill-world,
Let him mind his own business, let others alone,
Never rouse sleeping dogs, never throw the first stone!

When you travel, be sure to be hame by daylicht
And keep away frae kirkyards in the how o' the nicht!

In that poem you get echoes of Burns' *Tam o' Shanter*, as well as the ballad *Helen of Kirkconnell*, but usually Glendinning was very much his own master. Another poem is entitled *Davington Green School.* It tells you about a school football match but it's also a real Victorian blockbuster, casting light on the high days of the British Empire, the resurgent Border spirit and the warrior prowess of the Eskdale boys! The history of rugger in the Border counties goes back 3,000 years! Glendinning wrote this poem on hearing the news, in Canada, that his old school had won the annual football match against their neighbours from Hutton:

Well done, well done, my hearty cocks,
Young heroes yin an a'!
Well done – tae meet the Hutton folk
An' beat them at the ba'!

Puir though I be, upon my word,
I'd raither lose a cow –
Than here, in Canada, I heard
– That they had beaten you!

Such ploys bring back my boyhood's days,
I mind, just like yestreen,
The Sheriffmuirs we used to raise
On Davington School Green!

Aye, yince a year, at Candlemas
We'd met another school;
Dick Bell oor worthy teacher was
– and they had Mr Yule.

Oor trysting place was Johnston Holme,
Beside the Waterfoot:
Though forty years since then hae flown,
I mind those meetings yet.

'Good Day,' quoth they, 'Good Day,' we cried!
And each the ither scanned
– Then flung oor jaickets to the side
And mustered man tae man.

Up flew the ba', the strife began!
A curse he got, and he!
And there was many an anxious man
That day on Johnston Lee.

Now North, now South the hubbub sways
– they're at it tooth and nail!
And we, wi' a' oor energies,
Are passing on the hail.

Oh! Mony a dirty deed was done
And feet remembered lang!
Mony a weill run race was run
– The ba' got mony a bang!

And there was mony a heel flew high
An mony a kicket shin!
The heroes o' Thermopylae
– Stuck never better in.

My hert warms o'er each gallant feat,
I scarce can think it true,
But I'm thinkin' on a debt
– As auld as Waterloo.

And where are now my comrades fell?
Mony a good chiel's away:
Upon the rest, long summers tell,
Their beards, like mine, are grey.

And we are severed, far and wide;
I'm on the Axangle's Bluff,
And Christie's on the world's backside,
The place where men jump off!

Some wandered westwards many miles
Beyond the Kariboo!
And some are in the Australian Isles
Among the kangaroos!

Will Riddle, like a decent chap,
Clung tae his place o' birth –
He pounds the smiddie wrap for wrap
Beside his faither's hearth.

We've a' had mony a tug, I wot,
Muckle toil and strife,
And mony's the tumble we hae got
In the rough old game o' life.

But this I'll say, who ere would win,
The stakes be big or sma',
The patent virtue's stickin' in –
We learnt it at the ba'!

But I must stop – now boys be sure,
When next you play a spiel –
For the honour o' auld Es'dalemuir
Let's see you manage wiell!

Let Westerkirk and Hutton, baith,
Bring a' their bag o' tricks! ...
What need I talk? I take my oath
– You're into them like bricks!

My blessings on your hieds, dear lads,
It does me good tae ken
That you are worthy o' yer dads!
– And they were famous men!

That's great, don't you think? When I recite that poem it reminds me of Rudyard Kipling's *If.* But Glendinning wrote his poem long before Kipling wrote his and Glendinning was standing up for ordinary kids just as Kipling spoke up for the common soldiers. I sometimes think our own soldiers were used and abused far more than the colonial peoples they were sent out to control. They suffered like the industrial working classes and little thanks or reward either got ... I know a lot of Kipling. I think he's very good. Who now knows or cares he won the Nobel Prize? Very few. Kipling is a much better and more interesting poet than the modernists give him credit for.

Glendinning liked to have a 'reason' for writing a poem, and he liked to be asked to write a poem for an occasion. People here wrote to ask their 'Canadian bard' to compose poems for Eskdale weddings and, if he knew the bride or groom, he usually obliged. One I like is called *Wee Geordie-man*:

Wee Geordie-man I wish you joy
An a' the luck that's goin',
What think you of the world, boy,
Now you're a married man?

It seems an uncu strange affair,
Against season a' thegither,
For freeborn folk to remember what –
I can tell aboot *the other*!

I'll warrant she's a bonnie wife,
As ever yet was seen,
She'll be the comfort o' your life
– Till you call her Kate or Jean!

An is she short, or is she tall?
Or has she coal black hair?
Or does she wear the lint white locks
Like the belles o' Moffat Fair?

I wish you great felicity –
Your blessings come in showers,
The bard's best bevvy yet is raised
– To you and yours!

One of my own favourites is *Jeannie Bell*. It's a humorous tale about Glendinning's lifelong bachelor status. It's a poem about the hardships of emigration and the way in which Victorian proprieties undermined human nature, particularly where sex was concerned.

I cannae understand
How it has come –
That Jeanne Bell
Has never got a man!
Did ye nae like your faither's folk?
Did naebody like you?
Or did you boggle at the yoke
And wouldnae enter through?

If you come oot tae Canada –
Wheest – harken – dinnae tell!
If you come oot tae Canada
– I'll marry you mysel'!

I've bigg beside the Axelbluff
A snug wee summer shiel
– In Canada there's room enough
For two tae ploo the field!

I'm gettin' auld, the truth tae own,
But you're not young yersel'!
There's mony a summer sun gone doon
Since I kenned Jeannie Bell!

With white heid, tidying but an' ben,
I think I see ye yet,
I was the cooherd ca'd in then
– aboot the Barbon fete!

Frae times lang gang, we turn to this,
Oor dearest friens are gane;
And in this world's wild wilderness
We wander all alane.

We wander all alane, lady,
An' that's what shouldnae be!
– We'll totter on in company
If you'll come o'er the sea.

They say it's far to Canada,
That 'tis not worth the while,
'Tis but a tiresome trip, my heart,
'Tis but four thousand mile!

And crossing the wild sea is now,
Since steamers got so rife,
Like steppin' on the ferry boat
And sailin' o'er tae Fife!

Up, up and come tae Canada!
Come, come and be my wife.
If you stay there for twelve month more
– You'll ruin half my life!

'I'm diggin' for a wife,' they'll say!
An' one that's far awa'!
Ye'd better get a man like me
– Than get nae man at a'!

I'm no, although I sayest it mysel',
As daft as ye may think,
– But cracket like a cattle bell
That gives a curious clink!

I'm juist aboot as wiell theday,
As ever in my life,
Ye munna ca' a man, a fool,
Because he wants a wife!

When Adam frae his bower looked up
(A spruce well-titled lord!),
What signified his goodly cup
– Wi' naebody to share it.

Adam address-ed everyone,
(The animal couples were standin' round!)
He looked an' looked but there was none
In his own likeness found.

No upright form, no soul at a',
In all that group was seen,
He stood in lonely dignity
– a King, without a Queen.

Heaven gave him, for his bliss to find,
A helpmate young and fair.
– Yon sun, the world, has never looked
Down on a happier pair.

But then, somehow, maitters went aglee,
I couldnae tell ye how,
Mankind fell prey tae miserie
And toil and trouble now!

The road we hae tae travel through
Is full o' pits and snares:
– I still think them better though,
Who take the road in pairs!

Up, up and come to Canada,
You, the said, Jeanie Bell!
If you come oot tae Canada,
I'll marry ye mysel'.

That's a heartfelt poem in a light vein but rooted in *The Bible* and Milton's *Paradise Lost.* Milton went blind just like Adam Murray and for some reason I've always thought the two men must have shared similar powers of delivery. Of course, I didn't hear Milton, or Glendinning, but I did hear Adam Murray and I can well imagine him reciting Milton.

Of Man's first Disobedience, and the Fruit
Of that Forbidd'n Tree, whose mortal taste
Brought Death into the World, and all our woe,
With loss of Eden, till one greater Man
Restore us, and regain the blissful Seat,

Sing Heav'nly Muse, that on the secret top
Of *Oreb*, or of *Sinai,* didst inspire
That Shepherd, who first taught the chosen Seed,
In the Beginning how Heav'ns and Earth
Rose out of Chaos . . .

Adam Murray never composed verse of his own. He was just a great reciter. He became a walking library – like those men in Ray Bradbury's book, *Fahrenheit 451*, and there is no doubt that pure 'reciters' are important in the history of the ballad. And Adam Murray's life is relevant to the on-going dispute as to whether the great ballads are the corporate production of country people over many centuries, or, individual productions produced by bards of high talent or genius. My own feeling is that both theories have truth to them but the existence of people like Glendinning and Adam Murray give a third strand – to what is, essentially, one unified web. There are outstanding individual poets like Ossian, MacDiarmid, Hogg and Scott who make timeless, individual contributions – although much of their work is fuelled by the folk tradition. There is an on-going 'anonymous' tradition in which various minor poets, remembrancers, reciters and singers, like my father and myself, pick things, make things and polish them: over the centuries, this sifts the wheat from the chaff to such an extent that these poems also become part of the quality mainstream. And there are people like Adam Murray, pure conveyors of what they know to be good. Adam was like an electric current – he carried Glendinning's 'letters from Canada' back into the community from which he came and in doing that strongly influenced the next generation of folk balladeers. Murray became the voice of a bard silenced by emigration. Whether the Glendinning/Murray poems will, in the future, live or die, will depend on the merit future generations award them – whether they are spoken and enjoyed. And even great poets must suffer the same testing.

I have a magazine that quotes a man called George Martine who wrote a good deal about the continuance of the bardic caste in Scotland in a work entitled, *The State of the See of St Andrews* (1683). 'Up till our fathers' time and ours something remained and still does of this ancient order. And they are called by themselves and others *Jockies*; who still go about begging and use still to recite the sluggornes of the true ancient surnames of Scotland from old experience and observation. Some of them I have discoursed, and found them to have reason and discretion. One of them told me that there were not now twelve of them in the whole isle; but he remembered when they abounded, so that at one time he was one of five that usually met in St Andrews.' Another man, John Colvil, who died in 1605, recorded that when he was a boy he 'heard the beggarly *Jockies* recite certain homely verses ascribed to Thomas the Rhymer, a reputed prophet'.

It must of been these kinds of men and women, shepherds and drovers who gave so much border balladry to Sir Walter Scott. And the tradition of the wandering minstrel continues even today and, like Glendinning, such wanderers have never confined themselves to Scotland. In fact leaving Scotland made their need to sing greater, like Cornet Andy Morgan in Union Street, Plymouth! And, I recently found a beautiful piece in the biography of S.T. Coleridge, by Richard Holmes, which describes a Scots minstrel of the eighteenth century – influencing the author of 'The Ancient Mariner'. One of Coleridge's earliest memories was of being carried out by his nurse to hear a strolling musician playing ballads in the moonlight during a Harvest festival in South Devon:

To hear our old Musician, blind and grey,
(Whom stretching from my nurses arms I kissed,)
His Scottish tunes and warlike marches play,
By moonshine, on the balmy summer's night ...

I remember my father telling me a story about Sir Walter Scott. Sir Walter was travelling through Northumberland when he met up with a Scots doctor – whom Scott had previously known as a blacksmith, when he worked north of the border. On asking the man where he'd learned his medicine the man replied that his two prime cures were 'calomel and laudanum'. 'But surely', said Scott 'you'll be killing, not curing, half the patients you see!' 'Oh aye,' replied the smith, 'I kill a good few, but it'll tak an awfu lot tae mak up fer Flodden!' Whether he was joking, or engaged in some one-man war of revenge I don't know – but certainly many of our Elliots fell at Flodden.

To end on a cheerful note, Adam Murray had a beautiful poem of farewell. Here it is, Alexander Glendinning's *Adieu Bonnie Es'dale,* and I think there are few more moving poems about the Border country:

Adieu bonnie Es'dale amid moorland and mountain,
Be peace in the cottage and joy in the ha':
Adieu tae the hearth and the hame o' my childhood,
Frien's, comrades and kinsmen – farewiell tae ye a'.

How oft we light footstepped in life's early morning
And ran by Glen Derg and the Midkipple Lee:
To the scenes o' my youth the glad spring is returning
But winter, dull winter, is gatherin' on me.

Far up on Toon Law the bletter is crooning,
The lark sings his song on the bonnie Knowe Drie:
In Fooshie, the blackbird his whistle is tinning
But his notes hae lang syne made me weary and whey.

The Hugh MacDiarmid Memorial on Whita Hill, Langholm. Arthur Elliot was one of the men responsible for its erection. The sculptor was Jake Harvey of Maxton Cross, by Kelso. (TN)

Nae mair, nae mair shall I climb the Brown Mountain
To gaze on my native vale stretching beneath,
Nae mair in the corrie I'll sit by the fountain
And muse on my hirsel widespread on the heath.

The years shall roll on and my name be forgotten,
A stranger shall run in the cauldren's wild glen –
But I'll never forget till life's last tie is broken,
The friends o' lang syne and the breeze o' the Penn.

Overleaf:
Highland ponies begin their descent after a day's stalking, Blair Atholl, Perthshire; Jill, Skye, and John Steel, 1998. (John Tickner)

Part Four

Remembrancers and Orramen

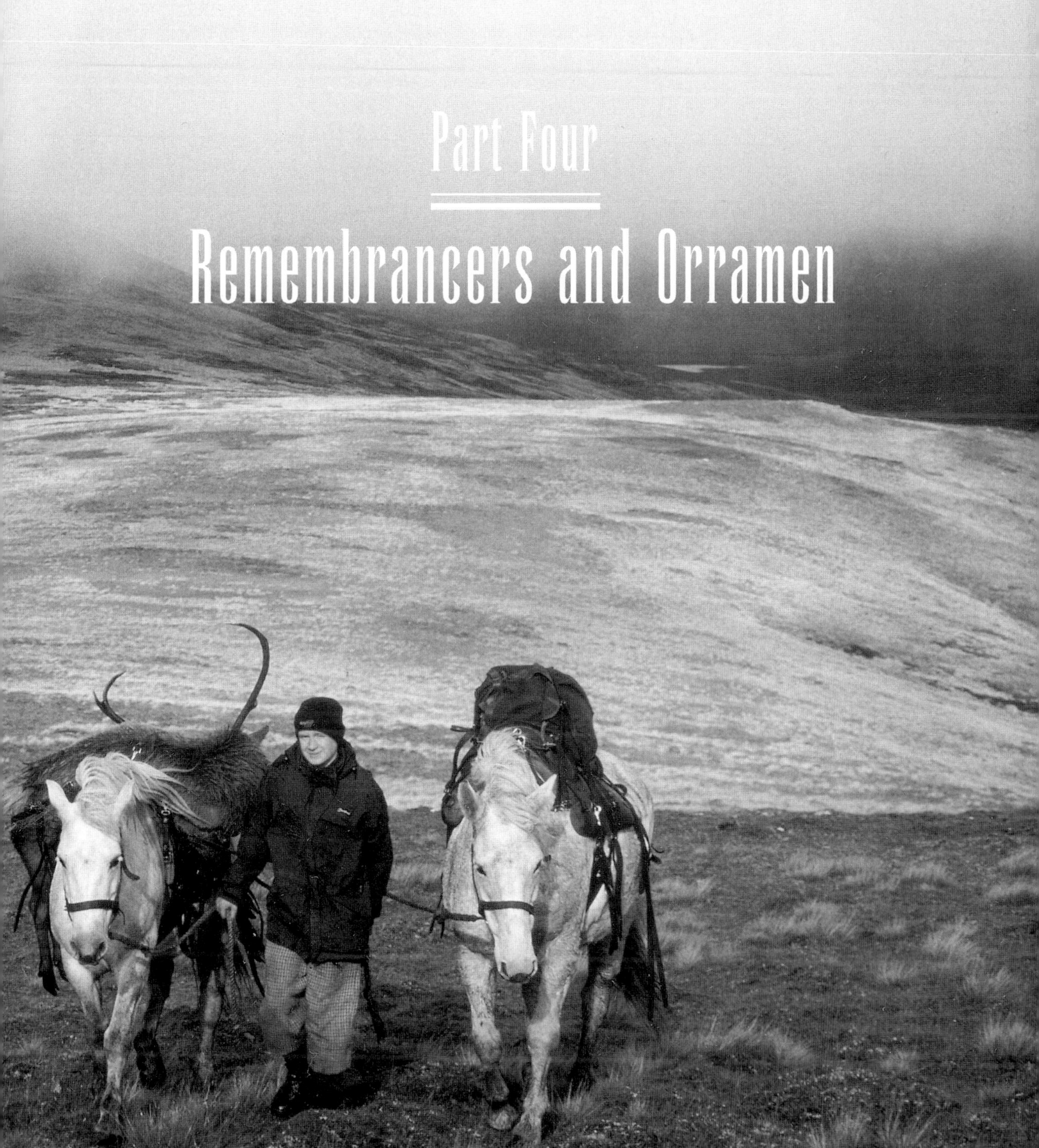

Alastair Livingstone

BARON of BACHUIL, LISMORE

The preamble to the Declaration of Arbroath describes where the leaders of the Scots nation, at the beginning of the fourteenth century, believed they came from. They saw themselves as direct descendants of the Scythians, the most powerful people to the north east of what was later to become the Greco-Roman empire. The Declaration documents that they had journeyed 'from Greater Scythia, by way of the Tyrrhenian Sea and the Pillars of Hercules and, after many years among the savage tribes of Spain, came to this land. They drove out the Britons, destroyed the Picts, resisted the Norsemen, Angle and Dane, and thereafter lived under 113 kings of their own royal stock – the line unbroken by a single foreigner!' That statement is based on folk memory, the recitations of bardic genealogists, the sheer wish to be different, and, perhaps, some remnants of historical fact.

The three outstanding claims to fame amongst the Scythians were their horsemanship, their skill at metalwork (particularly gold), and their free-roving, martial prowess. Twentieth-century thinkers like Hugh MacDiarmid and Compton MacKenzie gave some credence to this story of origination and various cultural connections have been made. Recurrent waves of Indo-European migration seem to have flowed out of the Scythian heartlands to the north of the Black Sea and it is quite possible that coherent groups of Scythians ended up in Ireland and Scotland. Having settled here they might well have re-established connections with their Scythian homeland – through the Baltic. Some scholars speculate that the vanished Pictish language had connections with Estonian, but there can be no argument about is that the Scots have

Anatolian farmers setting off for work, 1980. The combination of man, horse, wheel and metal remains a powerful reality, and a powerful symbol, even at the end of the twentieth century. (NT)

long had a special relationship with horses, inventive metalwork and martial enthusiasm.

This island, Lismore, was always a great island for horses and religious scholars. As a boy I knew horses as a natural part of life and the landscape – and knowing horses gives you a head start with camels! I started work with camels in 1938, in the Sudan. Dromedaries were still the best means of transportation in the African mountains at that time. I'd joined the Scientific Service and been sent off to Cambridge to learn Arabic, on a special one year course. Then I went out to Khartoum, to join the West Yorkshire regiment as a junior officer. I was twenty-three. The Italian occupation of Ethiopia was in full swing. It was a mixture of Alan Breck, Baden Powell and Lawrence of Arabia. I was involved mostly in map-making and reconnaissance. Then, during the war, I was moved to India, then Palestine and various Middle Eastern countries. In 1947 I was seconded to work for British Petroleum in Iraq and I stayed out there until I retired from the army in 1973. Then I came home to Lismore. And the very next year, in 1974, the staff of St Muluag, which had 'not' enjoyed a 104-year holiday in Inveraray, was returned to its traditional resting place, here at Bachuil, Lismore. It's the oldest Christian relic in Scotland and it's been in the custody of our family since the time of Muluag.

Certainly, our family have been the recognised keepers of 'the Big Staff', *am bachull mor*, since early medieval times. It's a plain blackthorn stick, thirty-four inches long, and curved at one end – like a crook or a shinty stick. It was the crozier of St Muluag. At one time it was decorated with embossed bronze and copper – jewels and gold leaf: because of this gold it was known as *am Bachull Buidhe* – the Yellow Stick. As freeholders and keepers of the staff we were 'The Barons of the Crozier', the Barons of Bachuil. Our family, the *Macdhunshleibhe, Mac-an-leigh*, or MacKinleys, are believed to have had special religious duties and responsibilities on Lismore ever since St Muluag established his first missionary church in 561. That was two years before St Columba settled on Iona and, although nobody would deny Columba's fame and greatness, there is good reason to believe Muluag's influence on Scotland was just as great as Colmcille's. Muluag is one of those men whose place in history has been overshadowed by received historical opinion – by repute and habit – rather than actuality. Thus, I am honoured and proud to keep *am Bachull Mor* here, at Bachuil, on behalf of the people of Lismore. And I am proud to have seen it returned to its rightful home – a point I'll return to, after I've explained the change of our name.

I was born, Alastair Livingstone, in Nyasaland, on 1 September 1914. My father went out to farm there in 1893. After a long correspondence my mother, Kitty, joined him and they were married in Nyasaland in 1908. She was from Appin, across the water here, and went out by sea, with a chaperone. Not withstanding that – she was a combative and strongminded

Alastair Livingstone, Baron of Bachuil, holding the ancient staff of St Muluag, outside his house on the island of Lismore, Argyll, 2000. (TN)

woman. When she heard that the best man was to be a black she insisted that she have a train of black bridesmaids. I was the third child and the first boy. Both my parents loved Africa. Their first daughter was named Nyasa. But out of the blue, in January 1915, when I was just five months old, my father was killed in a native uprising. Another Argyllshire, Duncan MacCormack was killed beside him. My mother soon returned to Scotland and we three children were brought up at Bachuil, our ancestral home – close to the broch of Tirfuir, the cathedral church of St Muluag, the Fire Hill Cairn and the old Smithy. Over the last two centuries the Livingstones have had continuous direct contact with Africa. Being brought up in the Highlands seems to give us a natural sympathy for life in Africa. The family of the great explorer, Dr David Livingstone, came originally from Lismore and when I went out to the Sudan I felt a little as though I was fulfilling a destiny. My leaving home and arrival in Africa evoked strangely similar emotions.

I am tall but my father was very tall, strong and athletic. Hunting was a natural part of his life, taming the bush. I grew up in the company of four leopards he'd shot. Like much of southern Africa, Lismore is open, rolling country, with plenty of caves and rock shelters. Geologically, Lismore is a limestone intrusion into the Highland landscape and it creates land of exceptional fertility. This island is famous for its quality grass. We exported hay. Lismore hay was in great demand at the coaching inns on the mainland. Calcium

Egyptian horsemen on Arab horses, viewed from camel-back, 1889. (TN)

nurtures strong bones and the Lismore people, and their animals, are known for robust health. In the old Statistical Account, McNicol describes the finding of fossilised bones of deer and 'elk horns of great size and cow horns of a still greater size in proportion. The pith of one of the latter, though much shrivelled and withered, is twelve inches in circumference at the root'. Besides deer and oroc, there were wolves, bears, wild boar and bison on Lismore and, since very early times, this island was famed as a place for hunting. The open landscape and the particular scale of the island, about ten miles by one, made it a perfect arena for organised hunting. In the Heroic Age it provided the Fiana with a prime game reserve. The name Lismore means the enclosure, or the great garden. Like Glasgow it's another 'dear green place'. Lying east west in the sound of Lorn, it catches the sun all day and all year long. In the *Book of the Dean of Lismore*, written in the early seventeenth century, there is a poem by Ossian, the last great bard of the Fiana, which describes the most successful deer hunt ever organised in the Highlands. One of the place names mentioned is *Sliabh nam Ban Fhionn*, a name retained to this day on Lismore; we also have Cnoc Fionn and Oscar's bay and Ossian's island, and it seems highly probable that this famous hunt took place here on this island. Three thousand hounds took part and six thousand deer were killed or captured – not including the hornless! Exaggeration?

For thousands of years Lismore has been a secure and pleasant place of habitation and it has played an important part in Highland and Scottish history. Strategically it controls the southern entrance and exit from the Great Glen. Ancient processional ways, burial sites, brochs and cairns are still visible all over the island. In the Christian period it became a 'hortus concludus' from which St Muluag and his followers broadcast their new religion across Scotland. After that, the Picts and Scots divided the island between them – the boundary wall running though the great cairn behind the house here. Intellectually, the island has a distinguished history with a powerful wish to evangelise, recurrently, displaying itself. It was from Lismore that Ossian argued for the retention of the old pagan ways. In the seventeenth century, the episcopal Dean of Lismore, Sir James MacGregor, collected and collated many ancient Gaelic texts here and he has provided scholars with invaluable written evidence about early Scots Gaelic literature. His book is the fulcrum on which various Gaelic revivals have rested. Lismore seems to nurture missionary zeal – like Raasay it looks out towards wild and bare mountains, and Lismore's history of evangelism might have been one of the forces that inspired Dr David Livingstone to go out to Africa. His grandparents left Lismore for Blantyre at the time of the French Revolutionary Wars and he personifies the historic virtues of the Liosach. In the twentieth century, Ian Carmichael is one of several distinguished men who have continued this heroic evangelising tradition. He was born in the United States of Lismore parentage, served with great distinction during the First World

War, returned as a minister of the Church and wrote a splendid history of the island, entitled 'Lismore in Alba'. I knew him well over many years and his life embodied the finest values of this island's human history – echoing that of Livingstone, the Dean of Lismore, St Muluag and, in a modified manner, the life of the Fiana.

Lismore has witnessed a continuing interaction between the values of the old Celtic world and the changing face of Scots Christianity and this has been, in my opinion, very much to the advantage of both. The connection is most dramatically demonstrated in the *Book of the Dean of Lismore* itself. For example, in the marvellous 'dialogues' between Ossian (last survivor of the Old Order) and St Patrick (first leader of the New Christian Order). This unusual literary form – argument as poetic narrative – is very old, probably Druidic. These dialogues are of great interest in themselves but the arguments and images give a fascinating insight into the historic collision between the pagan values of the Heroic Age and the visionary, mystical humanism of Christian Faith.

Ossian: Tell us O Patrick, you of the great learning – will the nobles of the Fiana be offered entry to your Heaven?

Patrick: No – Heaven will never be the resting place of the Fiana – nor of thy father, nor of Osgar, nor of Goll.

Ossian: These are sad tidings, O learned one – and I ask myself why I should be seeking knowledge of your philosophy, if there is no salvation for anyone who is a Fiana. However, I'll do a deal. If you describe to me the glories of Heaven, I'll describe to you the Battle of Gobhra.

Patrick: There is no thirst, no hunger, no poverty, no distress . . .

Ossian: Good. But answer me this – I know the Fiana to be noble – but what of the people of Heaven? Are they hard of heart, or would they reward poet bands?

Patrick: There are no similarities. The Angels in Heaven are not like the Fiana.

Ossian: O Patrick – in the name of honour and humanity – forget not The Men! Could you not, in secret, give grace to the Fiana – without the knowledge of your Heaven's King?

Patrick: No I will not – though little room they'd take! No – not one of your race will find shelter in the House of the Lord.

Ossian: O Patrick – how different is MacCumhail, Chief of the Fiana. All men are always welcome in his house.

Patrick: Be silent Ossian. Be at peace. Accept my rule and the King of Heaven.

Ossian: Ah Patrick – if you had seen the banners stream above the battle host – you too would exult in the joyous din – exalt in the Life of the Fiana.

Bachuil house, built c. 1860. (TN)

Patrick: Ossian – though you were born the son of a Prince – know this – your soul is in mortal danger. Remember not the battle joy – all that is vanity.

Ossian: Man – if you had but once been part of the chase, had heard the hounds belling the hill – you – like me, would long again to join the fray and leave the walls of your Heavenly City.

Patrick: Just one of God's Angels is worth more than Fionn and all the Fiana the world can muster!

Ossian: You have spoken – but if I was now as I was in my youth I would avenge the contempt you show for Fiana – I who was there at the Battle of Gabhra, Gabhra of the Great Blows.

That poem was given to the Dean of Lismore by travelling bards who remained direct heirs to Ossian heroic tradition and it is clear that the culture of the old pagan order remained socially dynamic for at least a thousand years after Christianity became the established religion of the Highlands. And, perhaps, it is not surprising that the British Foreign Service, the British Army and Secret Services have embraced an unusual proportion of Highland Scots. Also, Scots have played central roles in the Commandos and the SAS. Why should this be? Is it because Druidic powers of memory and habits of secrecy, combined with martial prowess and communal loyalty, produce a very special 'diplomatic' mix – that remains as effective today as it was long ago.

However, whilst it is right to recognise the romance and heroism of the old pagan world, one is bound to acknowledge the revelatory impact Christianity had on early Scots society. St Muluag was, undoubtedly, the most influential man in the history of Lismore. His transmission of Christ's message of love and mercy, his recognition of the dignity and potential of every individual – brought intellectual, spiritual and social hope to many hard lives, many brilliant minds. St Muluag honoured the plough and the pen and abhorred blood and the sword. The old Celtic Church proclaimed to all and sundry 'that the enslaved shall be freed, the common people exulted – for the Lord is accessible'. It was never elitist.

I never saw my grandfather. He died before I was born. He became a Baptist and a minister and he did much good work on Lismore. He failed, however, in one regard – it was he who lost custody of *am Bachull Mor*. We understand that the Duke of Argyll visited Lismore in 1870 and on being shown the staff he asked to borrow it for an exhibition at Inveraray Castle. My grandfather agreed but years passed and the staff was not returned. My grandmother and various Liosachs here asked him to act but he seems to have displayed a feudal subordination typical of the age and any mild request he might have made to Argyll was wholly ineffective. As the years passed my grandfather became holier and holier and seems to have persuaded himself that such 'a worldly' request was mere vanity. He died in 1906. My father would certainly have sought return of the staff but he was then in Nyasaland and unfortunately was never to return. My mother, however, on settling back into Bachuil made contact with the new duke. To her chagrin, he was most unhelpful saying, 'Even if I wished to return it, which I don't, I would not be entitled to return it.' Thus things remained until towards the end of the Second World War when I began to take a serious interest in the issue and a small stroke of fortune played into my hands. I was in the army and so was the Duke of Argyll. On leave, in London, we arranged to meet and, immediately, struck up a rapport. I explained to him the history of the staff, its importance to Lismore and the facts of its chartered custody within our family at Bachuil. After a good deal of discussion he agreed that the staff should never have left Lismore and promised that the staff would be returned to the permanent custody of the Barons of Bachuil – as soon as possible. However, we were both then stationed far from home and likely to remain so for some years so I insisted a written agreement be made – in case one, or both, of us 'should die tomorrow'. This was done and it was formally agreed that when I, or my descendants, returned permanently to Lismore, the staff of St Muluag would be returned to our perpetual possession. Thirty years passed but in 1973 I retired and re-established permanent residence at Bachuil. And the next year, on a wild and stormy day, *am Bachull Mor* was brought with due ceremony from Inveraray – back to its rightful place on Lismore. That led to a great sprey on the island. A loan of 104 years is a very long loan but, in the end, the resolution was amicable; honour was satisfied on all sides.

I hold *am Bachuul Mor* in the name of all the people of Lismore. It is not the property of any particular church; we regard it as a sacred relic for ecumenical use – as appropriate. There is a sense in which the Episcopal Church is the direct descendant of the old Celtic Church but the staff is non-denominational. I discuss all usage with the sennachies here on Lismore and we act by agreement. For instance, we took it to St John's Cathedral in Oban for the consecration of the last bishop. It is a crozier and the oldest Christian relic in Scotland, so what could be more appropriate. As with the staff, so with myself, things have come full circle. Not long ago I fell from the roof of the house here and badly fractured a leg – now I'm almost well again and back where I belong. We both look out on the world from our island enclosure – with great interest and a sense of great hope.

As a child, a horse and small carriage took me down to the ferry and, from the age of five, I went across to Port Appin School. There, all my best friends were Campbells – sons of the Port Appin smith. He had twelve children, they kept the school going! When his wife died he married again and started a new family. The smiths play a big part in the story of Lismore and Appin. Clan Pheidirean, the Patersons, had their smithy at Creagan Corrach, Fearrlochan in Benderloch. They were famous armourers, renowned for their swords and it may be they were direct descendants of the Pictish smiths of Ledaig. All metalworkers were respected craftsmen with direct links to the clan chiefs. There's a story of a clan feud. A baby boy, one of the Stewarts, was rescued by his nurse and hidden in a cave. The parents were killed but the child survived – fed on suet by the nurse and protected by her husband the smith. Time passed and the boy was reared in secret as one of their own children. He started work in the smithy and he proved himself a young man of quite unusual strength, with the gift of working two hammers at once. He became known as Donald Two Hammers. Then, in typical, mythical fashion, he learned the truth about his birth and hereditary rights – and went forth to regain his family's land and title. Here on Lismore the smithy stands just in front of St Muluag's well.

The Stewarts and the Campbells here were at each other's throats for centuries and our family's change of name probably had something to do with this feud. We were glad to be seen not to be in thrall to either and, overnight, in the mid-sixteenth century, it seems we changed our name from MacDhunshleibhe to Livingstone. It is a much easier name to spell, but MacDhunshleibhe is a version of Mac-an-leigh, which means son of the physician. Thus the name 'Living stone' retains some associative link with the original Gaelic but beyond that – family tradition suggests the name came from the south of Scotland, from one James Livingstone of Skirling. Whether he had land up here, or whether we established some personal contact with him down there, I don't know, but the name was taken. It is a Saxon name. A man called Leving was given lands at Skirling; over time the place became known as Livingston and the name spread. Today there are Highland and Lowland Livingstones; ours is the Highland line.

Names are a fascinating subject. In the Highlands most people need nicknames. In my time, at school and in the army, everybody had a nickname. They were usually based on some connection that somebody had with something. For example we had an officer called Elim; he was always called 'The Prophet'. I started off as Livinski but that soon got changed to Molotov. When I was with the Indian Division I was known as Molotov Sab. Quite recently I had reason to phone one of my old brigadiers. We had not been in contact for, maybe, thirty years. When I heard his voice I said, 'Good afternoon brigadier. Do you know who this is?' 'No,' he said. 'It's Alastair Livingstone.' 'Never heard of an Alistair Livingstone!' he boomed but as soon as I began to say, 'It's Molo …', he burst in – 'Ah Molotov! Why didn't you say!' Nicknames stick like glue and can have great associative power – like a Molotov Cocktail!

In my retirement, I became president of the 1745 Association and I was very pleased to able to oversee the completion of a book that documents all the regiments and men who fought at Culloden. The Livingstones fought with the Appin Regiment; indeed it was Donald Livingstone who rescued the Stewart Banner. We suffered some consequences after the battle. This house is not old, it was built by my grandfather in the 1850s as his family home and as the Baptist Chapel. I call it Bachuil Mark III. The original chieftain's house was burnt down in 1746 because of his role in the Rising. That was Mark I. It was replaced by a rather poor, stone crofthouse that stood for about a hundred years until it, too, was burned to the ground – this time by accident. That was Mark II. The present rather fine, stone house was then built. It looks like a tacksman's house but it wasn't. Originally, the Livingstones owned a modest amount of land on Lismore but this was gradually eroded away and since the eighteenth century few of us were able to make a living from the land – we went out to the colonies, into the Foreign Service, into the army, into the church – but our loyalty to Lismore has remained absolute.

We have always been happy in a spartan environment. We had to! But there's more to it than that. We have over centuries made a virtue of simplicity and hardihood and it produces results. This must go back to the earliest settlers here and to the ascetic tradition of the early Christian monks. They were not necessarily celebate and never subordinate. St Muluag and St Columba were devoted Christians but also in many ways highly competitive.

Cliff Valros, West Lewis, April 1938. The kind of Hebridean landscape within which the Eriskay breed developed over the centuries. (PC)

They behaved like clan chiefs. They taught their particular visions of Christianity, they sought advantage against each other but they remained 'brothers' within one, single Celtic church. Not surprisingly the followers of both men were deeply perturbed by the Synod of Whitby. It established the dominion of the Roman Church and whilst they might have celebrated the unity of European Christianity, they certainly resented the loss of the old ways and the truth – as they saw it – from their isolated, spartan perspective in Scotland. And, although the Celtic Church accepted the Roman dating of Easter, and some level of Papal authority, for hundreds of years after 664 AD, resistance lingered, independence continued and many leaders of Celtic Christianity withdrew to live private lives as hermits and saints.

Those isolated adherents of the old ways became known as the Culdees. The name comes from *Cele De*, which in Gaelic means Servants of God. Like Christ they went out into the desert, but they stayed. These were, perhaps, the first of 'the Men' who have, recurrently, evangelised Highland Scotland by ascetic example up till the present time. In the eleventh century Queen Margaret expressed high admiration for those 'who in different places, enclosed in separate cells, lived in the flesh, but not according to the flesh, in great straitness of life, and even on earth lived the lives of angels'. That description brings to mind the *Book of Kells* – which most people now recognise to have been produced on Iona. And, although the Culdees disappeared under continuing Roman pressure in the thirteenth century, in a real sense the Celtic Church has continued quietly, underground, to this day.

The Culdees, like the Druids, expressed something very deep in the Celtic and Scottish character – an independence, a thrawnness, a wilful strongheadedness, a commitment to ideological enquiry. They were exemplary custodians of attitudes and ideas still strong in Scotland and these kinds of attitudes have even affected the existence of the Eriskay pony! Did you know that this breed of ponies, which only a few years ago was on the absolute verge of extinction, is now protected and controlled by two separate Rare Breeds Societies! One organisation exists in the Hebrides and one on the mainland of Scotland and each is frequently savage with the other! It would appear to be a farcical situation. But such independence and prickliness is not necessarily foolish. Things are different in the most isolated places, differences of emphasis are important; and the recent revival of this vanishing breed might

Cliff Valros, West Lewis, 1938, showing buildings, a landscape and life style that has changed little over thousands of years: the Battle of Troy was fought in a landscape remarkably like this. (PC)

well owe something to the creative tensions that exist between the representatives of these two societies. Each feels it has crucial values to uphold – and they have upheld them! The revival of the Eriskay can stand as a symbol of the revival of Scotland. The Eriskay is not, however, a subject I know a great deal about. What you should do is speak to Alec McIntosh, an old friend of mine; a man who knows a great deal about this ancient, native horse – the Eriskay Pony.

ALEC MCINTOSH AND THE ERISKAY PONY

Many images of horses are carved and engraved on the Pictish Stones of Scotland. They portray medium size horses that look remarkably like the modern Eriskay Pony. The Pictish stone carvers who decorated these stones were, almost certainly, metalworkers – that was their day job. They had great naturalistic skills and a naturalistic sensibility that would seem to go back to palaeolithic times. The horses they represented were, obviously, once the common riding horses of eastern Scotland. Up till the mid-twentieth century the descendants of these Pictish horses continued to exist, with remarkable genetic purity, in the Outer Hebrides; most notably on the isolated small island of Eriskay. At the last moment, on the verge of extinction, in the early 1970s, the unique genetic, historical and cultural importance of these ponies was recognised – and moves were made to conserve them.

Historically, there are presumed to have been two major modern breeds of wild horse in Europe, what might be called the Asiatic and the Celtic. The Asiatic was larger and inhabited the Steppes of Russia and Scythia. The Celtic horse is generally identified with the Celtic peoples and is known to have inhabited the British Isles, Western Europe and Greece. The Eriskay is a classic representative of the Celtic horse in the modern world. It also represents a continuum within Scottish history. The fleet-footed and powerful small horse that carried the Bruce to victory in single-combat before the battle of Bannockburn was not an Eriskay pony but it was, almost certainly, a horse whose genetic make-up was very similar to a modern pure-bred Eriskay. They are an old and hardy breed that would have passed into extinction but for the work of the two Eriskay Pony Societies, and the British Rare Breeds Survival Trust. A few years ago we were down to a single stallion and a small scattered herd of mares and foals – many with a touch of Highland pony in them. Today they are a recognised facet of Scotland's heritage and the world's biodiversity.

There is less information about the early existence of the native horses of Scotland than one would expect of such a literate nation. *Burt's letters from the North of Scotland* contain some of the most riveting early facts. Burt travelled in the Highlands in the 1720s, when the new military roads were

Two Eriskay ponies, enjoying the snow at Kinross, Christmas Day, 1995. (AM)

being planned, and he documented various aspects of Highland life at a time of major climatic, economic and political hardship. In Letter XX he writes:

> Before I proceed to their Husbandry, I shall give you an account of an animal necessary to it; that is, their Horses, or rather (as they are called) Garrons. These Horse in Miniature run wild among the Mountains, some of them till they are eight or ten years old, which renders them extremely restive and stubborn. There are various ways of catching them, according to the Spot of Country where they chiefly keep their Haunts. Sometimes they are hunted by Numbers of Highlandmen into a Bog; in other places they are driven up a steep Hill, where the nearest of their Pursuers endeavours to catch them by the hind-leg; and I have been told that sometimes Horse and Man have come tumbling down together. In another Place they have been hunted from one to another, among the heath and rocks, till they have lain themselves down through Weariness and want of Breath.
>
> They are so small that a middle-sized Man must keep his Legs almost on Lines parallel to their Sides when carried over the stony Ways; and it is almost incredible to those who have not seen it, how nimbly they skip with a heavy Rider among the Rocks and large Moor-Stones,

A classic, grey Eriskay pony saddled with two traditional panniers, 1998. (AM)

turning zig-zag to such places as are passable. I think verily they all follow one another in the same irregular Steps, because in those Ways there appears some little Smoothness, worn by their naked hoofs, which is not anywhere else to be seen. When I have been riding or rather creeping along at the Foot of the Mountain, I have discovered them by their Colour, which is mostly white, and, by their Motion, which readily catches the Eye, when, at the same Time, they were so high above me, they seemed to be no bigger than a Lap-dog, and almost hanging over my Head. But what has appeared to me very extraordinary is, what when at other Times, I have passed near to them, I have perceived them to be (like some of our common beggars in London) in ragged and tattered Coats, but full in flesh; and that, even towards the latter End of Winter, when I think they can have nothing to feed upon but Heath and rotten leaves of Trees if any of the latter were to be found. The Highlanders have a Tradition that they came originally from Spain, by Breeders left there by the Spaniards in former Times; and they say, they have been a great number of years dwindling to their present diminutive Size. I was one Day greatly diverted with the method of training these wild horses.

A traditional cattle and horse sale on the machair, Uist, c.1920. Photograph by John Kennedy in the collection of Christie Matheson of Ullapool.

> In Passing along a narrow Path, on the Side of a high Hill among the Mountains, at length it brought me to a Part looking down into a little Plain; there I was at once presented with the Scene of a Highlandman beating one of these Garrons, most unmercifully, with a great Stick; and, upon a stricter View, I perceived the Man had tied a Rope, or something like it, about one of his hind-Legs, as you may have seen a single hog driven in England; and, indeed, in my Situation, he did not seem so big. At the same Time the Horse was kicking and violently struggling, and sometimes the Garron was down and sometimes the Highlander, and not seldom both of them together, but still the man kept his hold.
>
> After waiting a considerable time to see the Event, though not so well pleased with the precipice I stood upon, I found the Garron gave it up; and being perfectly conquored for that Time, patiently allowed himself to be driven to a Hut not far from the field of Battle …
>
> In the Western Highlands they still retain that barbarous custom (which I have not seen anywhere else) of drawing the harrow by the Horse's Dock, without any Manner of Harness whatever. And when the tail becomes too short for the Purpose, they lengthen it out with twisted sticks … When a burden is to be carried on Horseback they use two baskets called *Creels*, one on each Side of the Horse; and if the Load be such as cannot be divided, they put it into one of them, and counter-balance it with Stones in the other, so that one Half of the Horse's Burden is – I cannot say unnecessary – because I do not see how they could do otherwise in the Mountains.

That letter is well worth analysis – as literature it combines elements of Shakespeare, Bunyan and Johnson – as ethnography it is hugely informative.

First, the methods of early eighteenth-century hunting it describes are classic examples of pre-historic practice. Large numbers of Highlanders drive wild horses – down into a bog, or up to a steep hilltop, where they are to be captured (and killed). Others were driven hither and thither until they collapsed with exhaustion.

Second, the method of breaking these horses seems to have been remarkably close to that still used by Travelling horse dealers in Sutherland in the 1950s. They are first hobbled by a rope round one leg and then wrestled or smothered into submission (described in *The Summer Walkers*, Volume 1 of this Quintet).

Third, the colour of the horses described by Burt corresponds extremely well with the colour of mature Eriskays – dappled grey to white.

Fourth, the method of load carrying is of exactly the kind continued up to the present in the Western Isles – a creel on each side of the horse.

Fifth, the style of riding was, perhaps, the only style possible on such small horses but it was also remarkably similar to that depicted in the

Hibern-Saxon manuscripts and on various of the Pictish Stones.

Sixth, the local people seem to believe that these horses were the descendants of Spanish horses, greatly reduced in size because of the harsh environment. Factually this would appear to be historical and genetic nonsense but it equates well with other misconceptions – for example that their 'darkness' comes from Spaniards washed ashore from the Armada ... In fact the small white horses, like the dark-haired people of North West Scotland, are likely to be much more ancient and indigenous.

Seventh, with regard to size – it is obvious that horses are one of those creatures that, by feeding and breeding, can be bred large or small surprisingly quickly.

The Highland horses described by Burt are considerably smaller than present-day Eriskay ponies, but even in the eighteenth century, ponies, living on the good grass of the Machairs in the outer islands, would have been much larger than their Highland mountain brethren. Writing in 1549, Dean Munro had stated that there 'layes ane little ile, half an myle lang, callit be the name Eriche Ellannaneache, that is, in English, the Horse Isle, guid for horse and other store, pertaining to the Bishope of the Isles'. And in 1772 Thomas Pennant describes the Isle of Canna in these words:

> Here are very few sheep; but horses in abundance. The chief use of them in this little district is to form an annual cavalcade at Michaelmas. Every man on the island mounts his horse unfurnished with saddle, and takes behind him some young girl or his neighbour's wife, and then rides backwards and forwards from the village to a certain cross, without being able to give any reason for the origin of this custom. After the procession is over they alight at some public house, where strange to say, the females treat their companions of their ride.

The final statement there seems to suggest an annual, ceremonial, practice of 'out breeding' continuing on Canna long after one might expect. Michaelmas on Canna sounds like Carnival in Rio de Janeiro!

During the nineteenth century various 'improved' breeds of horses were taken out to the Hebrides to increase the size, strength and 'beauty' of the native ponies. There are records of Arab, Spanish and Clydesdale stallions being employed but the mass of Hebridean horses remained local and the breed tended to revert to type. With regard to gene and breed purity, isolation and a shortage of hard cash were great advantages, and the most isolated of all the great horse islands was Eriskay. There the breed remained ancient and pure into the 1960s. By that time numbers were dangerously low but, cometh the moment, cometh the men. And the three individuals to whom we really owe the preservation of the Eriskay are Dr Robert Hill, Father O'Neill of Barra, and Robert Beck who has codified the characteristics of the pure Eriskay.

Head:	rather large and broad without being coarse or ugly.
Body:	very wide, deep chest and abdomen.
Tail:	set low.
Height:	12.2 to 13 hands.
Legs:	fine boned, without feather; a small tuft in winter.
Action:	small, energy saving steps, especially at the trot; effortless 'lope' when cantering. This economical action, along with the large chest, means that they do not tire or sweat easily, and are quite swift for their size.
Colour:	normally charcoal-coloured at birth, gradually lightening to grey/white in adulthood.
Winter coat:	ample and waterproof without looking shaggy.
Disposition:	exceptionally amenable and easy to train; intelligent: willing and content in human company – the labradors of the horse world.
Use:	the Eriskay is an exemplary pony – good with children and the disabled, strong and speedy when required, gentle, characterful and lovable. What more could you ask?

These characteristics show how similar the Eriskay is to the Highland pony. The Highland is not a pure breed, in the genetic sense, as the Eriskay is, but the Highland is a recognised breed and it too is a descendant of Scotland's native horse population. Highland ponies, often known as garrons, have done varied work in the Highlands over many centuries. There is a man up at Blair Atholl, with the same name as myself, who worked for years with Highland deer ponies on the hill – Willie McIntosh. He comes from a different branch of the Mackintosh clan to the main family, based at Moy, Inverness-shire, but Willie will tell you a good deal about the work of the Highland on the hill carrying deer …

WILLIE MCINTOSH AND THE HIGHLAND DEER PONY

My father was a forester, a horseman and a ghillie, who worked on the Blair Atholl estates. He was known as the Chiefie. Why that was – I didn't know, till after he died. I thought it was just a nickname. But, one day a man from the west coast came over to tell us, after doing a great deal of genealogical research, that we were the last of the McIntoshes of Glen Tilt and Glen Fender and that my father had good reason to be called 'the Chiefie'. Charlie McIntosh was his name. We go back to the twelfth century in Glen Tilt and we contested the ground here with the Wolf of Badenoch – long before the Murrays and the Stewarts had anything to do with Blair Atholl. There are now very few of us left. My brother died eighteen years ago and I've been ill – with cancer of the brain, in here behind the eyes. I had five years of radium treatment, in and out of Ninewells Hospital, in Dundee. I think nobody thought I would survive but now I'm back at work fulltime with two years to go before retirement. I play a lot of bridge and I'm a corporal in the Atholl Highlanders. Thirty-two years' service. We're the only official private army in Britain and certainly the best looking.

Charlie McIntosh married a Wilson from Glasgow. Miners they were, and my mother was one of sixteen children. She moved up here and she became a good old country woman; always a livewire till the end. We lived at Pitagowan, by Calvine, and at the Milton of Invervrack. That was a beautiful wee cottage, with a walled garden all round. I grew up during the war with the Canadian lumberjacks – and prisoners of war. Austrians, hundreds of them, all around here. When I left school in 1953 I went straight into the forestry but

Willie McIntosh of Blair Atholl, hill pony man, 2002. (TN)

there was a great cry for ghillies every summer and my brother and I went out with the deer ponies, half the year. Ghillies were paid ten bob a week more than the foresters and we enjoyed being out on the hill. I did three seasons before my National Service and another three afterwards. All that was with garrons, in the old style. That was long before the quadbikes and the walkie talkies came in.

My first season was on the Home Beat, working from the kennels. The paths zigzag up very steep but the distances were relatively short. I had two ponies. I would lead, with one horse right behind me and the other on a rein following – Indian style. The next year I was selected for the Tarff Beat, working from the bothy at Forest Lodge. That gave you a long walk out to the Tilt. It was a long, long walk and a long, long day. Seven miles out and seven miles back and maybe ten chasing the deer. It's a wild, isolated area of ground and it was tiring work for the men as well as the ponies. There's a lot of water up there on the Tarff Beat and it all drains off into the Tilt. Then the Tilt runs into the Garry, the Garry runs into the Tummel and the Tummel runs into the Tay.

There'd normally be just three of us, myself, the stalker and a gentleman. The aim was to bring two stags back on each pony. The big stags – that's what the toffs on the Tarff were after – they would weigh in at about fourteen stones. None of the ground was easy, it was rough, or steep, or boggy and the stags might be shot anywhere across thousands of acres. The horses needed to be fit and they needed to be strong. What I liked was a nimble, sensible pony with a long slow step – a nice gentle big stride – so that the deer were more likely to stay on the saddles and the horse wasn't likely to go down in a bog. I had a lovely natured, strong pony called May but she was a half-breed and she had a short, sharp step and she was always liable to break through the peat and go down.

Loading a stag was never easy. You'd have to keep hold of the reins whilst you lifted. I normally had a hand from the stalker and sometimes the toft might hold the head of the horse. It was very important to get a stag balanced, and the girths good and tight, before you set off. If a stag with tines swung loose under the belly of your pony he was in trouble and so were you. Out on the Tarff Beat we liked to leave the heads behind, if we could, but many of the gentlemen would be wanting their trophy, wanting 'a royal' to take home. That meant us lugging the whole carcass. But then again, if you took the heads off, you had a lot more blood. And that was something the ponies never took to. They might be trained to it and get used to it but none liked the smell or the sight of blood. It must have spoken to something deep in their natures. It was as though they had a sympathy for their dead fellow creature or, perhaps, a fear – that they would be next. Anyway, some horses never got used to the blood and every time, during loading, they would kick up a fuss –

Blair Atholl: Headkeeper Reid, checks the strapping on a Highland pony with Ghillie, Calum Kippen, 1999. (John Tickner)

and coming home – and when we unloaded. Now a man can keep control of the strongest horse if he has him by the head, by the nose, by the nostrils but – if a horse is away from you, if you're down the side of a horse whilst unstrapping a carcass and that horse decides to bolt there's little you can do about it. I had a gelding did that to me – he lunged forward, rushed away and left me on the ground. He then started bucking like a Bucking Bronco, till he went head over heels – stag and all – backwards!

Horses might not have rational intelligence but they have well-honed instincts, they have timing and they have a memory. They will both retaliate and await their moment – payback time. May was like that. One December we were up at the hinds. Two keepers culling and myself with May and a legless wee nuisance called Princess. She caused me a lot of trouble and she'd caused May a lot of trouble. May, being the good one, was always loaded first. So, Princess just lounged about for hours whilst May suffered her burden. Well, at last, we had our four hinds, all loaded up, ready for the tramp home but first we had to cross the Tilt. The water was high and very cold. The two stalkers crossed first and waited. Not wanting to get wet, I decided to hitch a lift on May. I squeezed onto her rump, one hand grabbing the carcass of a hind, the other holding Princess on her rein. Into the river we went, May stepping out boldly with her short stride and her body pressed up against the flow of the river. Halfway across, Princess started to panic, she was pulling back and careering about. May came to a stop. I tried to urge her forward – whilst the ghillies were roaring with laughter on the bank. Suddenly, May decided she'd had enough. She reared up on her back legs, pawing the air like a stallion, and I, very slowly slid down her backside, arse-first into the water. She then plunged forward and up the bank whilst Princess and I were swept away, out of sight, round the bend. All that was very close to where there's a great boulder by the Tilt, where the Clan McIntosh gathered. The chief called his followers to meet at that stone. That was the McIntosh Rallying Stone, that was our Parliament Tree.

Today, the Blair Atholl ponies spend most of the year trekking and only some of them go out to the hills for the stalking but when I came in the trekking had not really started and the main role of Highlands was to work on the hill. The twelfth of August was the special day. The heather is just coming into its own. My brother and I would go up to the bothies and live there through the week, right through to the winter. We had to supply all our own clothes – boots and waterproofs in those days. And we had to supply our own food and cook it. We would normally lodge with one of the underkeepers. Three of us together, quite spartan. You had to get on. My mother would set us up with food for the week. We had very little money so it was beans, beans and more beans. Some bread and tea but that was it.

However, on the hill we got paid more than we got in the sawmill

Blair Atholl: David Steel announces his departure from Castle, 1999. (John Tickner)

and it was well worth it to us. We enjoyed our time out, learning life in the hills. We'd rise, shave, catch the horses. That wouldn't be easy sometimes because they knew they were in for another tiring long day. We'd feed them and groom them and saddle them. Then we'd have our beans and be ready to set off with the stalkers at about nine o'clock. They had to walk out in those days. No all-terrain vehicles. Once we crossed the Tilt, depending on the wind, the stalkers would go forward and I'd stay back with the horses – making sure we didn't disturb the deer. No walkie talkies then, so I'd wait till I heard a shot, or saw the stalker burning a handful of heather – giving us a glimpse of a wee wisp of smoke. Or, maybe, he'd wave, and I'd wend my way forward to the kill. Normally he'd have the stag gralloched and ready for me. We loaded the best of the ponies and then the stalker and the toff would go off after another. Then I'd wait and follow on again. It was hard work and we looked forward to the tip that came at the end of the season. That would be about ten pound. It cleared our debts and got us set up for the New Year. It was tipping that put an end to my life on the hill.

My brother and I stopped work at the same time and for the same reason. It would be about forty years ago, in the mid-sixties. We fell out with our employer, not Atholl estates but one of the tenants. For years Forest Lodge was let every year to a big family from the south. And it was them took us on and paid the ghillies and stalkers. Each year a different member of the family played host – brothers, sons, sons-in-law – it was a good arrangement but some were more tight with their money than others. That was the time that the five-day week came in but not for us out on the hill. Saturday remained a full day, the most important day. Because we were offered the usual wage but still had to work the sixth day, we two stood together and asked for a rise. We weren't popular but in the end, that year's toff agreed two things. We would have a small increase in our weekly wages and have access to a vehicle that would allow us to drive home each night and up in the morning. We were not delighted but we were satisfied and we put in a good season, but – come the end and come the tips – that toff, like May, got his revenge. Instead of a £10 tip we got £1! He reimbursed himself all he thought he had lost. The other stalkers and ghillies, who had not complained, got their usual £10. That man wasn't wicked but he was a man of his time and thought he'd teach us a lesson. Rub our noses in the mud – for our temerity in asking for a rise. He was a pleasant man and a wonderful shot but he wanted to keep us where he thought we were. We didn't complain but we weren't happy. He had insulted us as clear as day – and we never applied to go back to the hill. And by that time, wages off the estate were shooting up. The A9 was being built, there was plenty of work with the Hydro Board. My brother went away and I went into the sawmill and got married.

One thing I did miss was taking the ponies up to the grouse shoots. That was much easier work and much more civilised than killing stags. Each horse had two panniers, like creels, strapped over their backs and even if they got filled with a hundred brace – they were still light compared to a stag and the ponies would enjoy the trek home with the crowd. The older I grow, the more I love nature and see that nature is the best conservatory force that we have. I like things to balance out as nature not man determines. I like those who mind their own business. I don't thinks it's up to us, or the Americans, to run the world. What right, but might, have they got to bomb whosoe'er they choose? I believe in natural justice. There's something of this must run in our family. An ancestor of mine was Charles McIntosh, the botanist and naturalist. He was born and brought up in Glen Tilt. One day he saw a pressgang coming up – looking for men for the army. The Crimea War, I think it was. The Duke of Sutherland was recruiting as well. Well, Charlie McIntosh had no interest in being shipped off to fight the Russians for a shilling – so, he put on women's clothes and fled, hid and fled, across the hills and settled down at Dunkeld. He was a good fiddler and he loved nature and he loved the old ways. Beatrix

Potter used to come up to holiday there and she used a lot of him, and his ideas, in her stories. One of the old Gaelic rhymes he collected describes 'the three beautiful dead – a salmon, a blackcock, and a child'.

A dead stag may be noble but you couldn't say a dead stag is beautiful but, of course, the bigger a stag is, the more tines he has, the more some people want to shot him. People like to bring down that which is beyond them. I have a friend who got sent a letter, with a poem from the poet Hugh MacDiarmid which describes, exactly, that phenomenon. The poem is usually known as *The Royal Stag* but MacDiarmid later retitled it *Homage to the Poet W.S. Graham – In admiration of the long years in which he has always set a 'stout heart to a stey brae' and refused to be deflected from his creative purpose – despite all the pressures of Philistia.* It's very good.

The hornless hart carries off the harem.
Magnificent antlers are nothing in love.
Great tines are only a drawback and danger
To the noble stag that must bear them.

Crowned as with an oak tree he goes,
A sacrifice for the ruck of his race,
Knowing full well that his towering points
Will single him out, a mark for his foes.

Yet no polled head's triumph since the world began
In love and war have made a high heart thrill
Like the sight of a Royal with its Rights and Crockets,
Its Pearls, and Beam, and Span.

James Stewart

Balmuir Wood

I joined the army in 1937. Despatch Rider. Rough Riders – that was what we were. It was horses in those days. I did two years on horses and four years on motorbikes. On my two pins I went up to Perth Barracks from Dundee, to join the Black Watch, twenty-two miles. I was sixteen years old. I was living in a Home, a Children's Home, so I was glad to get away. There was a small gang of us gathered thegether. The sergeant said, 'Sit down boys' and he gave out papers and we all had to do a test, an intelligence test. He said, 'Just fill in the answers and put your hand up when you're finished.' Well, I found that test very easy, just wee sums to add and subtract, and as soon as I'd finished I shot up my hand. The sergeant came over, 'Finished Stewart, are we? Youse had better try something more difficult!' And he gave me a second paper. Easy! I shot up my hand a second time. 'Stewart,' he said, 'you're smart, very smart! What regiment is it you're wanting to join?' 'Black Watch, sir!' He said, 'Do youse like horses?' 'Yes sir,' I said, 'I've worked horses since I was four years old.' 'Stewart,' he said, 'stand up. No laddie like you should be joining the Black Watch!' 'Why not, sir?' I said. He leaned over and in a quiet voice he said, 'A smart lad like you should use his brain – the likes of youse should join a corps, learn a trade.'

All the boys were bent over their papers, trying hard not to listen to what the sergeant was saying to me! I said, 'What's a corps, sir?' 'Oh,' he said, 'there's the Medical Corps, the Transport Corps, the Royal Engineers, and there's the Signal Corps. You said you liked horse-riding, Stewart.' 'Yes sir, I like horse riding.' 'Well,' said the sergeant, 'youse could be a despatch

James Stewart of Balmuir '
2000. (TN'

rider – in the Signal Corps – like the Pony Express!' Well that sold it to me like, you know what I mean, and that very day – I signed on in the Signals. I got six shillings straight in my pocket; three days' wages at two bob a day. That was a lot of money for me in those days. They sent me down to Catterick camp. That's a very old army camp and it was a big place for horses in those days. I did three and a half months' basic training and map-reading. I was good at all that. Then, we each got our own horse and I became a 'rough rider'. That was a good life. The poet, Sorley Maclean, he was a signaller, he wrote a poem about going down to Catterick, after the start of the war, but his experience was different to mine.

I went down to yonder town
with the sentence of death in my hand
written with two wrongs:
the great wrong of the Nazis
And the great wrong of her misery.
I myself wrote it on my heart
As ransom for my darling's state;
I was going to a war
and she was bruised and wretched,
with no lover in the wild world
who would care for what she had of grace.

Of course, I didn't know that poem then, it wasn't even written then, and I don't know whether I've remembered it quite right. But when I did hear it, because it was about Catterick, I remembered it. Well, we soon got shifted further south, down into the Garden of England. I got sent to the barracks in Canterbury – so I could meet the Archbishop! Me, being a Catholic like – I tried to convert him! I asked him to sit an intelligence test and I asked him if he liked horses and wanted to join a corpse like me! Good times we had. Riding through the orchards with all the apple trees in blossom – oiling the leather, polishing the brass, polishing my boots, going out to the pictures – a girl on my arm. Then tragedy struck! Our horses got replaced by motorbikes! It was the Germans caused the trouble! We got sent over to France. I was there at Dunkirk – I ran – like everybody else! One incident sticks in my mind, sticks in my throat, I should have said! I had to take a message up to an 88 Field Battery, which was under attack by Tiger tanks. I came to a crossroads where I was stopped by a red cap, that's a military policeman. 'Where do you think you're going?' he said – a Glasgow man, he was. I said, 'Up to the 88 Field Battery.' 'I'll gie ye a tip,' he said, 'dinnae go. Five o' your boys hae gone up there and there's not one's come back. They've got snipers everywhere. If you want my advice, head for the beach, like ayebody else!' So I turned the bike and I said, 'Jump on!' He took off his tunic top, laid it on the bar at the back

Stewart boys outside their cottage, north Aberdeenshire, c1920. (JT)

of the bike and away to the beaches we went. We dug in on the sand and I came back on the same boat I sailed out on, the *Ben MacCrieve* from Southampton.

Three years later I was riding north from Salerno when bang, I was shot through the throat. A German sniper. That was our bogie, snipers. That was the bogie of the motorcycle men – I was flung off my bike! I never knew hit what me. One minute there I was – singing away – enjoying the road – the next minute I was in the dust with the bike all over me. The wound turned septic. My head swelled like a balloon, twice the size of a normal head. I started to look very impressive! After that I was invalided out, discharged. I was twenty-four years of age. My career was finished. Out there in Italy, singing on my bike and in the cafés I'd begun to think I might be an opera singer! But that bullet went straight through my throat, tightened the vocal cords, made me talk like a snipe and sing like a castrati! So that was that – when I came home I went out on the streets to make my living as a busker and all my life I've made half my living out of singing – like my father before me. I have an unusual voice – it reaches those parts other voices don't reach. It's old Traveller songs I sing, the bothy ballads and the songs of the road – a bit of roughness in the throat can help carry that kind of song.

My father was Davy Stewart. He was well known all over the north east. He was very popular in Dundee – he used to sing, with his accordian, to the cinema queues and when I was a boy in the Dundee Royal Infirmary – I used to listen and wait for his voice coming up to the ward windows. I never saw him in the Home – so that used to bring the tears to my eyes – anybody could recognise his voice – it was very particular and he played the accordian like nobody else. He didn't know I was in the hospital, but I knew it was my father singing outside. He went on to make records for the Tangent label. He was a tenor like me. He left my mother and went away to Ireland. He was away for twenty-seven years. Just sometimes he'd come back over in the summertime. Davy Stewart was one of the Perthshire Stewarts – even though he was born in Aberdeen and his mother was Irish, a McGuire.

My own mother was a MacAlister from Sutherland. The Wild MacAlisters, Gaelic speakers they were. There was a living to be made in the fishing towns in those days, before the First World War. There was money in the fisher towns and Travellers could make a living alongside the fisher people – so I was born in Peterhead and that's the first place I remember. We had an old horse-caravan down by the railway line. I was brought up with horses and carts and the old caravans. We went to school in bare feet. That was in Buckie. You could get the odd job and plenty free fish in those days and from the time I could walk I went busking with my father all along the north coast. I was going round with a bonnet, collecting the pennies. Davy sang with the big accordian and I'd pick up fifteen shillings, no bother. That all came to an end when the family broke up and my father went away to Ireland. I was put away into Baldowan, a big house and a Home in Downfield, Dundee. Baldowan Children's Home.

A lot of the Traveller children were being put into Homes in those days. If the mother had no man with her, or the parents were alcoholics, or just living rough out on the road – you got taken in. My sisters were taken away and I didn't see them again. I heard that, during the war, they went down to Coventry and Wolverhampton to work in the munition factories. And there they were both killed in the bombing. At least that's what I think must have happened because I never heard of either of them again. My brother, he was much younger than me, he stayed out with my mother and the new family she got. Later on he too joined the army. He went out to Burma and he was killed in the jungle, he never came home. One of my stepbrothers was drowned in a river up around Aberdeen, he was thirteen years of age, Hughie MacAlister to name. The Traveller life was always hard.

I was in Baldowan for nine years from 1928, when I was seven, until 1937 when I was sixteen and went away to join the army. Some hard times we had in Baldowan but not bad times and we were lucky compared to the boys put away on the *Mars*, that was the old sailing battleship moored out in the Tay. There were hundreds of boys out there and the discipline on that ship was iron. Five hundred boys – scrubbing the decks on their knees! Compared to that we had it easy; we had to work but we knew it helped earn our keep. We unloaded twelve tons of coal every week, we worked in the grounds and we worked in the gardens. We had our own horses and carts and that's when I first worked horses by myself. We were grooming and feeding, cutting grass, sawing logs, tidying up, moving things about. Everybody knew I had a good voice so I was put in the choir at Downfield church, under the eye of the Reverend MacKnight. I soon got to know all the hymns and psalms by heart and I enjoyed letting rip. At just the right moment he'd look across and give us the nod – 'Now, Jim,' he'd say, 'sing up!' And he'd get me to lift the whole choir and I could do that, at the drop of a hat, and the choir would then lift the whole congregation. I'm a Catholic yet and a singer till the end.

So, between my father and the Reverend MacKnight, I had a very good training and we had records to listen to in Baldowan. My two favourite singers were Count John MacCormack and Nelson Eddie. But I also liked Joseph Locke, the Irish singer. He was a cousin of Father Sidney McEwan in Aberdeen and he used to try to push Joseph Locke onto me. You wouldn't think a man of the cloth would be so partisan to his own family but Father Sidney couldn't but hear his cousin as the best; maybe he was, but I stuck to my opinion and I always told him that I thought McCormack shaded Locke – just that wee bit. You know what I mean! Father Sidney would go purple with rage! Another singer was Peter Mullen but who's heard of him today? I could go out and ask the people here on this campsite, 'Have you ever heard of Peter Mullen?' and nine out of ten would answer 'No!' What do you think of that?

When I was in Glasgow I used to drink with Calum Kennedy, the Gaelic singer; we used to be meeting there in The Politician, and he'd be singing and I used to sing with him. The Politician's the pub named after the whisky ship that sank off Eriskay and inspired Compton MacKenzie to write *Whisky Galore*. I was there very often with my cousin, Toby Stewart. He used to play the box for Calum. He's some box player. He was playing the streets in Ireland when he was six years old. Toby was like Willie Star was, brilliant! The only difference was that Toby was not an alcoholic! Toby plays a Shand Marina, that's the box that Sir Jimmy Shand plays – but Toby was always a better player than Shand! Toby married a haulier's daughter way down at Ecclefechan. That's where Thomas Carlyle was born. Toby used to play with me and he used to play for Chick Murray, the comedian; great times we three had together. Calum Kennedy had money, that was one of the nice things about singing with him – we never had money! Chick Murray sometimes had money but we never had money! Now Chick's dead and Calum's house burned down – but I'm here, at Balmuir, swinging the lead and Toby's still playing his box like a wizard! There's nothing fair in life – that's what the rich man said. But, for quality of music – on the box – I'd always give you Toby Stewart. He's one crack player, you take it from me! I never sold a bum steer – if you want great music – ask Toby Stewart to play. Brilliant.

I'm eighty-one. I'm no chicken but – I've never smoked, I look after myself and I've had plenty of time in the fresh air. You get some people are finished at sixty. But my people come from the north and they live to a great age. They like a drop of whisky like, you know what I mean, but they never smoked – not before Sir Walter Raleigh came back from America. Nor did a single one of us Stewarts inhale. Not like President Clinton, we don't! We smoke like a train – going so fast we leave the smoke behind on the wind. I still do my exercises. I've got three bikes – an old Hercules, a mountain bike, and a big three wheeler. I bike down to Dundee to get my messages.

I look after myself. That's what I tell my family – keep fit and look after yourselves. In the old days the Travellers looked after their horses but very often didn't look after themselves – now we don't have horses we have started to look after ourselves! One of my sons is a banker in Zurich, he did very well. First he was a kitchen hand, then he became a chef, then he went sideways into computers. He was good at exams – like his father! Then he went into banking and did very well. I have another son down in Leeds. He's done well – in another direction. He's father to twenty-five children. So far! Off different women like, I don't know how many, but he keeps a very close tally and he's still at it. When he got to twenty-one I told him 'that's over the score'. But he just kept going. I told him – we know the can's big enough – but don't stretch your luck. He said he was just keeping up the Stewart name! But I'm not happy – he's become far too modern for my liking. Make full use of your proper entitlements – that's what the politicians and the social workers keep saying! He's got himself a big family but it's not him who looks after it. And you know this – not one of the those kids is a singer, not one. You have to hear songs when you're young if you're going to be a singer and the kids in the the housing estates don't hear songs. Not down there, not up here. They go to discos – but I could walk around this camp today and not one soul would sing a Traveller song. It's all monkey music. All hip-hop, all modern rubbish.

O, 'twas in a place they call Dunkeld –
We had shelties for to seld;
And we filled our bellies wi' cauld ale
– Upon the Moss o' Borrowdale.

There were fighting men upon the green –
Brave MacAlister looked sae bra'
When he took aff his jaicket they a' ran awa'
– Over the Moss o' Borrowdale.

There were Stewarts, MacKenzies and MacPhies –
They'll flicket their tongues aboot their knees
And wallop it gently as you please
– Upon the Moss o' Borrowdale …

Loose-headed ponies being driven to the Ballinasloe Horse Fair, Ireland, 1990. (CR)

That's a real Traveller song but there's not many can sing that song today. People hide their songs. Maybe they have good reason. I can remember the time when if people knew you were a Traveller, they wouldn't serve you in a pub. If you came into a town with horse and cart – if the Tinkers came into town – the pubs would close their doors. I mind in the sixties, hawking with a horse and cart in Fife and coming to the town of Leslie. I was going slow and Willie MacAlister came by me on a big fast horse. I remember him shouting across, 'I'll see you when you come in – we'll hae a bucket o' beer – at the back o' the pub!' That's what it was in those days, a white enamel bucket of beer – put out at the back of the pub for the Travellers. It didn't matter how much money you had, Travellers weren't allowed in the bar and that was that. Like the blacks in the Southern States. Of course, we still had fun. We'd sit there on the grass, all around the white bucket, about ten of us, dipping our mugs. People passing would turn away – or maybe they might stand around and watch and listen to a song. I mind us saying that day in Leslie that, of the ten of us drinking from the pail, eight had served in the war. We had fought for what was called Freedom and yet twenty years later we couldn't get a drink at the bar – even of a rundown wee town like Leslie, Fife.

Of course, some of the Travellers were throwbacks, hundreds of years back, throwbacks to the olden times. My grandfather's sister, she was like that. I stayed with her up in Dingwall when I was working for the Hydro Board in the forties. She was six foot two when I knew her and she was seventy by then, so she must have shrunk a couple of inches. Tine MacAlister was her name. She was my mother's father's sister. She was banned from every pub in Dingwall. If she wanted a drink she had to walk to Strathpeffer, that was the nearest pub would serve her. Sometimes she went by bus. She couldn't read, she couldn't write, she couldn't tell the time. She went to bed when it got dark and rose when it got light. She always wore a shawl, a tartan shawl around her shoulders. My mother did as well. They both spoke Gaelic as well as English. She never bought food, she knew nothing about money. She went round the houses and she went round the shops. She'd just wait by the side of the counter, like a nun over in Ireland, and when the shopkeepers had time they'd go ben and bring out a box of food they'd put ready for her. Knowing she was coming. She never needed to ask, just like the nuns, and the food was offered as a gift – sometimes it would be old stuff and stale stuff but no harm would that bring to a good constitution. That was her life. Tine MacAlister was well known in Dingwall.

I stayed in her house and, at the end of the first week, I was going to offer her a pound for my lodging – she had the house to herself since her husband died – but my grandfather said, 'No, Jimmy! Gie her nothing. She'll only drink it, or lose it, or gie it awa'! Bring her in some bacon and eggs for a fry up. Bring her a bottle o' Guinness – but nae more. She's a woman never knows when to stop – never did, never will!' Tine Ann MacAlister, she was a big fighting woman. After a few drinks she'd challenge any man in the room to come out and fight. And, of course, many a man took her on and many got a battering. They'd hammer away in the darkness – thumping and grunting. The best thing was just to let them keep at it. Now they're all buried on the hill, above Dingwall. It's nearly all MacAlisters up there and you'd never know one from another: they all had these very long shanks, the MacAlisters all had these very long thighs.

I worked for the Hydro and I worked the farms and I learned a lot from the plough men. I've always loved 'The Dying Plough Boy'. It's a song that suits the tenor voice.

The cannie wunds are sighing saft
Noo aroon my lonely stable laft,
Through the skylight's dusty rays
The sunbeams wander roon my bed.

I minded stirks a week the morn
When I was weill and hierstin corn –
Somethin in my briest gaed wrang
A vessel burst and bluid it sprang.

Noo the doctor bids me hold guid cheer
But somethin tells me daith is near,
My time on earth will nae be lang
The time has come when I mun gang.

Sae its fare-thee-weill my dandy pair –
For it's you I'll yoke and loose nae mair,
Fare thee weill my cumrades dear –
My voice ye will nae langer hear.

I've served my maister weill and true,
My weill done werk ye munna rue
And yet it's true that I hae striven
Tae reach the pearly gates o' Heaven.

It's weill my Maister now kens my name –
Will he gie me a welcome hame?
And if you can in time afford –
Receive me in thy mercy Lord.

Now isn't that a beautiful song? The man – dying alone, up there in his loft – made up that song. He'd have TB, probably. I learned that song

Ballinasloe Horse Fair, Ireland, said to be the biggest in Europe, 1990. (CR)

from an old shepherd. He was just a wee man, five foot three inches high. He lived to be eighty-six, his name was Alfie McGee. It's a sad song but there's something there in the melody that suits my voice, an ecstasy comes through, and I love to sing that song. The last time I sang it, a Tornado from Leuchars roared over the caravan, at one hundred feet – a dummy run for Yugoslavia. They're blowing up the Hydro Stations, dropping cluster bombs, breaking the backs of men working the fields with horses – and they wonder why the IRA won't give up its weapons! I know plenty of the Rebel songs. I'm an Irish Nationalist.

When my throat was sorted out after the war, I went to work Clydesdales – up around the Gleneagles Hotel, Auchterarder. I was working for a farmer, Walter Westwood, who had three big farms on the north side of the Ochils. Ploughing, sowing, harvesting, cattle – I did all that for a year, but I liked the roving, busking life and I decided to strike out on my own – looking for a wife. And the woman I found was an Irish woman. Skinner was her name. We got together but we didn't get on, we never got on! She was a drinker – a heavy drinker – you know what I mean. I left her, away down there in Leeds and went away to Ireland, just like my father before me – though I didn't stay twenty-seven years. It was the time of the troubles and things had turned sour. Going into a pub, people would ask you, 'What are you?' I didn't like that, you never knew where you were. I was there near Ballycastle and I went down under a bridge to get a drink of water from the river and this farmer came up to me with a twelve-bore! 'What are you doing down there?' he shouted. 'I'm having a drink,' I said. 'Are you sure you're not planting a bomb?' Well, all that didn't make for a happy life.

I was travelling with Toby Stewart, he would be on the box and I would be singing and I remember once when a big ginger-headed boy came and shouted, 'Come on boys, give us "The Sash"!' He was testing us you see. We were in Lamnavaddy and Lamnavaddy's a Catholic town. He was just looking for trouble. Now, we weren't wanting to play 'The Sash' and our crowd wouldn't be wanting to hear it. That boy knew we came from Scotland and maybe he knew we were Travellers – he was tempting us – you never knew what people were wanting over there. They'd set you up to knock you down. Now – I was an Irish Nationalist, and I'm still very clear about that, but I also know the trouble is there on both sides. And I don't think there'll ever be peace in Ireland – the poisons come in from so many sources. The English are the most treacherous nation on earth. They've got the most underhand politicians in the world. They settled the Protestants from Scotland on Irish land and the Irish won't stop till they get it back! So I think there'll be plenty more trouble yet – and the same in Palestine. And I always loved Ireland, even though we always seemed to be unlucky there.

We made some good money busking but we were also always

hitting the buffers – farmers with guns, street fighters. We went to the big Horse Fairs. We had great times in Ballinasloe, in Galway, where you get all the Gypsy ponies and the Travellers come in from all over Ireland. Piebalds, skewbalds and the gypsy coloured. Some people don't like them, they say they're just a crossbreed, but I like them. They stand between thirteen and fourteen-and-a-half hands. They're certainly strong enough to pull a caravan. Owners like to see colours in the mane and in the tail as well as the body. Black and white, brown and white, roan and white – cream and white, that's the least popular, they're the 'poverty colours'. Black hooves are preferred but most have striped hooves. The head should be small and pony-like but some still have the bigger heads of the heavy horses with which they were crossed in the past. The neck should be medium but very strong, the carcass deep and well-sprung, the back short and hindquarters very strong. They should have short cannon bones, strong joints and plenty of feather from the back of the knee. I like them. They look like Indian horses and they comprise a breed just because they're unlike any other. 'The coloured gypsy cob's a horse' – it goes like a song.

I remember a place called Burnside, near Letterkenny in Donegal – we fell in with a madman! A man came up out of the crowd, his waistcoat all covered in slobber and green slime. We were singing and he started shouting and spitting and drooling and we couldn't understand a word he said or what he wanted! Then he came at us. He was like a vision – he made you think 'I've got to get out!' That man was the last straw – and Toby and I decided to head back to Glasgow. You have to be brazen, just stand there and do it and pass the hat round but you don't want nonsense. Back here I travelled all over Scotland and over England. I used to go into bookies and betting shops. I used to stand outside Woolies – singing for my supper. We were poor in the fifties and you had to make do. I have a relation, Jane Stewart, up at Mintlaw, in Aberdeenshire who has a lovely song. My father used to sing it and Jane, she always had these crippled legs, she sings it yet: she's eighty-seven.

Cauld blaws the blast
Down fell the snow
Nowhere for shelter
Nowhere to go;
No mummy, no daddy,
In their graves they lie low,
All cast out in the wide-world
Was poor little Joe.

A carriage was passing
With a lady inside
Who stared at poor Joe
As her own darling child;

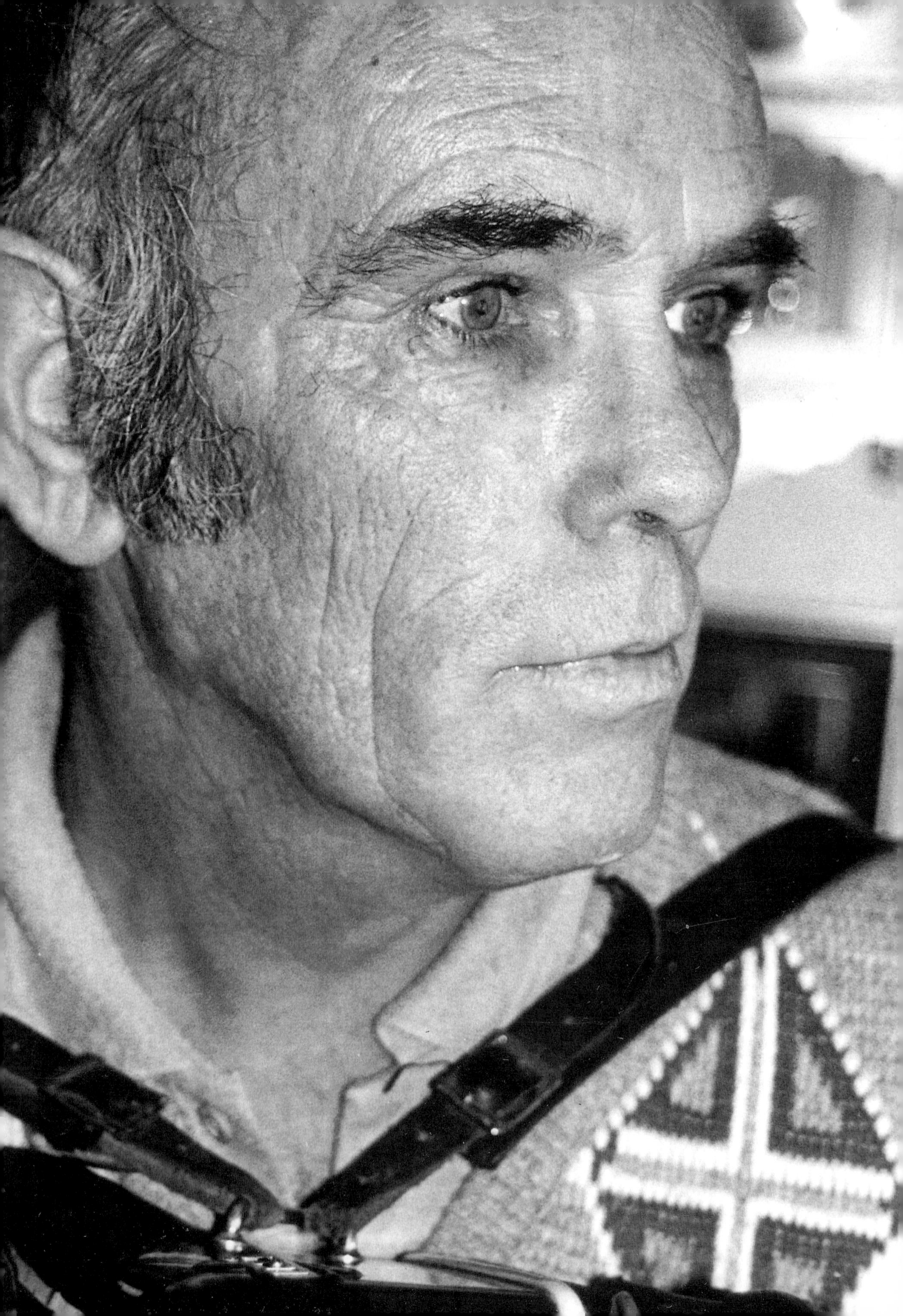

Joe followed the carriage
With tears in his eyes,
Although he was singing
He wished himself dead.

That was it. That was the Traveller life for many of the children when I was young. Today, in this camp, you see footballs left lying about. The kids just leave them – good leather footballs we would have walked a hundred miles to bring home. We went down to the knackery and we'd ask the men for a bladder, a pig's bladder. That was the best we ever did. What care we took of those piss bags! We used to blow them up as hard as we could, with our mouths, and tie them with string. Sometimes we tried with a bicycle pump. They were tough but after a bit of kicking they burst – even with bare feet. So, back to the knackery we'd go – and the men would be pleased to see us come in. 'Here,' they'd say, 'there you are, boys!' and sling over a bladder! They liked to see us play. Give us a bloody pig's bladder – and we were happy. And maybe, sometimes, they'd give us a scrag end of mutton to take back to the caravan.

Oppoiste: James Dodie Stewart of Alford, Aberdeenshire, 2001. Like his relative, James Stewart of Balmuir Wood, Dodie was brought up in a home for orphans. He is today a singer and musician and a stout defender of the rights of the travelling people and their traditional ways. (TN)

If we ever had spare pennies we got toffee from the shops – the shopkeeper used to break the slabs with a hammer and we'd savour every splinter. Here – the kids leave half-full cans of Coke, they throw down their bikes, they leave litter like snow, they leave their dogs running loose. Last week one of them came sniffing up here and Major went for him. Now, Major's a big Rottweiler – quiet as a ghost when he's left alone but he can be a tiger when messed about – you know what I mean. He went for this dog and – listen to this – two days later I had the warden up telling me that if Major went for another dog, I'd be off the site! Changed days. Today authority sows disorder! The social workers feed what feeds them, just as the sun breeds maggots in the dead dog! That's Shakespeare. You never saw wristwatches amongst the Travellers when I was young, it was just the big pocket watches, Smith and Ingersoll – now it's watches, headphones, mobile phones – changed days from the days of the tent and the cauldron. Goes like a song.

When the ale was only tuppence
And a tanner bocht a gill –
A beezum, or a tilly pan
A sheltie for to sell:
We all forgot oor troubles
O'er a pottie o' sma ale
As we gathered in the gloamin'
– O'er the Moss of Borrowdale.

Now big Jock Stewart he got up
Sure he thocht he'd hae a fecht –

Left: James Dodie Stewart with two of his sisters in an Aberdeen children's home, 1952.

Right: James Dodie Stewart, on a day trip to Cullen, taking part in a Sand castle building competition; his, looks very much like a hillfort, 1956. (JS)

When Squeekin Annie rushed at him
– She said, my mannie you are daft!
She runs over amang the tilly pans
For a wee bit iron pail –
And she skelpit him up wi' a swarm o' bees
– On the Moss o' Borrowdale.

Now the bra'st man upon the green
Was a man ca'd Jock MacQueen
He went and sought a set of pipes
He'd bocht in Aberdeen.
The moment he began to blaw
His sheepskin plock began to swell!
And awa flew Jock MacQueen across
– The Moss o' Borrowdale.

That's a real Aberdeenshire Traveller song. There's always a great lilt in the Aberdeenshire songs, a vigour and a verve. You don't get so much of that over in the west, that's the place for the melancholy songs but there's one man, I think, who makes the cross between the two – Rabbie Burns. I love the songs of Robert Burns – 'Bonnie Mary of Argyll', 'Bonnie Mary's Bonnie Belle', 'My Love is like a Red, Red Rose'. Burns was great at putting the words together; I have his Selkirk Grace up on the wall, on my tea towel.

Some hae meat and cannae eat
An some hae meat that want it
But I hae meat and I can eat
Sae let the Lord be thankit.

There's nobody today could write words like that. Nobody. But in a song, it's the way the singer links and lifts the words that's most important. And that's where the Travellers do well – we can make the songs jump up like stones. My father could do that. He made all the songs he sang his own. He was great on 'McGinty's Meal and Ale' and 'MacPherson's Rant'. That was his song! That was his swan song. I sing it myself but he was the master – with his accordian wheezing away like the breath of a dying man but – with his voice rising and surging, defiant to the last!

Sae rantingly, sae wantonly,
Sae dauntingly gaed he,
He play'd a spring, and danc'd it round
Below the gallows-tree.

Farewell, ye dungeons dark and strong,
The wretches destinie!
MacPherson's time will not be long
On yonder gallows-tree.

Untie these bands from off my hands,
And bring to me my sword,
And there's no a man in all Scotland
But I'll brave him at his word.

Willie MacPhee, up in Perth. He died last year, October 2001. I was at his funeral. He was another relative of mine and he was like me – he wanted to join the Black Watch. But he didn't get in either. He went to enrol on the day the war started, 3 September 1939. The place was crowded and they told him to go away and wait for his call-up. Well, he was a Traveller; he was out on the road. He had a wife and a big family. They were wandering and working all over the west and two years went by. He was down at Loch Winnoch, camping, when a police car stopped and came in and they asked him, 'Are you Willie MacPhee?' He said, 'Yes sir, is it my call-up?' 'No,' they said, 'it's just a message for you to come into the station. We can give you a lift down.' Well, Big Willie thought it was a letter he was getting – him being on the road. But it wasn't a letter. Now, Willie was a big strong man, and he didn't even say goodbye to the family. Those two policemen took him into the station and as soon as they got him inside the door – there were four more stood there – they shoved him straight sideways into a cell. Six of them. They stripped him and he was there, sky-naked, in that cell for fifteen hours before anyone came back. And when they came – it was four Redcaps – Military Police. He went down fighting but they got him in handcuffs and they put him in a van and took him down to Bradford, to a military prison – nothing to eat till he got there. He told them, 'I want to be a soldier – I want to serve my king and country!' They wouldn't listen to him and they kept him in that prison for eleven weeks. He told them he wanted to join the Black Watch, that he'd volunteered on 3 September. He couldn't read or write so his wife knew nothing of what had happened. At last they told him he would join the Scots Guards and he was sent up to Fort George at Inverness. He did his square bashing, they taught him to shoot and he was good. Then it was down to the Maryhill barracks in Glasgow, where they gave him a broom, splint new! Willie wanted to fight, and he would have been a good fighter – but he spent the whole war there in Glasgow – sweeping – on barracks duty! They knew he was a Tinker and they thought he wouldn't take orders! But Willie was a man of great potential – he might have seen the war over in days! He was a gentleman of the real old style – unrecognised like Joseph robbed of his coat of many colours.

Of course, there is some truth in the idea that the Travellers don't like taking orders. Who does? The Travellers can be a wild people but they have to be. They've always had to risk their lives to survive. Today we take a pride in that but there's more to it than this. Knowing that we're prepared to accept the ultimate sacrifice helps keep people off our backs. For thousands of years people have wanted us out of the glens – they've always had the power to drive us out but if they know they'll have to risk their lives in the process, they always think twice. They've always had to ask themselves, 'Is it worth losing two or three of us – just to get rid of the Tinks?' We don't do much harm but we'll fight with the blood pumping out of us. No surrender! We've got nothing to lose but our lives. Nothing to lose but our chains. So, when we're cornered, we fight. And we practise amongst ourselves. I keep the newspaper clippings. I've got them up in the cupboard. Look at this, 22 October 1931.

> DRUNK AT DRUMLITHIE.
> William Stewart, travelling musician; James Stewart, pedlar; and Mary Cameron or Stewart, all of no fixed abode and in custody, pleaded guilty before Hon. Sheriff-Substitute D. Grieg at Stonehaven to having on Friday night, within the village of Drumlithie, conducted themselves in a drunken and disorderly manner, and committed a breach of the peace. William Stewart, in pleading for leniency, said his father was buried at one o'clock that afternoon. Addressing the accused the Honorary Sheriff said it was his intention to send them to prison for thirty days without option, but under the circumstances he would let them off by ordering the two men to pay thirty shillings each, with the alternative of fifteen days' imprisonment. A month was granted to find the money. The woman was admonished and dismissed.'

Fighting was something that happened at funerals. Often enough there was no harm in it. It was tradition, it was like two families fighting over

James Dodie Stewart with a gelded Tiger-stripped British Spotted Pony, Alford, 2001. (TN)

a bride at once given and taken. It was like two brothers fighting. I've heard the Moaris do it in New Zealand. We've been a hunting and a hunted people for thousands of years. The Williamsons in Argyll have a great poem called 'The Warrior Haggis', it's a poem about a Haggis hunt but it also tells the story of how the Travellers have been preyed upon. I got it from Duncan Williamson. There was a man here said that this poem reads like a newspaper report of the extinction of the Neanderthal peoples!

High in the hills above Loch Fyne
Where deer and wildfowl stop to dine,
Where shepherds stop and draw the line –
There live the Warrier Haggi.

In his castel sma', a king is he,
His castel is just six foot three –
Of solid mountain granite.

He raided far across the land,
Hunted and cursed by every hand –
The lairds all swore they'd give half their land
To the man who killed the Haggi.

But of man – he has no fear –
He's fought and beat the royal deer
And the eagle – he, glides off in fear
When he encounters Haggi.

Now this noble beast, of noble grace,
Whate'er he hunts, kings' tables grace,
But hunters they – they soon turn face
When they go hunting Haggi.

This noble beast with skin of steel,
A heart of lights and liver meal –
Mony's the man his wrath did feel
When they went hunting Haggi.

No deerhound fast can turn the pace
Or take on Haggi in a race –
And hunters they, they soon loose face
When they go hunting Haggi.

Some hunters – drinking at an Inn:
They curse and swear they'll 'Take his skin!'
And off they rode in a terrible din –
With a death cry for the Haggi.

They took with them a horn or two
And one of them, his horn he blew
– A Death Cry to the Haggi!

O Haggi lay out in the sun –
His feet just itching for to run;
'Aha' he said, 'I'll have some fun –
For no horse can out-run Haggi!'

Then in among them Haggi ran,
The first bite made the first horse fall
– The first blood to the Haggi!

You never saw a sorrier sight –
As Old Haggi took them on in fight
– Nine horses down! Nine bloody men!
Haggi cried, 'I bet they beat a fast retreat –
Whilst I'm still healthy on my feet!'

So, off across the mountain, Haggi ran
– Shouting, 'There never was a horse or man
Could ever catch – a Haggi!'

The Travellers were always getting it in the neck – burnings, stabbing, accidents. Here's another newspaper report, from the 1950s I think.

TINKER CLANS GATHER AT CRIEFF
Strange scenes marked the burial at Crieff Cemetery on Tuesday of Donald Newlands, who died at Bridge of Earn Hospital from injuries sustained when he fell 100 feet into a quarry at Abernethy. Newlands was a forty-four-year-old contractor and member of one of the Tinker families scattered over Scotland. Over sixty of his friends converged on Crieff from every direction to pay their last respects to a comrade of the road.

When the coffin arrived Tinker families followed it into the cemetery in little groups, many having travelled miles to the funeral. One Tinker came all the way from Oban. There were also 'Irish' Stewarts, the Rileys from Pitlochry, and the Hutchisons from Auchterarder. The Newlands family arrived from Buchlyvie in Stirlingshire, and the Blairgowrie Stewarts and the Drummonds of Aberfeldy were also there. The Stewarts from Newton made the journey, too, and were met by the McAllisters of Crieff, and the Donaldsons from Auchterarder. Alex. Mackenzie came by bus from Aberfeldy, and the White family travelled from Rattray.

As the crowd of nomads gathered round the grave for the last service, taken by the Revd Mr Yule, of Crieff South Church, brown skinned men in well-worn clothes and multi-coloured scarves and mufflers reverently doffed their cloth caps or battered soft hats. Ill-clad women, some of them with gaudy headscarves, bowed their tousled heads. Some drew little shawls closer round their shoulders to keep out the north wind.

According to custom, each Tinker drops a sprinkling of earth on the lowered coffin, as a final act of parting. Hardened knights of the open road shed tears unashamed, and the women huddled closer as if they found comfort in the contact. As the service ended, and the last solemn rites were observed, they filed silently from the burial place, to return to little hovels of tattered canvas and open camp fires in some country lane.

Perhaps they will never meet again in such numbers until a similar occasion. When that comes their mysterious 'clock-radio' will let them know the name of the dead, the hour and the place. And if at all humanly possible they will be there.

So there you are. If ever you see two men on one horse, two to one – they'll be travellers! And, on their way to a funeral more than likely. And, euthanasia? The Travellers have it, already! Live well, die well, that's the Traveller way. They live – never afeared to outface oblivion.

The Travellers are thick spread along the Highland Fault line. Thainstone, Drumlithie, Crieff. Travellers live where the mountains meet the Lowland zones from Caithness right down through Dornoch, Bonar Bridge, Tain, Alness, Dingwall, Beauly, Inverness, Elgin, Keith, Huntly, New Deer and Mintlaw, Inverurie, Kemnay, Aberdeen, Brechin, Kirriemuir, Alyth, Rattray, Blairgowrie, Dunkeld, Perth, Amulree, Crieff, Logierait, Aberfeldy, Callander, Aberfoyle, Dumbarton, Dunoon, Lochgilphead and Campbeltown. That's the thin red line. That's where we settled down – along the Highland line. So that we could move and trade between the two sides and maybe find protection here or there, or in the no-man's land between Highland and Lowland. We'd go west, up into the Highlands for the summer and back down to the low ground for the winter. Selling horses, both ways, till the horse trade died out, in the fifties.

Duncan Williamson, he's written a book about horses called *The Horsing Ma*n. He's a genius. Another of his poems that I love to hear is called 'Beside Ungathered Rice He Lay'. Where he got it, nobody knows.

Beside ungathered rice he lay,
His scycle in his hand,
His breast was bare,
His matted hair
Lay buried in the sand.

And again, in the mist
And the shadow of sleep –
He saw his native land:
He saw, once more, his dark-eyed queen
Among her children stand.
They clasped his neck,
They kissed his cheek,
They held him by the hand;
A tear burst from the sleeper's lids
And fell into the sand.

Wide through the landscapes of his dream
The lovely Niger flowed –
Beneath the palm trees on the plain,
Once more a king, he strode;
And heard the tinkling caravans
Descend the mountain road.

And then at furious speed he rode,
Along the Niger banks
His bridle reins were golden chains,
And with the martial clan.
And with each leap
His scabard smote
His stallions shining flank
And then –
Upon the plain he rode,
Where the great flamingo flew,
And morn till night
He followed their flight
To the land where the Tamarind grows.

O he did not feel the driver's whip,
Nor the burning heat of the day,
For death had illumined in the land of sleep,
Where his lifeless body lay,
A worn-out fetter round his sole
And the chains that he had thrown away.

Traveller Stewarts on the road near Callander, 1932. (JS)

That's me. That's the Travelling People: out on the road, always breaking free of their fetters. Imagination can transform slavery. Imagination shows death itself to be a paltry thing. 'Sae dauntingly, sae wantonly, sae wantonly gaed he! He played a tune and he danced it roond – below the gallows tree!'

Charlie Barron

the ORRAMAN, MINTLAW and BALMERINO

The heavy winter, 23 February 1947, that was when I was born. I was made of the hard stuff, I had double pneumonia but I survived. There were no antibiotics for the likes of us in those days. My mother, she had pneumonia too. I was the fifth son, two others had died. Three years later my sister came along and that was the family finished. My father was second horseman at Kininmount Farm, Mintlaw, Aberdeenshire and I was in the stable with him from the age of five. In the evenings, on Saturdays, in the school holidays. By the age of eight I was working my own horse; light work, schimming the turnips, driving the carts. The schim's a small grubber, very light and easy for a boy to handle, it dances through the weeds – does a shimmy, like Jimmy Johnston leaving a trail of devastation behind. The horses were well trained, you just followed on. I was what they called a penny loon. That was what they called the boy who did these kind of jobs – weeding, bird scaring and watching the horse in the roundel house. I was never big but I took to work like a duck to water – light work, hard work, I enjoyed it. Forking the dung was hard work for a boy. Straw was still long in those days, before the new seeds came in and the combines, it would be tangled and straddled two or three feet of the byre floor; you had to rack it off the face of the midden. It was all pitchfork in those days, no forklift trucks. We had fertilisers but we used to mix our own. Two and a half hundredweight bags – ammonia, nitrates, potash – they were couped on the floor, mixed up like cement and sent out to the fields. The farmers planned everything with economy in mind and the tied cottage was part of the equation.

Charlie Barron, orraloon, at Ackey Brae Fair, 1961. (CB)

The tied house was handy but it gave the farmers a second hold on their men. When you left a farm you left your house. You had twenty-four hours to get out. If you had a family that made you think twice. My father got short shrift once or twice. You had to work, you had to do what you were told and any theft was sat on with a ton of bricks. At Kininmount the house of the second horseman was closest to the stable. We knew who was coming and going and we would see what they had on their backs. Food for the horses was being stolen from that stable. My father knew it. Every horseman had a kist for bruised oats, to feed his pair. You filled your kist and the oats would last a certain length of time. One morning my father was grooming his horses when the farmer came in, looked around, lifted the lid of the kist and went out. He knew what he was looking for and my father knew what he was checking, and this annoyed my father. If the farmer, that was old Gauld, was looking in his kist when he was there, what would he be doing when he wasn't? My father decided that if Gauld did the same thing again, he'd have it out with him. So the following morning my father stayed, grooming the horse nearest the door, and he kept grooming. He'd decided that he'd groom that horse till Gauld came in – or there was no hair on it! Well, he did come in and he did the same thing again – he looked in the kist. My father stepped into the doorway and asked him, 'What are you looking for?' 'Nothing,' said Gauld. My father knew what he was up against and he said, 'I'm not a bloody thief!' And Gauld said, 'And I never blamed you! I was checking the bruised oats.' 'I know,' said my father 'and I'm not a bloody thief.' Gauld said, 'I know it's not you but there's somebody at it – and we need to find out.'

Well, my father knew what was going, even we kids knew what was going on, but he wouldn't be telling, nor would we. What he did was, he gave Gauld a clue. He said, 'There's a lot of food goes passed my door but I canna tell you where it goes – it's up for me to know and you to find out!' It was a man called Middleton, an orraman, I think, he was. He had a cottage with a yard and sheds and he was keeping a small menagerie! Pigs and chickens and ducks and he was feeding them all off corn from the stable. Well, it's surprising that old Gauld didn't know what was going on, because Middleton had been at it for years – he had a small farm! Anyway, next day, Gauld caught him redhanded and he had to be out of his house in twenty-four hours. And Gauld was decent, he gave Middleton a shot of two horse and carts, to help with the flitting. Two horses and two carts. And they both got used several times that day. Middleton moved his furniture first, then his stock and, finally, he came back to clear out his attic – which was crammed full of bags of bruised oats and corn. It was market day and Gauld was away, but Middleton had a cheek going out past the farmhouse with his carts laden with booty. And he'd saved money – he soon took on a croft of his own.

Charlie Barron, looking like a gaucho and sporting an eye-injury, takes a ride on his maister's horse, Forfar, 1967. (CB)

Middleton was only an orraman but he was a good worker and maybe Gauld didn't want to be rid of him till he had a man, at least as good, to replace him. That was my father. Those farmers were hard but they always worked in their own interest and some of them would be pleased to see a man set himself up ready to strike out on his own. Theft was a serious thing in those days but my father respected old Gauld because he sorted things out, he didn't go to the police. Today, everybody goes to the police but nothing gets sorted out.

It didn't take a Sherlock Holmes to find the Kininmount thief. Middleton was the orraman, he had the key to the gristing house. He bruised the oats and oversaw the roundel house – where the horse would circle round, like slaves of old, dragging a pole on a shaft, that drove a gear, that drove a pulley with belts, that drove the threshing mill, or the hammer mill – and Middleton could filter off whatever grain or cut vegetables he wanted. He had the motive and the opportunity. He had the cheek of the good-natured thief. Middleton could have starred in a good silent film. A comedy – he was Laurel and Gauld was Hardie!

My father worked on farms all his life, always with horses, but he had a mechanical cast of mind and he could turn his hand to anything. He repaired everything. With him on a farm you didn't need a smith. He found things, he bought things, he hoarded things – for the farm. He wanted to set himself up with a scrapyard and go into the motor business. In the end he never got the capital together. After he left Kininmount he moved south, he worked at Banchory, Stonehaven, Glenlethnet, and he finished up at Forfar. I remember working with him and my brother Sandy at the turnips, for Lord Stonehaven – pulling and cutting and throwing the neeps up into the cart. Now most farm horses were very good – they were used to the turnips flying about and the odd one landing on their backside – but, Sandy hit this one and he bolted! Away across the field with the cart behind him! And he didn't stop. He kept going. He went right back to the stable and crashed out. The door wasn't wide enough to take the cart. The shaft was shattered, both wheels sheered off at the axle. A joiner came in and he and my father fixed it together. Everybody knew how to do these jobs. That runaway horse was a big strong horse, a full Clydesdale. He brought home the firewood. We'd go out to cut birches, maybe thirty feet long and ten inches across at the base and make a big drag, three or four feet in diameter, and that horse would pull the load home, with me on his shoulders. Once he got going he knew not to stop – he had great style – he'd lean forward at an angle of thirty degrees, putting his whole body-weight onto his collar. He had a quick step and if you were down you'd have to be trotting to keep up beside him. Maybe his mind went when he got hit by turnip! He must have thought he was out in the wood and it was time to go home and he was away – no holds barred.

I saw the last of the three-horse binders. Three horse yokes. You had to know how to hitch a thing like that. Your two horses went on the short end of your three horse yoke and your one horse went on the long end, with a pivot between – the one horse then worked as the equal of the other two. Some farmers might have worked with one horse in the middle and one each side but that created problems and we always worked with the three-horse yoke. Who invented that, I don't know but it will have been a blacksmith and it was a good invention. Wooden yokes and metal swivels and hitches. A single swingletree was behind the one horse, and the theats, the two chains, came back behind. A double swingletree was behind the two horses. And the same swingletrees would be used for the plough and the drill plough. I worked every kind of field tool – we had equitine cultivators, we had spring teeth grippers with rachets and bushes at the end, that allowed you to vary the depth of the soil you were breaking. You had to work slow if you wanted a good deep tilth – what you didn't want was big lumps coming up to the surface and drying to cannonballs in the sun. The farmers gave the orders but the men who knew the most were the horsemen. On most farms you'd have one horsemen to two loons or orramen and on big farm like Kininmont, you had six horsemen. We had a good song about the orramen. It was called 'The Horseman's Gripping Word'.

O first I got for Orraman
And then I got on for Third –
The first thing that I had to learn
Was the Horseman's Gripping Word!

Wi a loaf o breid to be my piece
And a bottle fir drinkin drams –
While I buckled doon, belay me nee
A pair o nicky tams!

O I courted Bonnie Annie,
Jock Tamsin's kitchen maid –
She was five and forty
And I was seventeen!

Now she maks me a muckle piece
Wi ilka kind o jam –
But I cannae get to the Cattle Show
Wi-oot me nicky tams! ...

Just once I remember my father getting a rollicking. He was on a tractor taking the potatoes from the field to the shed. The truck had a tipper but because the potatoes were being stacked up to ten feet deep, only about a third of the spuds would tip off – the rest had to be forked. So it was hard fast work – he being needed back in the field to keep up with the pickers. Well, he had a bad stomach and he was taken short and he had to rush ben the shed for a tom-tit! When he got back to the field the pickers were stopped – waiting for him and the farmer went for him. When my father explained, the farmer lost his temper and shouted, 'I didn't put flush toilets in your bloody cottage for you to start going home for a crap! You're paid to work and keep these pickers picking! Not to sit about crapping! Can ye no do that in the morning, before you come to work!' Now my father hadn't gone home, he'd shot around the back of the shed and done his business fast as possible, like a dog. But there you are, there was no point in arguing – you just got on with the work.

My grandfather belonged to the Green of Udney and he spent most of his life around New Deer and Old Deer. He worked on farms, he worked on the roads as a foreman with Aberdeenshire County Council. He also worked in the quarries – the granite quarries sending the stone down to Aberdeen. He had an accident that led to a thrombosis, which led to gangrene and one leg had to be amputated. So, then he got himself a croft at Spittal of Rora. That was his retiral. But my father never got his scrapyard; he went in for motorbikes. First of all he got himself a BSA 500 Slopper, with a sidecar he built himself. It looked like a boat with a little wooden hand rail all round the top. I was still a loon but we travelled thousands of miles. He had it for

Charlie Barron, welder and salmon netter, outside Loom Cottage, Balmerino, Fife, 1987. (TN)

twelve years. My mother would be on the back, my sister and me in the sidecar. On Saturdays we'd go to Aberdeen, shopping. On Sundays we'd go away up into the hills or down to Linlithgow to see his sisters. Heading back to Banchory one day the back wheel came off at the North Water bridge. The spokes had fractured but he always carried spares. So, it was off with the wheel, out with the broken spokes, in with the new spokes, the tube back on, the tyre back on, the wheel back on, and away down the road as though nothing had happened. He enjoyed all that and I learned as he went along.

We came down to Banchory because the tenant farmer there was a Mr Davidson, a man who'd come back from the Argentine. He rented land from Durris estate but he wasn't a good farmer and he was going to be put off – for neglecting the land. The Government was very strict on that after the war. So Davidson looked around for a good man who it was known would make a go of the farm and he was told he should choose my father. And after six months things were so much improved that the Arbitration Board gave Mr Davidson the right to stay on.

The school I remember best is the Garrolhill up at Banchory. We had to walk three miles, then we got a car the rest of the way. Six miles a day. We enjoyed it. Later on we got pushbikes and every afternoon I liked to stop at the blacksmith's shop. Noam Legge was his name. He liked to see us standing there in the doorway. 'Charlie,' he'd say, 'it's bra you've come just noo – I've got a wee job. Could you just get a hold of this . . .' And, of course, I was keen to help and keen to learn. He'd give me a few taps, and I'd put on goggles to braze or help gas weld a fitting. And I liked to hold the horses whilst he was shoeing. He was on the Slug road if you were going up from Stonehaven to Banchory. The smithy's there yet and it's a nephew of my mother's that has it now, Arthur Strachan. His father was killed by a horse, kicked in the stomach.

My mother, she was a Strachan, from the Turriff area, and her people were farmers. Her father was at Leadmill Farm, King Edward, near Turriff – he too was killed as the result of an accident. He was repairing a roof in a storm, the ladder went down and he died of his injuries. That meant the family had to leave the farm and my mother's brother went out to Australia. He was a millwright.

When I left school I started an apprenticeship with Pert, the builders, from Montrose. They had the contract to build 'the monkey cage' for the early warning radar at Edzell. The poles came in by boat from America, hundreds of feet high. I swung about putting them up. All that was to keep the Russians at bay. I went down on my bike, five miles in the glen and three miles on from Edzell to the base. I was fit and I enjoyed it. They even say the wind got tired of me hurling myself against it day after day! I did that for eighteen months – then Pert let me go. They went bankrupt. The US payments were coming through too slow, so Pert was sacrificed on the altar of freedom. I swung from wire to wire, gave a great cry like Tarzan, then dropped like a stone and went back to work on the farm. The farmer's name was Ken Finley.

Now, Finley had a bad reputation as an employer but my mother had this saying, 'You always speak of people as you find them – if you do your work there shouldnae be a problem.' So I went in with Finley and he gave me £13, in my hand, every fortnight. That was a good wage in those days, it was only ten bob a week less than my father was getting. Finley only had the one horse so I went straight on to tractors – sowing the barley, neeps, potatoes. He had sheep and he had cattle and I was there with them all. I used to go into the stable before coming home just to get a smell of the harness – it made you feel alive, part of the history of the place. Up at Kininmont going in to the stable, the sight of the haunches of the six big Clydesdales with their heads looking round over the tops – that used to thrill me. I used to hope that Finley would go back to horses but, of course, it was impossible – but everything else was still done in the old style, and Finley was very good to me. We swept the hay with an old Fergie tractor and we stacked it in cones on poles. That allowed the hay to dry and it cured much better in a natural draught. Some would then be stored in lofts and some would go into the rucks. As the horses disappeared from the farms, more and more hay was fed to the cattle beasts.

Then there was the corn harvest. We were still stooking in those days and you still had the big threshing days when the men would come in from farms round about to have one big day on this farm or that. The boys and the old men would be there with a terrier and the collies – ready for the rats. We finished all our rucks with a sheave of wheat straw on the summit, tied-in like a Scottish thistle, and each ruck would be founded on rocks brought in from the fields. We liked to see the big traction engines coming in with the threshers. Sometimes it was the American International tractors. The boys would stand about waiting for a job, waiting to be asked to join in. Threshing was a job you couldn't do in the wet but one thing about farm work – you were never short of a job, you were never sent home. There was always something and even if the rain was coming down hard you might be sent out in oilskins to work on the walls – drystane dykes, fencing, scrub clearing. Finley had a lot of hill land at the back of Drumcairn. We were still breaking-in new land in the sixties – heather, rushes, gorse. We drained and re-sowed – rain or shine. You might grumble but you never complained.

I worked the sheep on the hill and it was a big acreage we covered. You'd take one dog in the morning and another in the afternoon when the first was worn out. Shearing and dipping, we did all that. I didn't do much shearing; contract clippers were coming in by that time. I knew Charlie Downie, the flockmaster, or floatmaster – he used to bring float loads of sheep in from the west each year. He then wintered or fattened the sheep over here. He was a very busy guy, rushing here and there, buying, selling, letting, driving, checking – he never stopped. A twenty-four-hour day he was working and summertime he did contract shearing to give himself a break. He came in with six men. I was seventeen-and-a-half by this time. My job was to catch the sheep and deliver them to the seven shearers just as soon as they'd finished the one before. It was all hand clipping, not electric shearing, but those men worked fast and that was some job. Each ewe had to be set down on her hip, half-seated ready for clipping. Two other guys were rolling up the fleeces. All would be there, in their vests and a dungaree jacket we called 'a greaser'. As each clipper finished he'd shout out, 'Sheep!' And I'd have to be there. They were all racing to keep up with each other and Charlie Downie liked to keep himself two or three ahead of the field. He was very good and very strong but he also had method. Some sheep are 'a good clip' and some sheep are 'a bad clip'. What you wanted was a sheep with a good rise – a nice smooth coating of new wool, maybe an inch long, next to the skin. What you didn't want was a scrawny sheep with no rise and matted wool all down its belly. And when I first took one of those to Charlie Downie, he grabbed hold of my hand on top of the horn and gave it a squeeze – and say, 'dinnae bring these ones to me, laddie!' He'd show me the hairy belly, 'I dinnae like these!' Then when I brought him a sheep with a good rise, he'd look up and say, 'This is good'n, laddie' and he'd maybe get a

Charlie Barron playing 'the moothie', preparing for his part, as Bruno, in the film Play me Something, 1988. (Jean Mohr)

couple of Jelly Babies out of his pocket and put them in my hand. It was like bribery but he was the boss, he was like the head horseman – and you did what was wanted. Even if it meant the least skilled shearers getting all the worse sheep. Cha was his nickname and his sons now carry on the business. I can feel his hand, on my hand, to this day.

After that we moved to Forfar to work for Chick Nicol. He was another man with a hard reputation but we got on well and when my father retired he got a free cottage on the understanding he would do light work and look after the cattle. That suited him and it suited my mother, and I went away to Fife to work in the garage at Gauldry. Seven years I did there – cars, trucks, lorries, Moffat and Williamson buses, tractors, combines – I did the lot. Then I went into sea salvage with Alec Crawford of Balmerino. He gave me a tied cottage by the salmon station and I took responsibility for the Naughton salmon beat, fishing the shore and the sandbanks from Balmerino Abbey down to Wormit Bay. Net and cobble that was and there were still fish to be caught in those days – now it's away down to almost nothing. Bill Imrie keeps it going but he'll be the last, I think.

Alec Crawford of Naughton estate, slowly got into salvage – fulltime. He bought the rights to HMS *Argyll*. She was 380 feet long – one of the best cruisers in the British fleet. She sank off the Bell Rock, 1916 – a navigational error of 1.5 degrees and a propeller was ripped off. With the war on, the Bell Rock Light was not working and the ship hit the rocks. That was hard work, heavy lifting, long hours, bad weather. We worked with the tides, two tides a day, out of Tayport. I didn't dive. Alec worked mostly with explosives. Some of the armour plating was fourteen inches thick but all beautifully put together with double dovetail wedges that we could still ease off after sixty years in the sea. It was valuable iron, free of the radiation that's permeated the air since the atomic bombs started being exploded. There was plenty of gunmetal brass down there and white metal that was ninety-five per cent pure tin.

After that I went out to the Black Sea on the oil rigs; now I'm cleaning boilers and heaters. In hospitals and the big chicken houses. I don't know which is the dirtier work – but it has to be done and somebody's got to do it. It pays well enough for me to now have a house and garden and a wife to boot – Christyna McNeill. She tends the plums trees and takes in dogs. It was through her I got involved in film work and television. First I was a driver and odd-job man then I got invited out to Venice to act in a film for the cinema. You never know what's round the corner! I appeared in a set of photographs that helped tell the story of the film. I played a farm worker from the Alps who goes out with his village band for a day in Venice. My name was Bruno and in Venice I met this girl called Marietta. The film was called *Play Me Something*. It won the Europa Prize as the best film at the Barcelona Festival. Then I came back to work in the flues.

It was Jean Mohr, from Switzerland, who took the photographs. The actress was called Lucia Lanzarini. She came from Bologna and we got on very well. The story was written by this man John Berger who lives in France. He was the star of the film. So we were all there in Venice for a week, on the island of the Giudecca. Bruno arrives at the bus station, then goes up the Grand Canal on a *vaporetto* – that's a waterbus. He has this trombone with him and a moothie in his pocket. Later on he meets a girl who works in a chemist's shop in Mestre. That's Lucia. And the pictures tell the story. The director was a man called Tim Neat, you'll know him yourself.

PLAY ME SOMETHING

The following photographic essay is comprised of stills taken by the great Swiss photographer Jean Mohr for the film Play Me Something*. This film, set on the Isle of Barra and in Venice, won the Europa Prize, as best film, at the Festival de Cinema de Barcelona in 1989. These photographs were taken during the course of a single day – and form a suitable, memorable, conclusion to this Highland Quintet. To Jean Mohr, high thanks.*

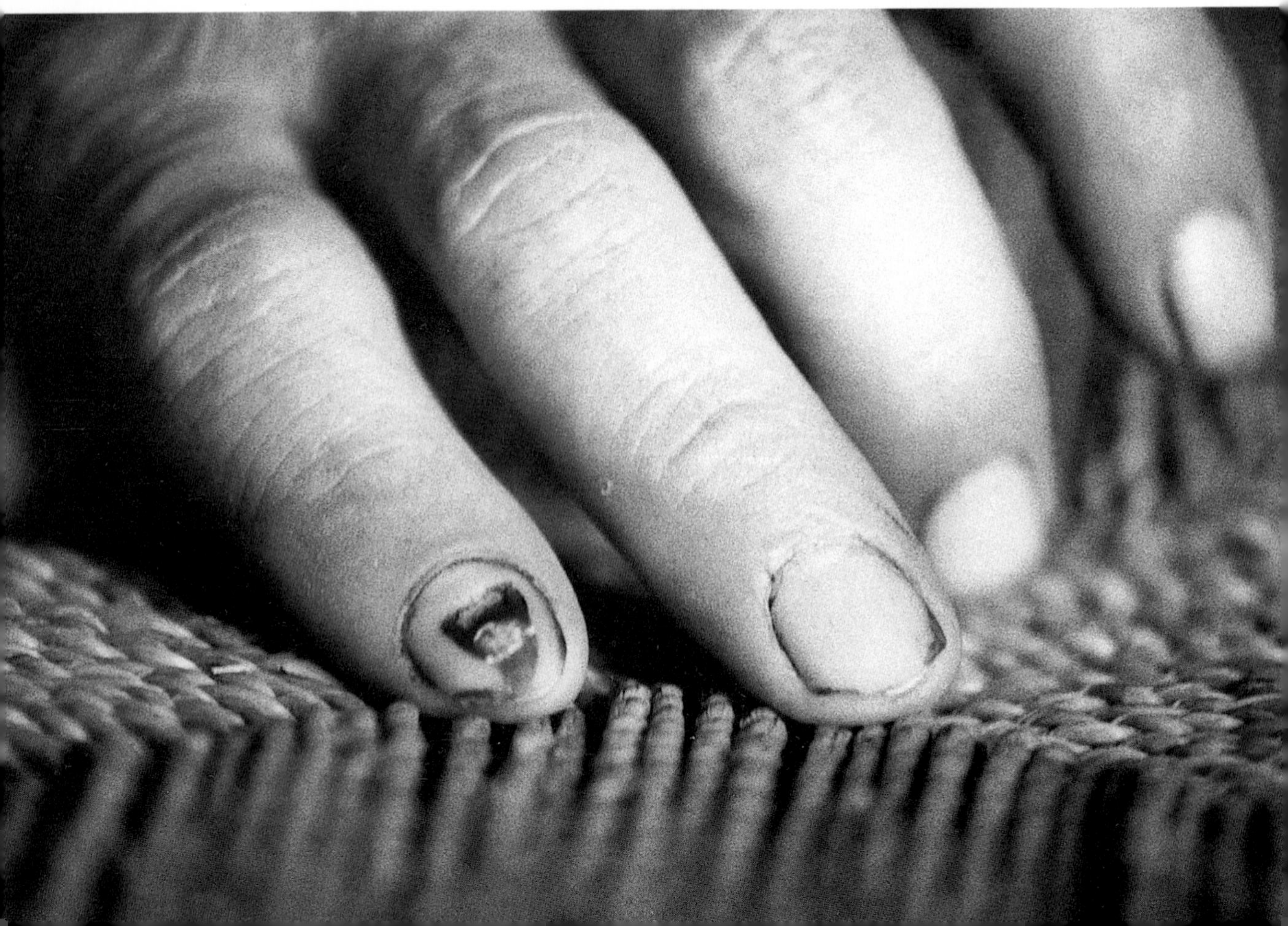

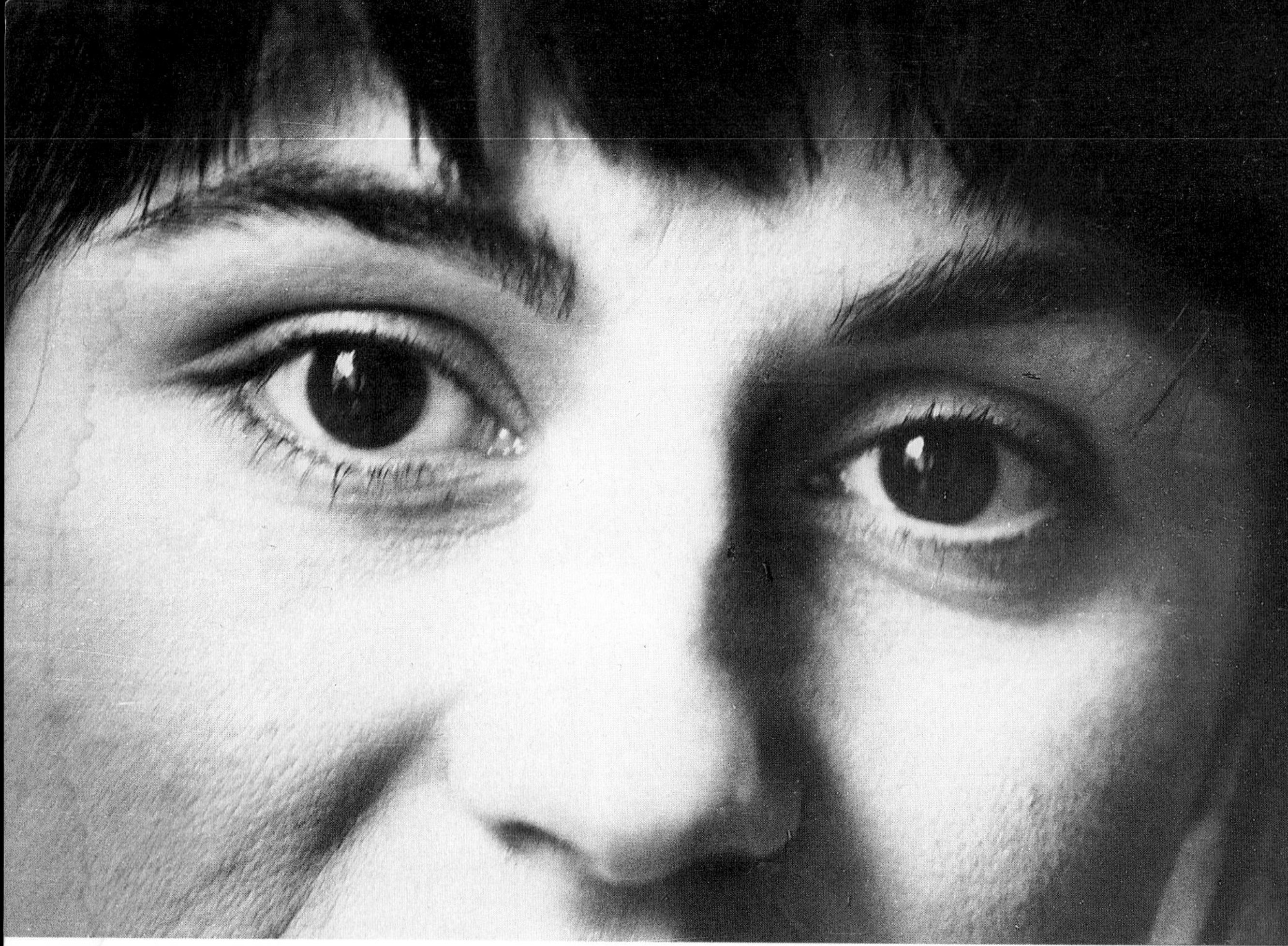

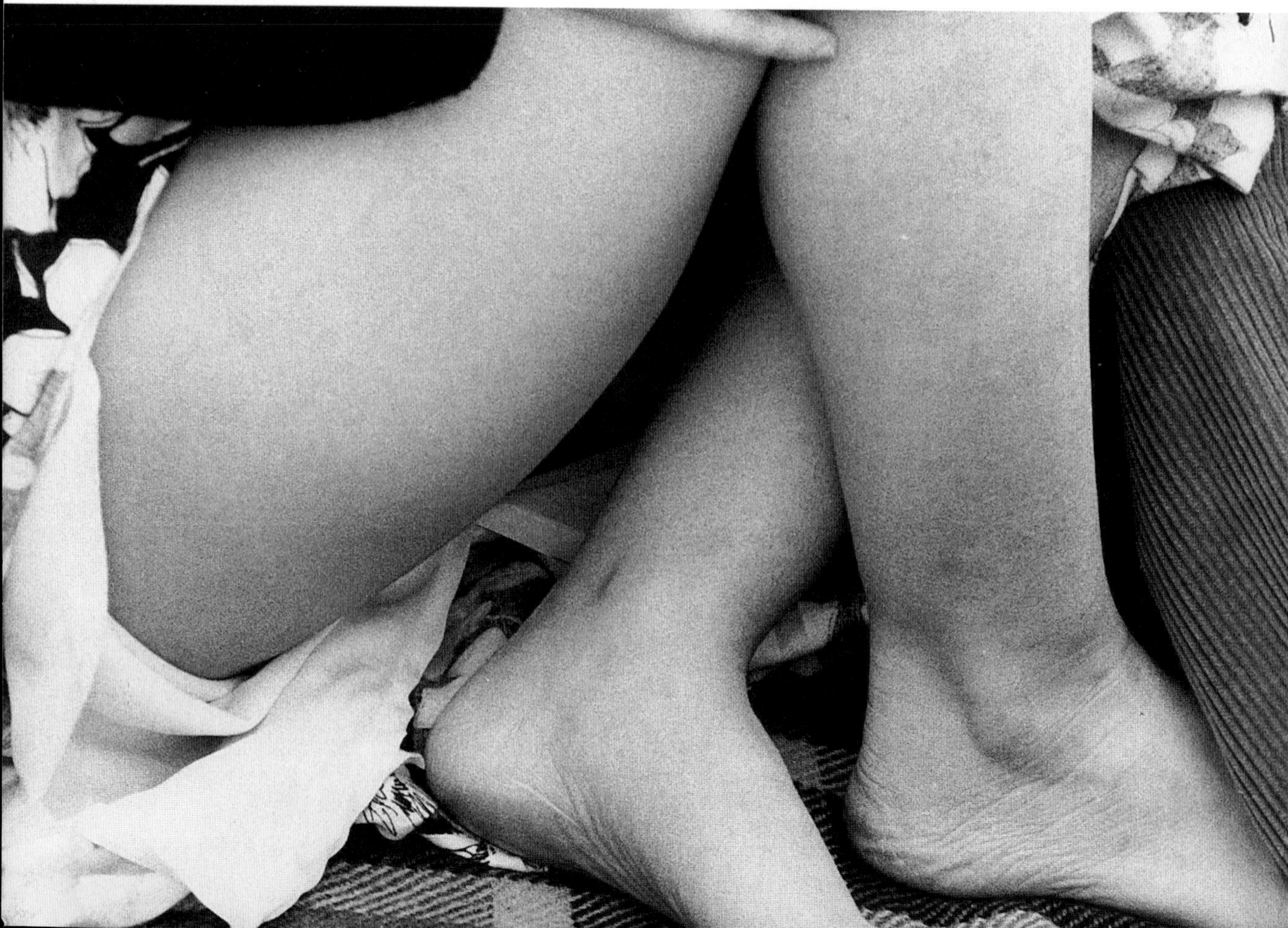

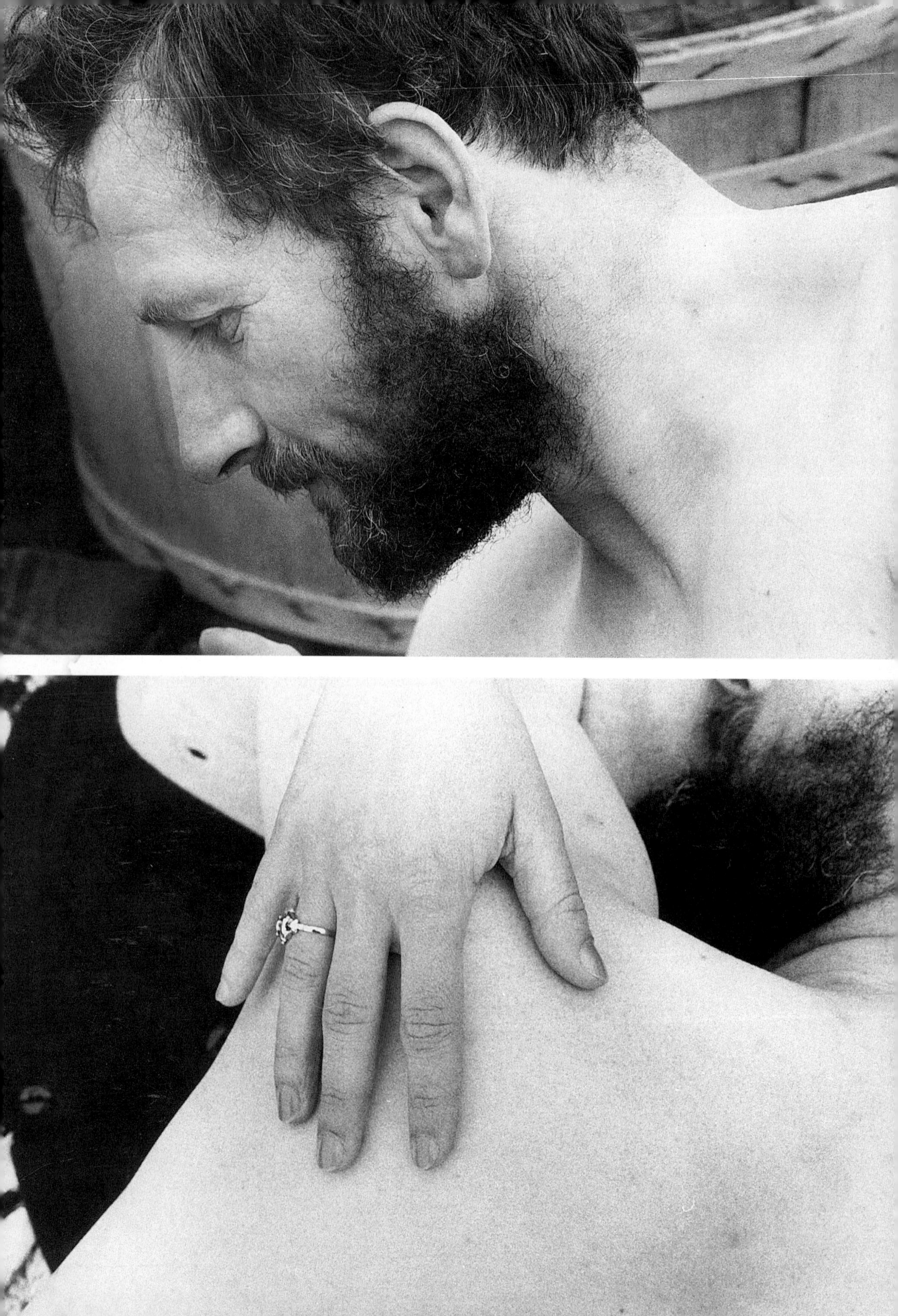

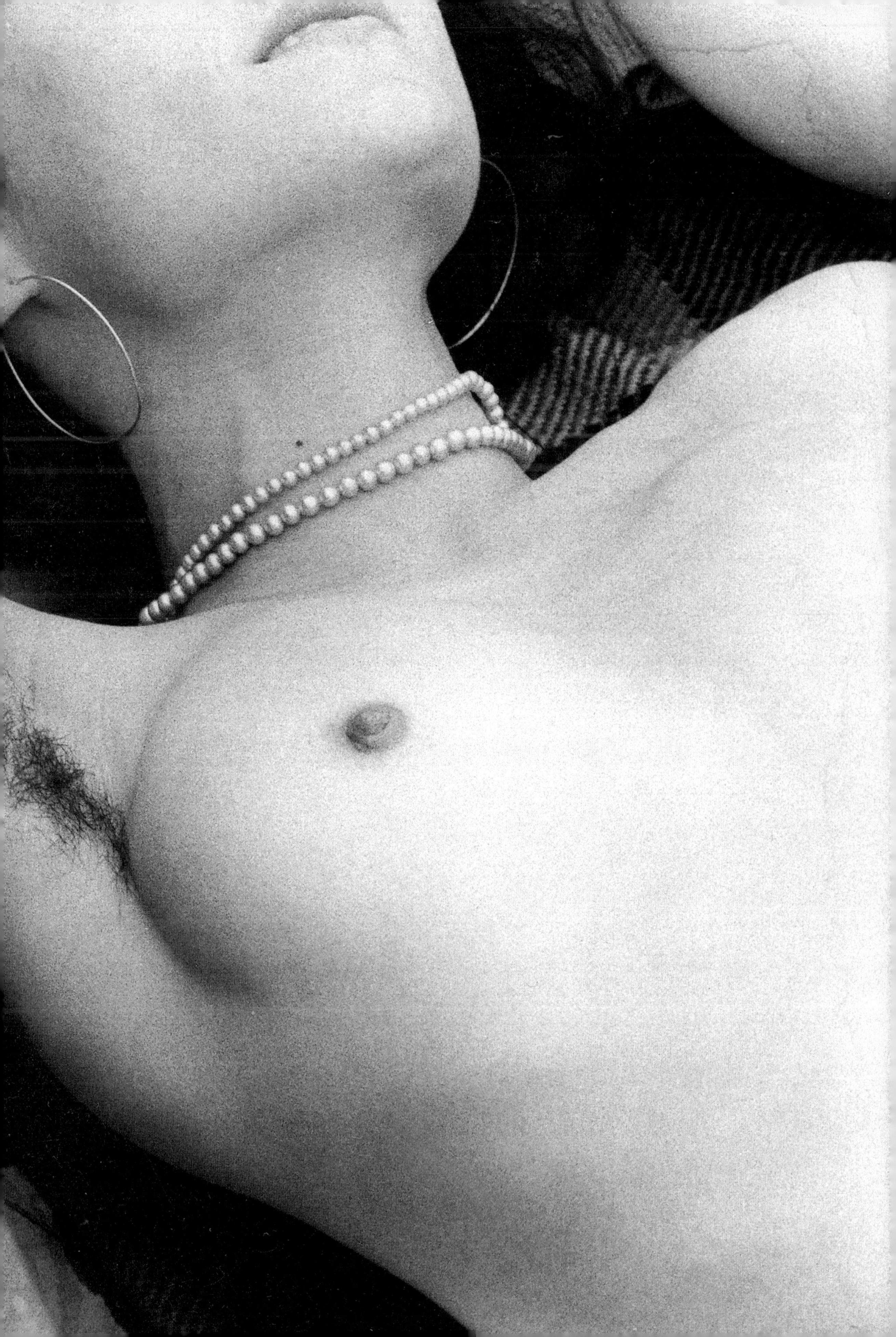

CHINA DUNHUANG

EDIT DUNHUANG RESEARCH ACADEMY

PHOENIX PUBLISHING & MEDIA GROUP
JIANGSU FINE ARTS PABLISHING HOUSE

CHINA
DUNHUANG

CHINA
DUNHUANG

CHINA
DUNHUANG

图书在版编目(CIP)数据

中国敦煌/樊锦诗主编. —南京:江苏美术出版社,
2006.4(2010.8 重)
ISBN 978-7-5344-2082-5

Ⅰ. 中… Ⅱ. 樊… Ⅲ. 敦煌石窟—壁画—简介—
英文 Ⅳ. K879. 412

中国版本图书馆 CIP 数据核字(2006)第 023715 号

Editor-in-Chief: Fan Jinshi
Deputy Editor-in-Chief: Gu Huaming
Executive Editor: Zhou Haige Mao Xiaojian
Layout Designed by Zhou Haige
Cover Designed by Zhou Yang
Text by Fan Jinshi
Photographs by Wu Jian
Photo Captions by Ma Jingchi
Translated by Fan Rong
Proofread by Zhao Wei
Printing Quality Supervised by Wu Rongrong Zhu Xiaoyan

ART OF DUNHUANG CAVE SHRINES

– A Splendid Achievement by Fan Jinshi

GEOGRAPHY AND HISTORY

Dunhuang is located at the western end of the Hexi Corridor in Gansu Province, China. Sandwiched by the Horse's Mane Mountain (also known as North Mountain) to its north and the Qilian Mountain (also called the South Mountain) to its south, Dunhuang is an oasis formed by constant floods of the Ji River (present day Dan River) which flows from the South Mountain. Scattered around this oasis are deserts and sand dunes. In the Han Dynasty when the famous Silk Road first opened it held a strategic position on the trade route. It came to be known as the "throat" of the Silk Road. From Dunhuang going east through the Hexi Corridor, the Silk Road led to the ancient capitals of Chang' an and Luoyang. Going west, the road split into two routes – one to the south and one to the north. The southern route passed the Yangguan Pass, stretched southward along the northern foot of Kunlun Mountain through Ruoqiang, Qiemo, Yutian, Shache, and climbed over the Chong Ridge (the Pamirs), and entered the countries of Da Yue Shi, Anxi, and others. The northern route of the Silk Road started from Dunhuang, passed the Yumenguan Pass, extended along the southern foot of Tian Mountains, through Turfan, Yangzhi, Kuche, Kashir, climbed over the Chong Ridge, and finally entered Dawan, Kangju, and Daxia. With two passes, Dunhuang controlled the flow of the traffic between the east and west, and served as a hub of east and west trade. The goods traded included silk and porcelain from Central China, precious stones from the west, camels and horses from the north, and local grain products. Besides being a business center, it also became a central melting pot.

▼ The Ruins of the Great Wall
The Western Han Dynasty (206BC–AD22)

During the Han Dynasty, the culture of Central China started to take root in Dunhuang. Meanwhile, because of its proximity to the western regions, the Buddhist culture of India also greatly influenced Dunhuang's growth. Furthermore, the eastward movement of Buddhism also brought the cultures of Western Asia and Central Asia. Here in Dunhuang the traditions of China and western countries met, collided, and merged. As Mr. Ji Xianlin, a renowned Dunhuang scholar, rightly states, "Although the world is large and its history is long, only four countries and regions have established their complete cultural systems which have exerted a far reaching influence in the world: China, India, Greece, and Islam. But there is only one area in the whole world where these four cultures once met; that is Dunhuang and Xinjiang in China." Mr. Ji's statement summarizes well the importance of Dunhuang's historic geographic location.

Dunhuang has a history of more than 2,000 years. Before the Qin the Han Dynasties (221 BC–AD 220), Yuezhi and Wusun tribes lived in the area. In the beginning of Western Han Dynasty (206 BC – AD 24), the Xiongnu of northern deserts drove out of Yuezhi

▼ The Ruins of the Yumen Pass
The Western Han Dynasty (206BC–AD24)

▲ The Ruins of the Yumen Pass
The Western Han Dynasty (206BC–AD24)

and occupied Dunhuang (121 BC), armies of the Western Han defeated the Xiongnu and took Dunhuang and the Hexi Corridor into its territory. In the six years of reign of Yuanding (111 BC), the Western Han made Dunhuang a prefecture along with Jiuquan, Zhangye, and Wuwei. These four prefectures came to be known in history as the Four Prefectures of the Hexi Corridor. As part of Dunhuang' s defense scheme, a long wall (which later became part of the Great Wall) was erected to its north and two fortresses, the Yangguan Pass and the Yumenguan Pass, were built to its west. From then on, Dunhuang became a doorway to the Hexi Corridor and Central China and served as a vital military outpost.

To further strengthen Dunhuang' s strategic position, the Court of the Western Han moved people from the Central Plains to settle in Dunhuang and also stationed troops to farm and guard the frontier. During the Western Han Dynasty Dunhuang' s important place in Chinese history was established. During the Eastern Han and Northern and Southern dynasties, Dunhuang developed further and enjoyed an relatively long period of stability. It grew into an important commercial and trade center as well as the grain production based on the Silk Road. Here the culture of Central China took root and continued to develop while Buddhist scriptures and India' s Buddhist culture were introduced into the area. The famous great translator of Buddhist scriptures, Dharmaraks, also known as the "Dunhuang Budhisattva," was in Dunhuang actively translating scriptures and propagating Buddhism in the Western Jin (AD 265 – 316).

During the period of the Sixteen Kingdoms, Central China was in turmoil, and war was frequent. Only Dunhuang escaped the ravage of war; it continued to enjoy peace and prosperity. Many people of the Hexi Corridor and Central China fled to Dunhuang, thus dramatically increasing Dunhuang' s population and helping to preserve the cultures of the Han and Jin in Dunhuang and the Hexi Corridor. At that time a group of eminent Confucian scholars opened schools, wrote books, and developed their ideas in Dunhuang. In the meantime, Buddhists of the west who came to China to teach the Dharma (Buddhist Law) to the Chinese and those of China who went to the west to quest for the Dharma had to pass through Dunhuang on their respective journeys. These traveling Buddhists established a growing Buddhist community in Dunhuang. As The Book of Wei– A History Buddhism and Daoism indicates, "Dunhuang is on the border with the western regions, where clergy and the lay population interchange. Although their traditional villages are quite similar to ours, there are numerous stupas and temples."

While the development of Buddhist culture in Dunhuang was inevitable, cave construction at Mogao in Dunhuang started quite accidentally. According to Buddhist Shrines in Mogao Caves by Li Kerang, "Mogao Caves started in the begging of the second year of the reign of Jianyuan of the Qin (AD 366) when a travelling monk named Shamen Lezun, arriving one day at Mogao Mount,suddenly saw golden lights appearing from the spot as if they were the thousands Buddhas. He then dug a cave from the Mogao Cliff and built a shrine. After him came Chan (Zen) Master Faliang from the east, who hollowed a second cave next to it." Thus began the trend of cave building in Dunhuang that was to last for more than a thousand years. After these humble beginnings, more serious endeavors supported by local authorities ensued. Two early magistrates of Gua Prefecture (Dunhuang) need special mention here. Yuan Tairong, a royal clansman, and Prince Dongyang and Yuyi, a noble man and Duke of Jianping of the Northern Zhou. Both of them were Buddhist devotees and greatly encouraged excavating caves and building shrines at Mogao.

In the Sui Dynasy, both Emperors Wen and Yang initiated a national movement to spread Buddhism and ordered that stupas built in every region of the nation. Accordingly, Gua Prefecture (Dunhuang) built its stupas in Chongjiao Temple (now Mogao Grottoes). Handwritten copies executed in the central court of Buddhist scriptures also reached Dunhuang. During the relatively short Sui Dynasty, carving caves became a fad which continued into the Tang Dynasty. The Tang court strengthened Dunhuang' s security by establishing the Anxi (Pacified Western Region) Garrison and four towns. The Tang court raised ten armies and stationed them in Dunhuang and the Hexi Corridor. The military strength in the area guaranteed a continued and steady development of Dunhuang' s economy and culture with an unimpeded traffic along the Silk Road. As is documented, "from the west of Dunhuang to the east of Persia, [the Silk Road] saw no end of envoys of the west bringing tribute to the court and no end of merchants and travelers as well." The peaceful environment and continued cultural and economic exchange between east and west were conducive to cave building in Dunhuang, which reach new heights in the Tang Dynasty. Unfortunately, in the fourteenth year of the reign of Tianbao of the Tang Dynasty (AD 755), a large uprising (Anlushan Rebellion) broke out in China leading the Tang to its decline.

Tibetan Powers (Tupo) took advantage of the weakening Tang and overtook Longyou and Hexi. In the second year of the reign of Jianzhou of the Tang, the Tibetans occupied Shazhou and enforced its administrative, economic, and cultural system. Since the Tibetans were for the most part Buddhist supporters, the development of Buddhist culture and art in Dunhuang was unimpeded under the Tibetan rule. Cave building at Mogao even increased swing. In the second year of reign of Huicang (AD 842), an internal rivalry broken out in Tibet and weakened its political clout in the western regions. Seizing this opportunity, Zhang Yichao of Sha Prefecture staged an insurrection and successively recaptured eleven prefectures including Yi, Xi, Gua, Su, Gan, and Liang from Tibetan hands. Zhang sent an envoy to the Tang court to pledge his allegiance to the Tang, which was accepted, and he himself was conferred the rank of general of the insurrection Army. Thus began more than two hundred years of administration of Dunhuang by the "Insurrection Army Government (Guiyijun)." Zhang's administration reintroduced the Tang system

▲ The Mogao Grottoes

and enforced Han culture. Dunhuang again regained its political stability. Under the protection of Zhang' s rule, Buddhist devotees continued to build temples and cave shrines on a large scale. In the Five Dynasties, Cao Yijin took over Zhang Chengfeng' s government. Cao maintained a close relationship with the court of Central China and received their support. He made good use of the strength, reputation, and prestige the old Tang court had enjoyed among the people of the Northwest to strengthen his position among powers to the west in Inner Asia. Through strategic marriage alliances, he struck good relationships with the Moslems of Gan Prefecture. Moslems of Xi Prefecture, and Yutian (Khotan). Cao' s efforts to build good relations with the central courts and surrounding minority nationalities were effective; they contributed not only to peace in the central plains, but also to the safety of the Silk Road and growing exchange between Dunhuang and the Buddhist culture of the west. Moreover, they created favorable political conditions for the development of Dunhuang' s Buddhist art.

▲ The Yulin Grottoes

In the third year of Jingyou of the Song Dynasty (AD 1036) and the third year of Baoqing of the Southern Song Dynasty (AD 1227), Dunhuang was occupied by the Dongxianqiang and the Mongols respectively. Since both of these people were devout believers of Buddhism, they regarded the Mogao Grottoes in Dunhuang as an important Buddhist sanctuary to be protected and improved. Therefore, there were still a few new cave additions to Mogao Grottoes during these periods. Then the development tapered off. With the rise of an "Ocean Silk Road" and expansion of the Mongol Empire, Dunhuang consequently started to lose its strategic position as a hub of east and west transpotation and the gateway of the Chinese west. Along with it, Mogao Grottoes fell into decline.

After the Yuan Dynasty, no new caves were excavated and Dunhuang gradually was forgotten. In the seventh year of Jiajing of Ming Dynasty (AD 1528), the Ming court closed the Jiayuguan Pass, turning Dunhuang into a frontier herding ground. Dunhuang did not see its revival until the first year of Yongzheng of the Qing Dynasty (AD 1723), when an outpost was set up again in Dunhuang. Three years later (AD 1725), the outpost was upgraded to a garrison, and many immigrants were brought in from every prefecture in Gansu

to farm and rebuild Shazhou City. In the twenty-fifth year of Qianlong of the Qing Dynasty (AD 1760), Shazhou Garrison became Dunhuang County. Dunhuang became alive again and Mogao Grottoes also began to attract people' s attention. In the twenty-sixth year of Guangxu (AD 1900) of the Qing Dynasty, the world famous Dunhuang Library Cave was discovered. Unfortunately, the Qing government was so Corrupt and incompetent that Western Powers could avail themselves of Chinese treasures at their will. Not long after the discovery of the Library Cave Marc Aurel Stein, a Hungariana, followed in turn by Paul Pelliot of France, Zuicho Tachibana of Japan, and Sergei Oldenberg of Russia, and other western adventurers came to the site. Using unfair means, they spirited away a large number of the Library Cave deposits from Daoist Wang. Most of these materials were then scattered around the world and are now in the collections of private individuals and national museums in England, France, Russia, Japan, and other countries. Only a small part remain in China. This misfortune is a tremendous loss for China, unprecedented in the history of Chinese culture.

ART OF DUNHUANG CAVE SHRINES

"Dunhuang Cave Shrines" is a general term referring to the live groups of cave shrines in the greater Dunhuang area. These five groups are : Mogao Grottoes outside the town of Dunhuang, The Western Caves of a Thousand Buddhas, Yulin Grottoes in Anxi County, the Eastern Caves of a Thousand Buddhas, and the Five–Temple Grottoes in Shubei County. Although different in scale, these cave shrines are all located within the boundary of the old Dunhuang Prefecture and are similar in content, style, and artistic expression. This is why they are generally grouped together and called Dunhuang Cave Shrines. There are 812 caves in all. Mogao Grottoes has 735, the Western Caves of a Thousand Buddhas has 22. Yulin Grottoes has 42, the Eastern Caves of a Thousand Buddhas has 7, and Five–Temple Grottoes has 6.

Among these cave shrines, the most magnificent are those of Mogao Grottoes which have been recognized as one of the most important sites in world cultural heritage. Mogao Grottoes lies at the eastern foot of the Mingsha Dunes (Dunes of the Singing Sands), 25 kilometers southeast of Dunhuang town. It faces east toward Sanwei Mountain, one range of Qilian Mountains, and in front of it runs Shiquan River. From the 4th century to the 14th century, cave construction and Buddhist image production was continuous, and the result is the spectacular cluster of caves stretching 1680 kilometers south to north. All together 735 caves are dug out of the cliff with a height rising from fifteen to thirty meters and distributed on four different levels. Mogao Grottoes can be divided into two areas: the southern area and

▼ The West Thousand–Buddha Caves

▲ The North Section of the Mogao Grottoes

the northern area. The south consists of 492 caves, more than 2,000 painted sculptures, more than 45,000 square meters of wall painting, and five wooden porticos. The north consists of 243 caves, which were religious practice and living quarters for monks. These caves have earthen beds, hearth pits, smoke ducks, wall shrines, lamp stands, and other practical elements. There are no painted images or wall paintings in these caves.

Since the cave temples were dug out of the sandstone cliff, fine sculpturing was impossible at the entire site. Therefore, painted clay stucco sculptures and murals became the major artistic media. Artists conveyed skin tone, facial expression, fluffy hair and beard, and costume texture through painted additions rather than carving. To make a painted clay stucco sculpture, the artist built an armature first of bound straw, and then stuccoed it with the mixture of dried reed and clay. Amural was executed on a treated wall, on which two or three layers of reed and clay mixture were first applied as a base. Then the process of composition selection, layout, sketching and coloring ensued. The art of Dunhuang cave shrines is a comprehensive art, which unifies architecture, painted sculpture, and wall painting. The architectural shape of a cave is determined by its content and function. The painted sculpture is a cave is the majar focus of worship placed in a wall niche or in a central pillar stupa or on a prominent position on an altar. It is coordinated with the surrounding wall paintings in theme and color coordination. The wall paintings depict a complex narratives or detailed decorative visual statement. These colorful wall paintings occupy the whole cave covering niches, the four walls, and ceilings, complementing the sculpture that sits at the focal point. Together, they set off each other and form a complete and unified expression of Dunhuang' s cave art.

The art of Dunhuang cave shrines is Buddhist with Chinese national and folk art characteristics. It is based on the artistic tradition of the Han and Jin Dynasties and has drawn rich inspiration from the arts of other lands. With its long history, large scale, profound content,splendid art, good condition, and domestic and international fame, the Dunhuang cave shrines are a treasure trove of Chinese as well as world Buddhist art.

◀ The Nine-storey Pagoda

▼ The Mount Mingsha and the Crescent Moon Lake

▲The Mount Sanwei

▶ Poplar

▲ The Daquan River

► The White Horse Pagoda

► The Wuwa

▼ Camels in the Desert

I. Cave Art of the Northern Dynasties

During this period, Dunhuang' s cave art was in its early stage of development. Its theme and style show a strong presence of the Buddhist art of the west along with deep roots in the cultural plains (Central China). Dunhuang' s Buddhist art, from its very beginning, bore strong characteristics of the art of local Jin and Wei regions. However, a dominantly Chinese Dunhuang Buddhist art did not take shape until the late Northern Dynasties.

A. Architectural Forms of the Caves

Chan (Zen) meditation caves. Chan caves were built for monks to practice meditation. The main chamber of the cave is oblong or square. In its front wall a niche is dug for a painted image, which was to be used by Chan monks in meditation. In either of the side walls are two or four small cells, each big enough for only one person to sit in meditation. The ceilings of these caves were either flat or recessed. The early models were plain, but the later ones had paintings on the walls and ceilings (Cave 267, 268, 269, 270, 271, and 285).

1. Caves with a central stupa. These caves were also called Central Pillar Caves or Stupa Caves. Originating from Chaitya Halls of India, they were the most popular caves in this period. A stupa is built as the cave' s center for worship. The main chamber is oblong. Just behind the cave' s center a square stupa column is connected to the ground and the ceiling. On each side of the column is a niche for a painted image to be worshipped by devotees. The ceiling in front of the stupa is gabled in the Han architectural style, and the ceilings surrounding the stupa are flat.

2. Assembly Caves. These are the places of worship. The form of this kind of cave was influenced by Chinese traditional assembly hall architecture. The main hall is square. In its front wall, a niche is dug for a painted image, or a painted image was erected without a niche. The other three walls are filled with paintings (murals). There are several assembly caves that have niches for images on the side walls. The ceilings are either recessed or gabled (cave 249 and 275).

B. Painted Images (sculptures)

The painted image in the Northern Dynasties can be classified into two groups: full-bodied images and attached, low-relief images. The full-bodied images were high reliefs connected to the walls. They were images of Buddhas, Budhisattvas, and disciples. The images of Buddhas included those of Maitreya, Sakyamuni, and the Sakyamuni and Prabhutarama. The images of Sakyamuni are further divided into those of a meditating Buddha, a practicing Buddha, a preaching Buddha, an enlightened Buddha, and a thinking Buddha. The early images of Sakyamuni have two attendant Budhisattvas, but in later ones his disciples Kasyapa and Ananda are added.

► Central Stupa-pillar Shape of Cave 288
The Western Wei Dynasty (535-556)

◄ Meditation Cave Shape of Cave 285
The Western Wei Dynasty (535-556)

428

▲ Budhisattva (the northern outside of an east-facing niche built into the central pillar)
Cave 432
The Western Wei Dynasty (535–556)

▶ Group of Painted Clay Figures (the eastward-facing niche built into the central pillar)
Cave 432
The Western Wei Dynasty (535–556)

▼ Buddhist Monk in Dhyana (chan) (the south side of a niche built into the west wall)
Cave 285
The Western Wei Dynasty (535–556)

◀ Central Stupa-pillar
Shape of Cave 428

432
C.216 P.127

▲ Hall With Inverted Funnel Shaped Ceiling Shape of Cave 305
The Sui Dynasty (581–618)

► Central Stupa–pillar Shape of Cave 303
The Sui Dynasty (581–618)

303

The attached, low-relief images include attendant Budhisattvas, apsaras, and the thousand Buddhas. They are modeled from clay models and then affixed to the walls of the central stupas or the wall of the caves. They resemble low relief images on the walls used to set off the full-bodied images. The Buddhas made in the early Northern Dynasties generally wear robes leaving the right arms bare or round-necked robes covering both shoulders. The images of Budhisattvas appeared with high hair buns and crowns of precious stones. Their hair is shoulder length; their upper bodies are bare or are covered with silk robes and their lower bodies are dressed with skirts of fine folds. Round or full-faced, wide-shouldered, and flat-chested, they sit looking robust, dignified, natural, peaceful, clam, and thoughtful. In this period, the art of painted images had its foundation in the art of the Han and Jin of the Central Plains. But at the same time it greatly absorbed influence from the artistic tradition of western Buddhist art. In the Western Wei of the late Northern Dynasties, as Chinese-style costumes were introduced to Dunhuang from Central plains, the Chinese artistic style of "delicacy and elegance" became fashionable. The images produced in this period started to wear Confucian-style high-collared and large sleeved robes with small knots on the chests, topped with garments that had buttons down the front. These figures have square and thin faces and narrow, flat bodies. Appearing more Chinese.

C. Wall Paintings

The wall paintings of the Northern Dynasties follow a fixed layout. The upper borders of the four walls are surrounded by heavenly dancers and musicians. The middle part of the walls are filled with pictures of Buddhas in different postures and settings, such as the thousand Buddhas, a preaching Buddha with a thousand Buddhas, Jataka tales and other Buddhist legends. The lower borders of the wall are surrounded by vajras or decorative patterns. The ceilings of the early Northern Dynasties are painted with decorative designs

▲ Cross-legged Maitreya (the west wall) Cave 275
The Northern Liang Dynasty(397–439)

▶ Meditating Budhisattva (a southward-facing niche built into the upper part of the central pillar) Cave 257
The Northern Wei Dynasty (439–534)

◀ Budhisattva (the southern outside of an eastward-facing niche built into the central pillar) Cave 432
The Western Wei Dynasty (535–556)

► Budhisattva (the south side of the central pillar) Cave 259
The Northern Wei Dynasty (439–534)

◄ Warrior (the northern outside of an eastward-facing niche built into the central pillar) Cave 435
The Northern Wei Dynasty (439–534)

▼ Buddhas (the west wall) Cave 259
The Northern Wei Dynasty (439–534)

▲ Meditating Buddha (the westward–facing niche built into the central pillar) Cave 248
The Northern Wei Dynasty (439–534)

► Buddha in Meditation mudr (the north wall) Cave 259
The Northern Wei Dynasty (439–534)

► Buddha Preaching the Law (in an eastward–facing niche built into the central pillar) Cave 248
The Northern Wei Dynasty (439–534)

▲ Group of Painted Clay Figures (the west wall) Cave 297
The Northern Zhou Dynasty (557–580)

◀ Relief Sculpture of Celestial Being (the west wall) Cave 297
The Northern Zhou Dynasty (557–580)

while the gables or recessed of the late Northern Dynasties are painted with Jataka tales. Buddhist legends, and a thousand Buddhas. According to their content, these wall paintings can be classified into five types.

1. Paintings of deities. This includes all categories Buddhist deities. Compositions of preaching Buddhas are composed strictly according to canonical rules. An example is the repetitive but colorful paintings of the thousand Buddhas. Paintings of donor Budhisattvas dance in an orderly and graceful fashion; compositions of joyous heavenly dancers and musicians are also common. Strong, fiercely-looking vajras, defenders of the Law (or Dharma, the Buddhist doctrine) and destroyers of evil spirits populate other works.

2. Paintings of Jataka tales, Cause and Effect, and other Buddhiast legends. Jataka tales record Sakyamuni' s various meritorious deeds from his former lives as a Budhisattva Cause and Effect tales tell stories of how Sakyamuni preached the Dharma to enlighten transient beings after he became a Buddha. Other Buddhist legends include episodes from the life of historical Sakyamuni Buddha. The main themes of these legendary stories feature tenets of Buddhist doctrine such as renouncing the householder' s life to enter monkhood; practicing giving, forbearance, and self-discipline; doing good and punishing evil; cause and effect of actions; and the power of the Dharma. The narrative paintings of the late Morthern Dynasties gradually incorporated more Chinese themes, including Confucian ideas of loyalty, piety, humanity, gentility, and familial harmony. These narratives assume a range of layouts. Monoscenic or synoptic paintings illustrate one particular scene in the history. These are also multiple-theme murals; these encompass several scenes from the same story in one picture; further, continuous narratives are composed of a series of pictures illustrating a complete story.

▲ Musicians in a Heavenly Palace (the northern side of the ceiling) Cave 272
The Northern Liang Dynasty (397–439)

► Jataka of King Bi–leng–jie–li (the north wall) Cave 275
The Northern Liang Dynasty (386–439)

▲ Sakyamuni's Wanderings (the south wall) Cave 275
The Northern Liang Dynasty (397–439)

◀ Attendant Budhisattvas (the southern section of the west wall) Cave 272
The Northern Liang Dynasty (397–439)

3. Paintings of mythical figures. These murals did not appear until the late Northern Dynasties. They originated with depictions of Daoist mythical figures such as Xi Wangmu (Queen Mother of the west) and the Lord of the East who ride on dragon phoenix and carriages, the snake-bodied and human-faced Fuxi and Nuwa, the flying Green Dragon (eastern deity), the winged, galloping White Tiger (western deity), the soaring Red Sparrow (southern deity), and Xuanwu (northern deity). These are also monsters such as the immortal winged man with two raised, pointed ears and long feathers growing on his arms; the god of thunder with an animal head and a human body; and the god of lightning, who also has an animal head and a human body.

4. Paintings of donors. Many donors and their family members wished to be depicted in procession on the walls they dedicated. They were usually painted at the bottom of the main murals in small scale, no higher than a foot. The donors are positioned according to gender with monks and nuns leading and laymen and laywomen following. The donors include kings, nobles, and their attendants.

5. Decorative Patterns. In the period of the Northern Dynasties, decorative patterns are used to embellish architectural aspect of the caves. They are pointed on the gabled ceilings, rafters, lintels, bracket sets, and the flat ceilings of the caves with central stupas,

▲ The Jataka of the King of the Nine-Colored Deer (Deer and King) (the west wall) Cave 257

The Northern Wei Dynasty (439–534)

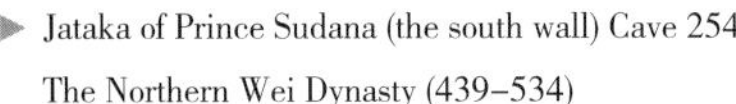

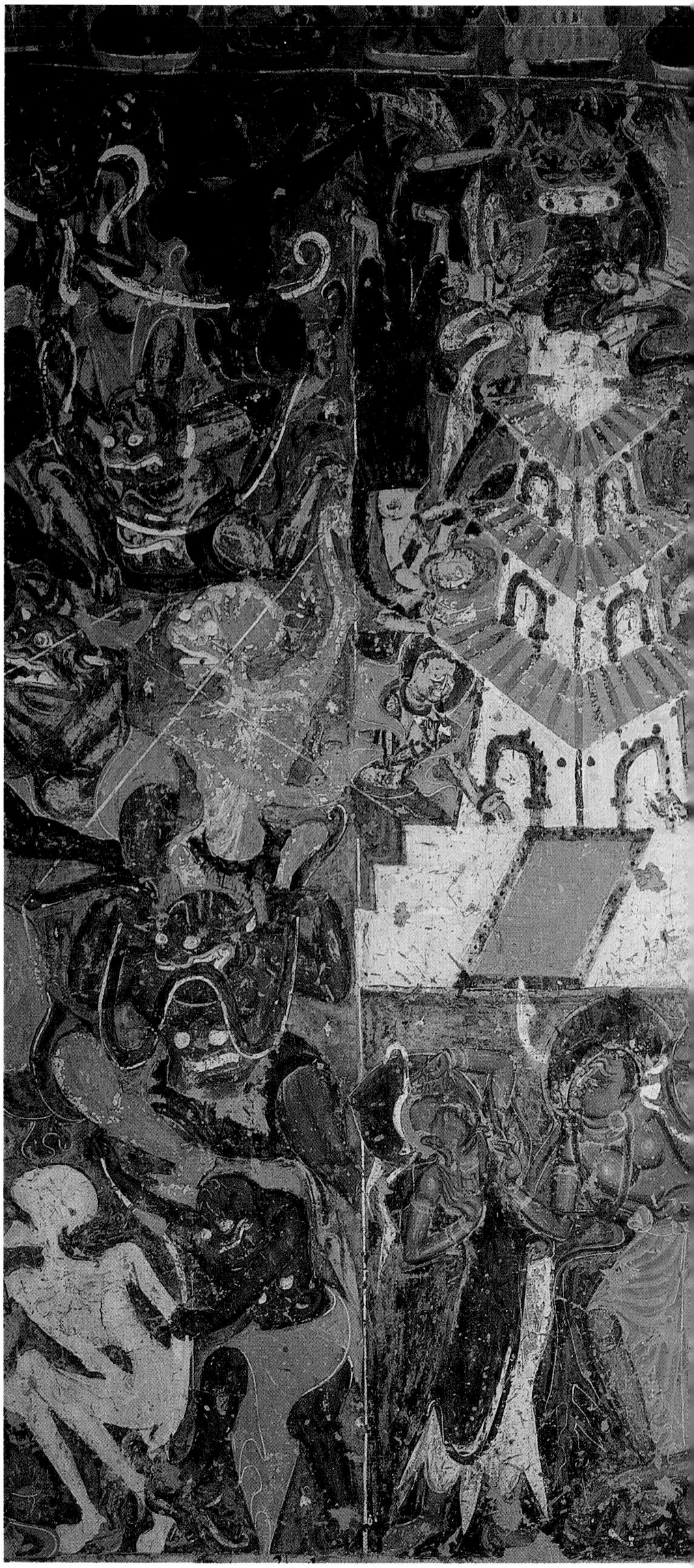

► Jataka of Prince Sudana (the south wall) Cave 254

The Northern Wei Dynasty (439–534)

on the sunken ceilings of the assembly caves, and on the frames of the niches, painted nimbuses, and the borders of the walls of various types of caves. The flat ceilings are covered with cavern-ceiling patterns. In the center of a flat ceiling large lotuses are painted, and the borders are decorated with flames, apsaras, and acanthus, designs. The center of the recessed ceilings are decorated with a canopy design. In it' s the center is a large lotus and its borders are embellished with acanthus, cloud, and flame patterns. Surrounding the recessed hanging banners and painted bells are depicted. On the rafters of a gabled ceiling, the borders of the walls, and the frames of the niches are covered with designs of lotus, acanthus, auspicious animals, clouds, geometrical forms.

▼ Jataka of Prince Sudana (the southern section of the east wall) Cave 428
The Northern Zhou Dynasty (557–580)

► Jataka of Prince Sudana (ride back to the palace) (the southern section of the east wall) Cave 428
The Nothern Zhou Dynasty (557–580)

▲ The Story of Five Hundred Bandits Becoming Buddhas (banished to the forest) (the south wall) Cave 285
The Western Wei Dynasty (535–556)

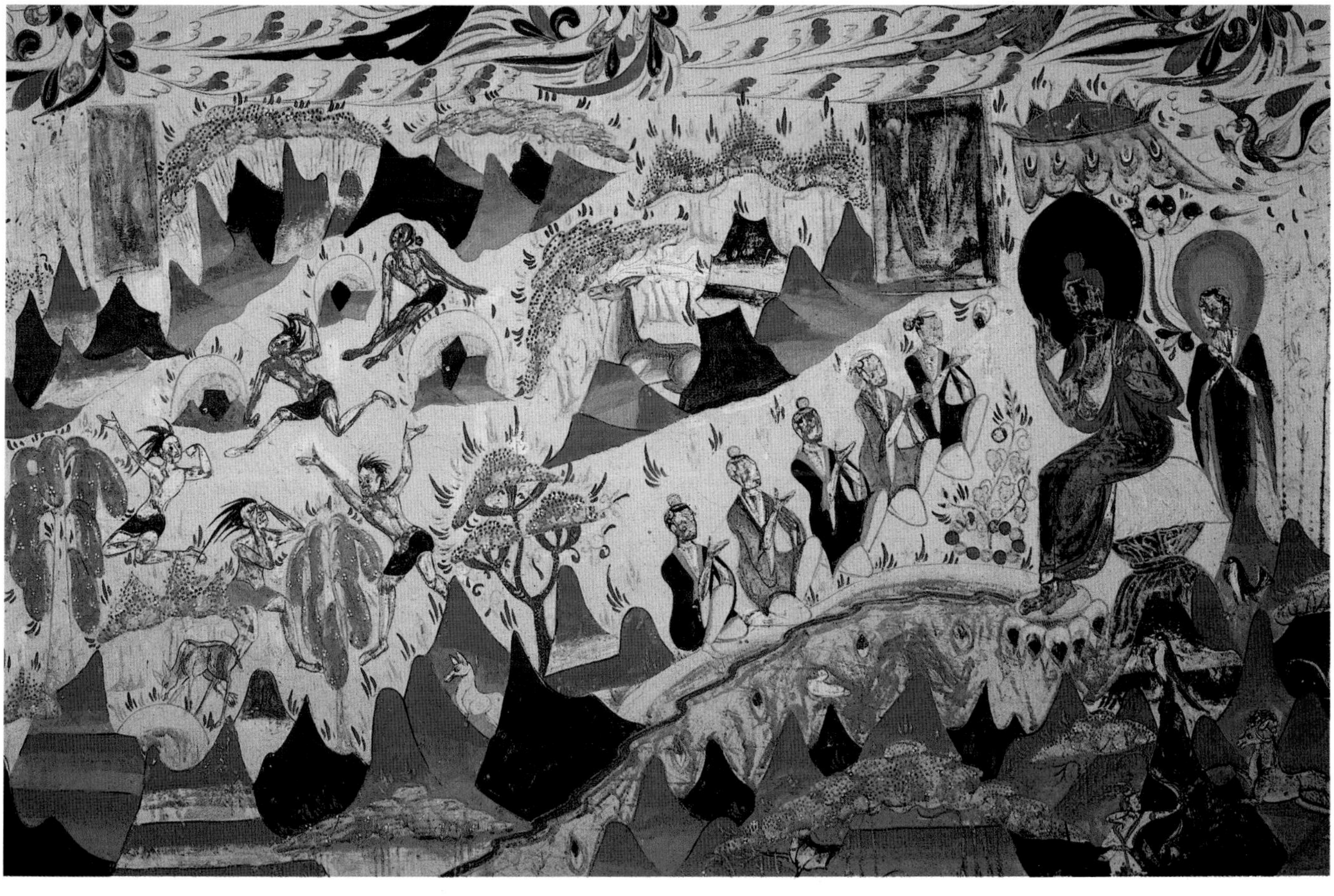

▲ Hunting with Bow and Arrow (the northern part of the ceiling) Cave 249
The Western Wei Dynasty (535–556)

◀ Apsaras (the north wall) Cave 305
The Sui Dynasty (581–618)

▶ The Story of Bhiksuni Patacara (section) (the north wall) Cave 296
The Northern Zhou Dynasty (557–580)

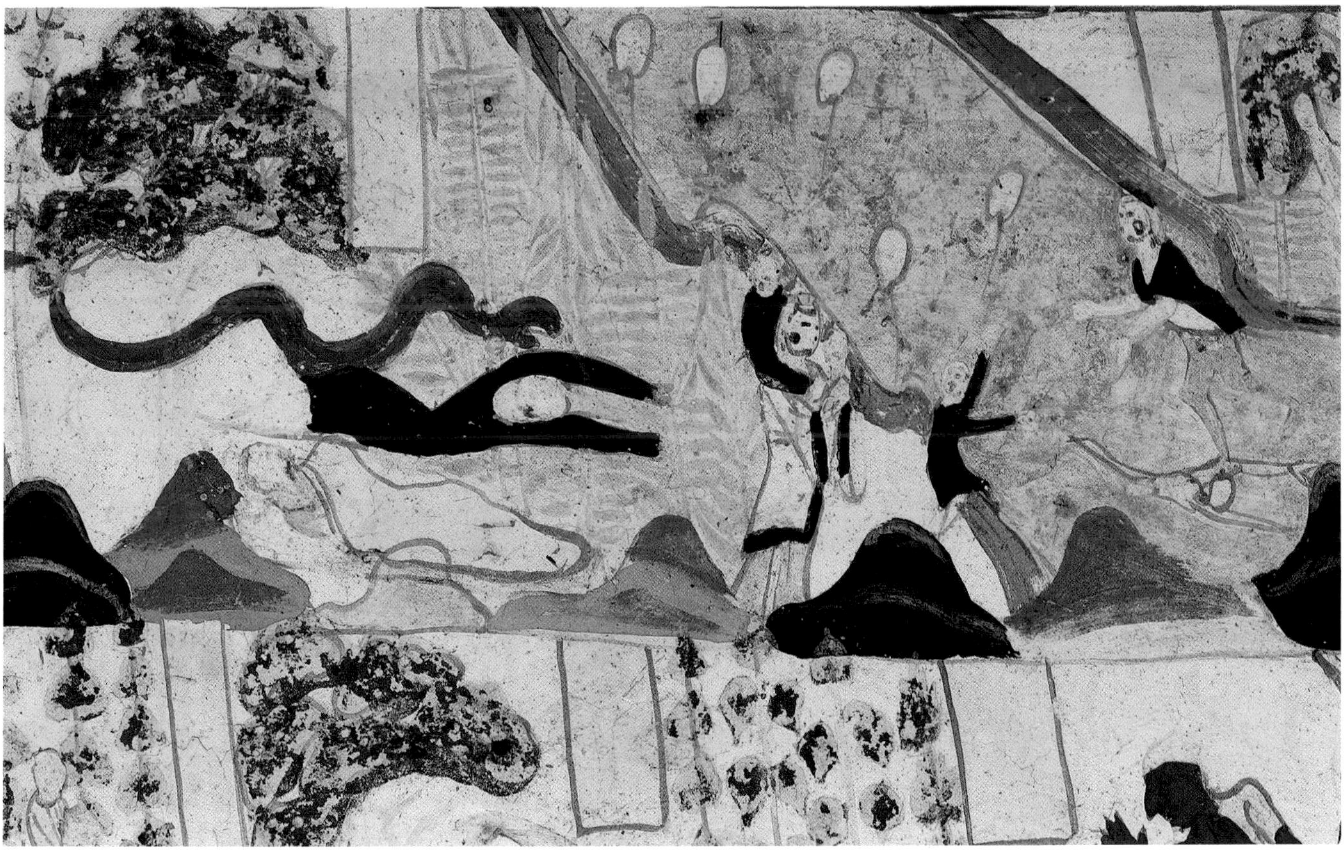

▲ Cart (the lower part of the east wall) Cave 6 of the Xi Qianfo Grottoes
The Northern Zhou Dynasty (557–580)

▶ Pattern (ceiling) Cave 407
The Sui Dynasty (581–618)

In early wall paintings artists use red ochre as the ground color; the figures in these paintings assume strong, well-proportioned masculine, features dressed in the western style costumes. Their faces and bodies are painted with shading (typically found in Inner Asian and Indian painting) to increase the effect of three-dimensionality and rotundity of the body. The colors are simple and unadorned, and the lines are thin, but forceful. Two different styles are employed. One is a continuation of the style of the early wall paintings, improving them with shading technique. In the second style, white is used as the ground color and the figures are thin, delicate, and elegant, with well-defined brows and eyes and a natural and unrestrained expression; they are dressed in the Chinese-style square collared, dark-colored robes. The faces are shaded with red according to the Chinese tradition. The colors are fresh and bright, and the lines appear quick, rhythmic, unrestrained, and elegant. This latter style is greatly influenced by the newly-arrived Chinese material.

▲ Pattern (ceiling) Cave 329
Early Tang Dynasty (618–704)

▼ The Lintel of the Niche (the upper part of a northward-facing niche built into the central pillar)
Cave 7 of the Xi Qianfo Grottoes

► Swimming (the ceiling) Cave 257
The Northern Wei Dynasty (439–534)

II. Cave Art of the Sui and Tang Dynasties

Buddhism and Buddhist art greatly developed in China in the Sui and Tang dynasties and formed a unique tradition with Chinese characteristics. In this favorable environment, Dunhuang Cave art reached its peak of artistic achievement. The secularization, popularization, and diversification of cave architecture, painted images, and wall paintings during this period demonstrate a successful Chinese acculturation of Buddhist art.

A. Architectural Forms of the Caves

In this period, the cave designs moved toward diversification, localization, and secularization. The majority of the new caves were of assembly caves. The niches in the caves became wider and deeper and had three different forms. In the Sui Dynasty, a typical niche had two layers, an inner layer and an outer layer. In the early Tang period, the niche had a smaller interior, but a wider opening. In the later Tang period, the niche was modeled on the style of a secular canopied bed. In this kind of niche, a horse hoof shaped pedestal was set, on which was placed a painted image (for example, caves 329 and 384). Although small in numbers, some assembly caves built in both the Sui and Tang dynasty had niches open in the back walls and side walls of the main rooms for painted images of Trikala (for example, cave 420). Caves with altars were new additions in this period. In the Sui and early Tang periods, an oblong or U–shaped pedestal was carved out of the back wall of the main room, while in the late Tang period a square pedestal was carved out in the center of the main room of large caves. In the back of the pedestal stood a screen that connected to the top of the recessed ceiling. Stairs led to the pedestal stop where painted images were on view for believers to look at from all directions. This kind of cave was an assembly cave and resembled the main hall of the temple or a royal palace (for example, Cave 196).

Paranirvana caves and seven Buddhas caves. These caves are so named because they contain images of the Buddha entering Paranirvana or images of the seven Buddhas sitting together; both types typically have pedestals. The main room of this kind of cave is oblong, and out of its back wall a cave–length bed is carves, on which rests a sculpture of a reclining Buddha (for example, Cave 148 of the High Tang and Cave 158 of the Mid Tang), or in the other case seven Buddhas (Cave 365 of the Mid Tang) are seated. The ceiling is either sunken or arched.

▲ Budhisattva (the south side of the central niche) Cave 420
The Sui Dynasty (581–618)

► Budhisattva (the northern part of the central altar) Cave 196
Late Tang Dynasty (848–906)

017
821
900 AD
晚唐
151

◀ Hall with Inverted Funnel Shaped Ceiling and Central Stapa-pillar (Cave16) Commemoration Cave (Cave 17) Shape of Cave 16-17
Late Tang Dynasty (848-906)

▶ Big Buddha Cave 130
High Tang Dynasty (705-780)

▼ Buldha in Nirvana Cave 158
Mid-Tang Dynasty (781-847)

Caves with large images. These caves are thus named because they contain colossal, seated images of Maitreya (Mogao Cave 96 of the early Tang, Cave 130 of the late Tang, and Yulin Cave 6 of the Tang). These caves are large and tall, and their main rooms were square with a smaller top and a larger bottom. A large, stone-bodied and clay-stuccoed sculpture is erected against the back wall. A U-shaped passage is carved out from behind the statue for circumambulation. In the middle and upper part of the front wall a large window is open for light. The ceiling is either receded or vaulted. On the exterior, multi-storied wooden verandahs are built.

During this period, caves with central stupas greatly decreased and fell into a decline because of simplification of liturgical procedures

▼ Nirvana Cave Shape of Cave 158
Mid-Tang Dynasty (781–847)

and the expansion of lay worship of Buddhism. The central stupas lost their favor as the center of worship, and in their place arose the sculptural altars of the assembly caves.

B. Painted Images

In the Sui and Tang period, the painted images placed in niches or on the pedestals were full-bodied, three-dimensional sculptures, completely separate from the wall. Along with the development of Buddhist ideas, painted images of deities also changed and developed in number and content. The number of images placed in a niche or pedestal ranged from three to eleven with seven and nine being the most common. In the Sui Dynasty, the main deities were expanded to include the Buddha of the past; Sakyamuni, Buddha of the present;

Maitreya, Buddha of the future; Dharmakaya, embodiment of truth and the law; Nirmanakaya, incarnation of the bhutatatthate; and Nirmanakaya, the meramorphisized body. Sakymuni, Amitabha, and Maitreya were the most popular images worshiped in the Sui and Tang. During this period, images of the four deva-king and vajras, all defenders of the Buddhist (Dharma), were added to the antechambers; in the late Tang they were moved into the main rooms to be grouped with images of Buddhas, Budhisattvas, and disciples. A typical layout is the Buddha positioned in the center flanked by Kasyapa and Ananda, Manjusri and Samantabhadra, standing or sitting, deva-kings of the south and north, and Vajrapani. In some of the groups small images of

▲ Budhisattva and Kasyapa (the north side of the central niche) Cave 419
The Sui Dynasty (581–618)

◀ Budhisattva and Ananda (the south side of the central niche) Cave 419
The Sui Dynasty (581–618)

▶ Budhisattva (the south side of the inner section of the central niche) Cave 328
Early Tang Dynasty (618–704)

▲ Group of Painted Clay Figures (the west wall) Cave 419
The Sui Dynasty (581–618)

► Attendant Budhisattva (the north side of the central niche) Cave 328
Early Tang Dynasty (618–704)

▲ Ananda (the south side of the central niche) Cave 328
Early Tang Dynasty (618–704)

▶ Buddha (the niche built into the west wall) Cave 328
Early Tang Dynasty (618–704)

▶ Kasyapa (the north side of the central niche) Cave 328
Early Tang Dynasty (618–704)

▲ Group of Painted Clay Figures (the central altar) Cave 205
Early Tang Dynasty (618–704)

► Avalokitesvara (the north side of the central niche) Cave 328
Early Tang Dynasty (618–704)

▲ Budhisattva (the north side of the central niche) Cave 159
High–Tang Dynasty (765–780)

► Budhisattva (detail) (the south side of the central niche) Cave194
High–Tang Dynasty (765–780)

▲ Big Buddha Cave 96
Early Tang Dynasty (618–704)

► Budhisattva (the north side of the central niche) Cave 194
Mid–Tang Dynasty (781–847)

► Budhisattva (the south side of the central niche) Cave 159
Mid–Tang Dynasty (781–847)

► Budhisattva (the southern part of the central altar) Cave 205
Early Tang Dynasty (618–704)

◄ Ananda (the south side of the central niche) Cave 45
High Tang Dynasty (705–780)

▼ Group of Painted Clay Figures (the niche on the west wall) Cave 328
Early Tang Dynasty (618–704)

▲ Heavenly King (the north side of the inner section of the central niche) Cave 46
High Tang Dynasty (705–780)

► Ananda, Budhisattva and Heavenly King (the south side of the central niche) Cave 45
High Tang Dynasty (705–780)

► Warrior (the northern outside of the central niche) Cave 194
High Tang Dynasty (705–780)

▲ Group of Painted Clay Figures (the niche built into the west wall) Cave 45
High Tang Dynasty (705–780)

► Budhisattva (the north side of the central niche) Cave 45
High Tang Dynasty (705–780)

▲ Hall With Inverted Funnel Shaped Ceiling Shape of Cave 322
Early Tang Dynasty (618–704)

► Kasyapa (the northern side of the central niche) Cave 45
High Tang Dynasty (705–780)

▲ Heavenly King (the north side of the central niche) Cave 322
Early Tang Dynasty (618–704)

▶ Statue of Hong Bian (the Hidden Library)
Late Tang Dynasty (848–906)

▶ Sariputra (the west side of the inner section of a niche built into the south wall) Cave 46
High Tang Dynasty (705–780)

▲ Group of Painted Clay Figures (the niche of the west wall) Cave 322
Early Tang Dynasty (618–704)

► Kasyapa Budhisattva and Heavenly King (the inner northern side of the central niche) Cave 45
High Tang Dynasty (705–780)

donor Buddhisattvas in kneeling positions with palms together in reverence were also added.

The Paranirvana scenes were the largest image groups. In Cave 148 of the High Tang, a 15.8 meter long image of Sakyamuni lying on his right side was constructed in the main room. Surrounding it stood seventy–two one meter high images of Budhisattvas, disciples, vajras, earthly kings, and high officals of the courts. Cave 158 of the Mid Tang was similar to Cave 148 in scale.

Cave 96, built in the second of Yangzhai of the Tang Dynasty (AD 695), and Cave 130, built between the ninth year of Kaiyuan of the Tang (AD 721) and Tianbao of the Tang (AD 742–756) have drawn attention. Both contain colossal images. The image in Cave 96 is 35.5 meters tall while the one in Cave 130 is 27.3 meters tall. Their bodies are constructed of rock at their core, followed by layers of clay stucco and colors.

A transitional period, the Sui Dynasty was comparatively short. Though the art of painted sculptures had made important achievements, there remained many areas for improvement; the heads were large, shoulders wide, legs short, and the sculpture lacked dynamic rhythm, and uniformity. These inconsistencies all disappeared from Tang sculptures. The Tang figures are better proportioned, more elegantly and colorfully dressed, more individualistic, and truer to life.

▲ Buddha Preaching the Law (the south wall) Cave 57
Early Tang Dynasty (618–704)

C. Wall Paintings

The wall paintings of the early Sui Dynasty adhere to the three register (top, middle, and bottom) layout of the Northern Dynasties. In the late Sui and early Tang period, the layout changed to a two–register format. The upper register typically contains either a picture of a preaching Buddha, the thousand Buddhas, or an illustration of a Buddhist s ū tra; the lower register contains donors. Some cave walls in the early Tang were fully occupied by huge illustrations of Buddhist s ū tras. When Buddhist art became more secularized in the late Tang period, the layout of the cave changed dramatically. Traditional screen painting was introduced. The walls of the cave contain illustrations of two to four different Buddhist s ū tras. Each illustration is divided into two portions: the upper portion, which represents a scene of a Dharma sermon and lower portion, which narrates stories from a Buddhist s ū tra in a style of a screen painting. Portraits of donors fill the walls of the corridor connecting the anteroom and the main room; they are also found at the lower portion of the front wall of the main room.

The wall paintings in this period are very rich in content and can be classified into the following categories.

▶ Avalokitesvara (the south wall) Cave 57
Early Tang Dynasty (618–704)

▼ The Illustration of Amitayurdhyana Sutra (the north wall) Cave 217
High Tang Dynasty (765–780)

▲ Apsaras are sweeping in and out through Windows (the upper part of the north wall) Cave 217
High Tang Dynasty (765–780)

► Parable of the Illusory City of the Saddharmapundarika Sutra (the south wall) Cave 217
High Tang Dynasty (765–780)

1. **Images of the Buddhas and Budhisatvas.** Besides depictions of preaching Buddhas, due to the growing diversification of Buddhist beliefs, there emerged numerous portrayals of other deities, such as the Medicine Buddha, Vairocana, Avalokitesvara (Budhisattva of Compassion), Mahasthamaprapta, Ksitigrbha, and Tantric bodhisattvas (Esoteric Buddhism).

2. **Sūtra Illustrations.** These depict the content of a specific Buddhist S ū tra in narrative form. There are more than thirty themes in Dunhuang caves, including Amitubha Sūtra (the Sūtra of Buddha of Boundless Light), Amitayus Sūtra (the Sūtra of Buddha of Boundless

Life), Amitayur-dhyana Sūtra (the Sūtra of Meditation on Amitayus), Maitreya Sūtra, the Sūtra of medicine Buddha, etc. The center is occupied by a Dharma sermon by the Buddha, flanked Budhisattvas and other divine beings; lively apsaras, heavenly musicians, and dancers.

3. Paintings of Buddhist Legends. These are paintings of historical Buddhist stories. They began in the Sui Dynasty and reached their zenith in the late Tang. These stories or legends came from India, Nepal, Pakistan, and Central China. There are more than ten kinds of stories, including those of miracles, eminent monks, divine appearance, and the Pure Land and other sacred settings.

4. Donors Portraits. Donors include monks, nuns, local lords and nobles, civil and military officials, craftsmen, herders, travelers, attendants, servants, maids and other devotees. During the Sui and Tang period, portraits of donors grew gradually larger and reached life-size proportions in some caves built in the late Tang. These portraits were painted with close attention to details.

5. Decorative Patterns. The decorative patterns during this transitional period in the history of Dunhuang decorative art developed

▲ Conception of Prince Siddhariha (the northern part of the ceiling of the central niche) Cave 329
Early Tang Dynasty (618–704)

► Attendant Budhisattva (the north wall) Cave 71
High Tang Dynasty (765–780)

◀ The Illustration of Zhang Yichao on the March (the south wall) Cave 156
Late Tang Dynasty (848–906)

▶ The Illustration of Song Guo Furen on the March (the north wall) Cave 156
Late Tang Dynasty (848–906)

from the "architectural style" of the Northern Dynasties to the "ceiling panel style" of the Sui and to the "fabric style" of the Tang. They grew in variety and in complexity and reached the peak of their development in the Tang Dynasty when decorations were modeled on the complicated patterns used on fabrics such as brocade, satin, and silk.

▲ Siddhartha Crosses over the Wall at Night (the southern part of the ceiling of the central niche) Cave 329
Early Tang Dynasty (618–704)

◀ Dancers and Musicians (the north wall) Cave 220
Early Tang Dynasty (618–704)

▶ The Illustration of the Bao' en Sutra (the north wall) Cave 112
Mid–Tang Dynasty (781–847)

▲ Dancers and Musicians (the south wall) Cave 112
Mid-Tang Dynasty (781–847)

► Musicians (the northern side of the niche built the west wall) Cave 159
Mid-Tang Dynasty (781–847)

▲ The Illustration of the Maitreya Sutra (the north wall) Cave 25 of the Yulin Grottoes Mid-Tang Dynasty (781–847)

► An Old Man Get into Tomb (the north wall) Cave 25 of the Yulin Grottoes Mid-Tang Dynasty (781–847)

▲ The Illustration of Amitayurdhyana Sutra (the south wall) Cave 25 of the Yulin Grottoe
Mid–Tang Dynasty (781–847)

▼ Tonsuring the Royal Consorts of the Illustration of Maitreya Sutra (the south wall) Cave 159
Mid–Tang Dynasty (781–847)

▶ Buildings (the south wall) Cave 25 of the Yulin Grottoes
Mid–Tang Dynasty (781–847)

▲ Two Buddhas (Probhutaratna and Sakyamani seated side by side) Preaching the Law (the ceiling of the central niche) Cave 45
High Tang Dynasty (705–780)

► Worshipping Heavenly Kings (the north wall) Cave 25 of the Yulin Grottoes
Mid-Tang Dynasty (781–847)

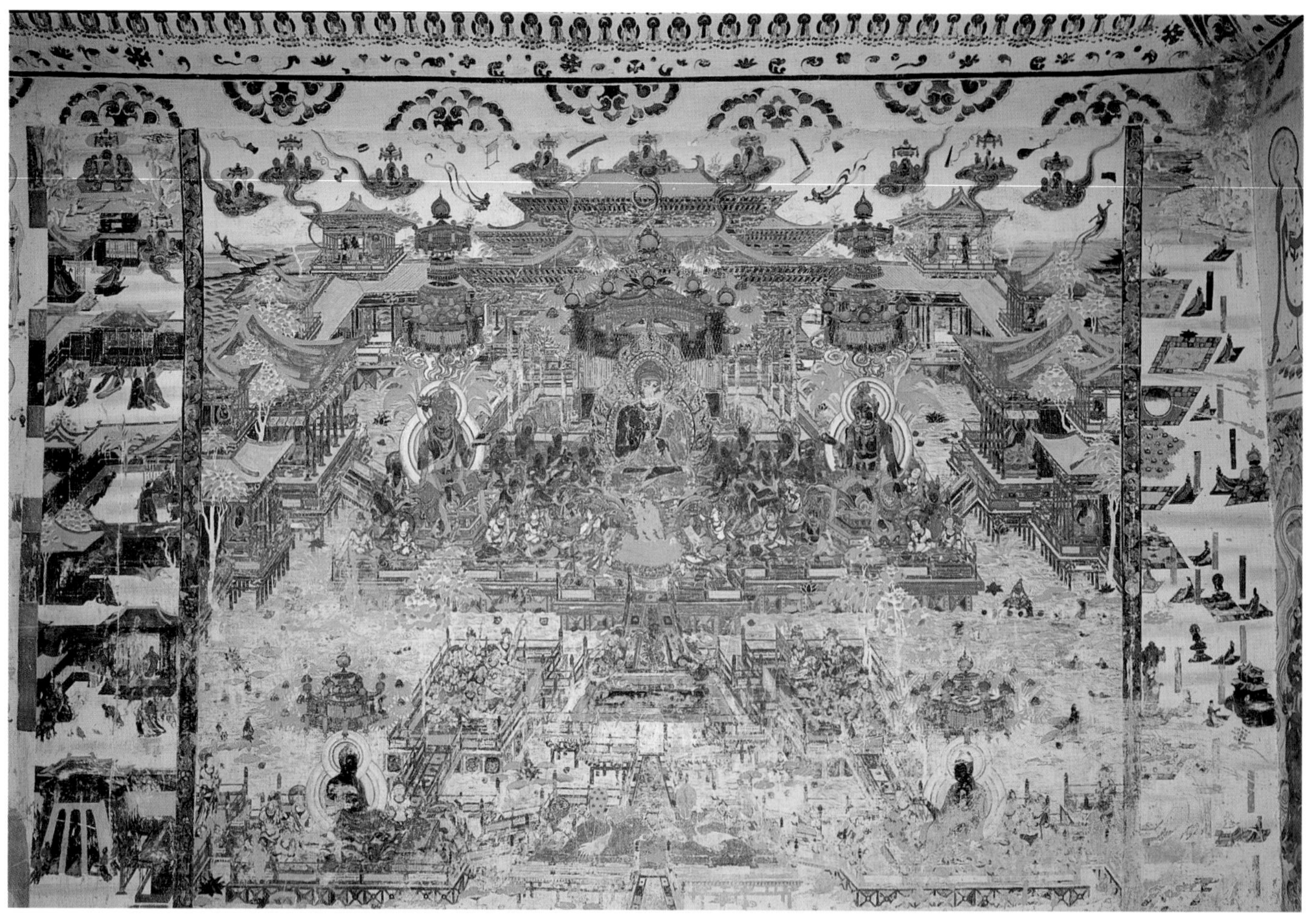

▲ The Illustration of the Amitayurdhyana Sutra (the north wall) Cave 172
High Tang Dynasty (705–780)

► Buddha Preaching the Law (the south wall) Cave 320
High Tang Dynasty (705–780)

◄ Tonsuring the Royal Consorts (the north wall) Cave 445
High Tang Dynasty (705–780)

▲ Playing the Zheng under a Tree (the south wall) Cave 85
Late Tang Dynasty (848–906)

► Thousand-armed and Thousand-eyed Avalokitesvara (the south wall) Cave 14
Late Tang Dynasty (848–906)

▲ Battle Scene of the Illustration of the Saddharmapundarika Sutra (the south wall) Cave 12
Late Tang Dynasty (848–906)

► Amoghapasa–avalokitesvara (the south wall) Cave 14
Late Tang Dynasty (848–906)

▲ Heavenly King and Warrior (the southern part of the central altar) Cave 55
The Song Dynasty (960–1226)

◀ The Illustration of the Saddharmapundarika Sutra (the south wall) Cave 12
Late Tang Dynasty (848–906)

III. Cave Art of the Five Dynasties, Song, Western Xia, and Yuan

A. Architectural Forms of the Caves

The cave architecture of this period continued the style of the late Tang assembly cave with a niche in the back wall of the main room or a square altar set up in the middle of the room. The caves with central pedestals built in the Five Dynasties and the Song are larger than those of the previous period (Cave 427, 431, 444, 437). In the Western Xia and Yuan Dynasty, the pedestal in an assembly cave became round and multi-layered (Mogao Cave 465 and Yulin Cave 3).

B. Painted Images

Most of the images made in this period have been severely damaged. What is left are only those in Cave 261of the Five Dynasties, Cave 55 of the Song Dynasty, and Cave 246 of the Western Xia. The images of this period carried on the theme and the style of the Tang tradition, but lacked the Tang spirit. There were some new materials, such as the principal image in Cave 55, a maitreya in three forms, and a heavenly donor girl in Cave 491 of the Western Xia.

C. Wall paintings

The majority of the wall paintings in the Five Dynasties and the Song are large compositions. Although their contents remained the same as those of the previous period, their size increased due to larger dedications. Some of the new subjects include the depiction of Manjusri in Cave 220 and the illustrations of Avalokitesvara Sūtra and the Eight Stupa Sūtra in Cave 76. Although declining in number, type, and variety, a new feature was added to the wall paintings in this period. Almost every painting has cartouches that describe the content of each anecdote. In the Western Xia and the Yuan period, most of the illustrations of traditional themes fell into decline, and some ceased to be depicted. The composition of the painting became more schematic. Some of the paintings show the strong impact of the painting style of the Song Dynasties of Central China (Yulin Cave 2, 3, and 29) and the arts of Tibetan Esoteric Buddhism.

1. Paintings of Buddhist Legends. This kind of paintings continued to develop in this period. More than forty caves contain this kind of the paintings. Depictions of auspicious things and omens are painted on the ceiling of the corridor linking the antechamber and the main room of a cave (Mogao cave 98 and 454). In some caves, multiple narratives share the same wall (mogao Cave 72). Paintings of Buddhist sacred places reflect strong influence of landscape painting of Central China.

2. Deities. During the Five Dynasties and the Song large images of the Four Heavenly Guardians, Eight Divine Beings, Eight Dragon Kings–all defenders of the Law were executed.In the Song and Western Xia, large paintings of processioned donor Buddhisattvas and sixteen Arhats were new additions.

3. Paintings of Jataka Tales. Avadanas, and historical anecdotes. Although small in number, these paintings are gigantic compositions; they were painted in the lower portion of the wall in some of the large caves

▲ Auspicious Deity (the north wall) Cave 3
The Yuan Dynasty (1227–1368)

▲ The Illustration of the Bhaisajya–guru–vaidurya–raja–sutra (the north wall) Cave 220
Early Tang Dynasty (618–704)

built in the Five Dynasties and Song.

4. **Portraits of the Donors.** Donor portraits increased in number in the Five Dynasties and Song period, and they appear much larger than those in the previous period. For example, the king of Khotan (Yutian) in Cave 98 is 2.9 meters tall. In the donor paintings of the Western Xia and Yuan, personages of other nationalities appear in costumes indigenous to their kingdoms.

5. Decorative Patterns. The decorative patterns in the Five Dynasties, used for ceiling panels, were inherited from the Tang. In the apex a lotus flower is encircled by writing dragons; the borders are decorated with scroll designs and fret patterns. In the Song and Western Xia, some of the dragons are gilded, raised in relief. Some apex are decorated with floral designs. Among the flowers are intersecting vajras and Dharma wheels; on the edges are fret, scroll, and pearl patterns. The decorative motifs of the

Yuan Dynasty, in addition to employing Western Xia features, show influence from secular culture and Tibetan Esoteric Buddhism.

In short, from the Five Dynasties to the early Song, the art of wall painting carried on the Tang creative tradition, producing many worthy works of landscape, narratives, and portraits with individual characteristics. The paintings of this period are characterized by full figures, warm colors, and unrestrained and dynamic lines. During the Song Dynasty, wall

▼ The Story of Manjusri (the northern section of the west wall) Cave 3 of the Yulin Grottoes

The Western Xia Dynasty (1036–1226)

▲ Worshipping State Priest of Western Xia (the eastern section of the south wall) Cave 29 of the Yulin Grottoes

The Western Xia Dynasty (1036–1226)

► Avalokitesvara Cave 2 of the Yulin Grottoes

The Western Xia Dynasty (1036–1226)

▲ The Stories of Li Shake (the south wall) Cave 72
The Five Dynasties Period (907–959)

► The Story of Samantabhadra (the southern section of the west wall) Cave 3 of the Yulin Grottoes
The Western Xia Dynasty (1036–1226)

paintings fell into a decline. The figures look less than animated and stereotypical; the colors are monotonous, and lines weak. The figure paintings of the Western Xia combined the style of Central China and Dangxiang nationality. The art of the Yuan Dynasty consists of two different styles. One is represented by the image of the thousand–armed and thousand–eyed Avalokitesvara (Budhisattvas of Compassion) in Mogao Cave 3. The figure is drawn with the tremulous strokes, and bent–reed strokes and

◀ Hall With Inverted Funnel Shaped Ceiling and Central Stupa-pillar Shape of Cave 61
The Five Dynasties Period (907–959)

▲ Worshipping King of Khotan (the southern section of the east wall) Cave 98
The Five Dynasties Period (907–959)

unfluctuating, continuous line; colored lightly and elegantly with wash, it reveals the standard, high skills of Chinese Painting. The other style appears in murals in Mogao Cave 465. These show a strong presence of the art of Saskyapa, a Tibetan Buddhist order. The figures bear some characteristics of Indian and Nepalese painting. They are painted with straight, clean iron-wire line and colored with black white, green and other rich, heavy colors. They evoke a feeling of mystery and awe. This style originated in the artistic tradition of Tibetan Esoteric Buddhism.

▲ Donors and Boys (the eastern section of the south wall) Cave 29 of the Yulin Grottoes)
The Western Xia Dynasty (1036–1226)

▲ Thousand-armed and Thousand-eyed Avalokitesvara (the north wall) Cave 3
The Yuan Dynasty (1227–1368)

► Esoteric Buddhist Deity (the middle section of the west wall) Cave 465
The Yuan Dynasty (1227–1368)

▲ Light-emitting Buddha (the south wall of the corridor) Cave 61
The Five Dynasties Period (907–959)

► Heavenly King Preaching the Law (the south section of the east wall) Cave 465
The Yuan Dynasty (1227–1268)

▲ Brick with Camel Design
The Tang Dynasty (618–906)

◀ Esoteric Buddhist Deity Mandala (the east section of the south wall) Cave 465
The Yuan Dynasty (1227–1268)

Ⅳ. The Significance of the Art of Dunhuang Cave Shrines

Although the art of Dunhuang cave shrines is largely based on Buddhist literature for its content, it can not be severed from its historical and social circumstances. From this perspective, what the art of Dunhuang reveals is life of more than a thousand years of a rich cultural tradition. Dunhuang cave-temples are not only a treasure house of art, but also of medieval history and culture.

A. Historical Significance

Although little has been written about Dunhuang' s long history, its local influential families have left accurate information about themselves and their relationship with neighboring nationalities and the western regions in thousands of donor images, paintings, and donor inscriptions. From these images and records we learn of the deep involvement of the local eminent families-Yin, Shou, Li, Ju, Zhan, and Cao-in cave construction, complex inter-relationships and connections with neighboring nationalities. They are invaluable materials for the study of Dunhuang under the reign of Zhang and Cao' s insurrection Army Government. We can also learn about the extent of involvement of neighboring powers in the life of Dunhuang. These images and paintings also provide information about yiwei and servant system of the Tang Dynasty, the Tibetan official system, and the insurrection army' s administrative style.

The ancient economic life in Dunhuang, including farming, harvesting, fishing, and domestic animal breeding, and hunting, is evident in motifs depicted in paintings of Jataka tales, Buddhist legends, Maitreya' s Paradise, Futian Sūtra, Lankavātara Sūtra, and donor portraits and inscriptions. Indications of the art industries can be found, including casting, wine brewing, pottery, weaving, knitting, leather processing, shoe making, painting, sculpting, carpentry, masonry, cave excavating, jewelry making, and bow making. Commercial enterprises evident in visual and written records include slaughter houses, meat markets, wine houses, inns, gold and silver trade, lumber mills, and archery workshops. According to the manuscripts in the Library Cave more than twenty kinds of crafts practiced. The cave-temple murals and the Library Cave manuscripts together give us a clear picture of the handicraft industry and commerce in medieval Dunhuang.

The illustrations of the Lotus Sūtra and Parunirvana Sūtra present information on ancient military training, expeditions, conquering, defense and offence, and weaponry. The wall paintings also provide details on ancient sports, including horse archery, target shooting, equestrian techniques, mounting, wrestling, weight lifting, chess, material arts, swimming, feather ball kicking, etc.

Dunhuang was once a hub of the east and west trade on the Silk Road. Some paintings recorded this historical role. For example, Cave

▲ Details from the Illustration of the Punya-ksetra Sutra (the north wall) Cave 296
The Northern Zhou Dynasty (557-580)

◀ The Illustration of the Saddharmapundarika Sutra (ceiling) Cave 420
The Sui Dynasty (581–618)

▲ The Illustration of Zhang Qian Visiting the Western Regions (the north wall) Cave 323
Early Tang Dynasty(618–704)

296 of the Northern Zhou has a painting depicting a foreign merchant with a prominent nose and deeply set eyes leading a loaded camel on one side of a bridge while a Chinese merchant riding on a horse, escorting a team of loaded donkeys, rides on the other side of the bridge. The Silk Road was not always safe. The illustration of the Lotus S ū tra in Cave 420 of the Sui tells a story of another side of the Silk Road, a horror story of highway robbery: merchants with teams of camels and donkeys loaded with silk being robbed by armed bandits.

The Silk Road was not only a trade route, but also a channel of diplomatic and cultural exchange. Some murals depict these activities. Cave 323 dated to the Tang Dynasty has a painting of Zhang Qian, a famous Western Han diplomat who was dispatched to the western regions. Cave 98 of the Five Dynasties and Cave 454 of the Song have wall paintings portraying Wang Xunche, Tang ambassador to India. Caves 231, 237, 98, 61, and 72 contain the deeds of Liu Shahe, an eminent monk who ventured west in search for the Buddhist Dharma. Cave 126 of Mogao and Cave 2, 3, and 29 of Yulin Grottoes tell the famous story of Xuanzang, a high monk of the Tang. There are also wall paintings depicting the activities of abbots from western China, such as Shigao, King Shenghui, Fu Tudeng in Cave 329, 9, 108, 454 of the Tang and Song Dynasties.

Scenes of daily life in ancient society can be seen in various murals. These include daily living activities such as births, weddings, and funerals. The illustrations of Maitreya S ū tra generally include scenes of weddings. There were two marriage customs widely practiced in Dunhuang in the Tang and Song period: one is rooted in the Han Chinese tradition in which the man would send betrothal gifts to the bride' s family and bring the bride home to marry into his family; the other is influenced by the custom of the western regions in which the groom would marry into the bride' s family. The mural scenes of wedding and marriage usually include the whole wedding process.

From the narratives of Buddhist legends and the illustrations of Paronirvana S ū tra of the Northern Zhou through the Song, one can find scenes of funerals and burials: body visitation, memorial service, funeral process, burial, and mourning after the burial.

Most of the painted images and wall paintings in Dunhuang caves depict Buddhist content. The sculpture and wall paintings of Buddhist deities, Jataka tales, Buddhist historical anecdotes, illustrations of various s ū tras, and numerous paintings of mythical figures provide us with a large body of material for the systematic and comprehensive study of Buddhism, including its ideas, orders and sects, beliefs, propagation, and especially its influence on Chinese life and its assimilation into greater Chinese culture. They also provide valuable information about India, Western Asia, Central Asia, and Xinjiang.

▶ The Story of Putting out a Fire of You Zhou City (the north wall) Cave 323
Early Tang Dynasty (618–704)

B. Artistic Value

The art of Dunhuang cave shrines, with more than a thousand years of history and development, is rich in content and style. It is a combination of the local artistic tradition of the Han and Jin, the imported styles of the Southern and Northern Dynasties, Tang and Song styles from Central China, and the foreign artistic traditions of India, Central Asia, and Western Asia. It is a product of cultural and artistic exchanges between Dunhuang, Central China and the west.

The wall paintings in Dunhuang caves fall under the following genres: figures, landscapes, animals, and decorative patterns. Each genre can be studied on its own because each has had a history of more than a thousand years of development. The most valuable works are the paintings done before the Song Dynasty. They are extremely rare. No museum in the world has any collection of these paintings.

There are more than two hundred caves that have murals containing themes. There are more than five hundred musical ensembles of various kinds, thousands of musicians, and more than forty kinds of musical instruments depicted in the wall paintings in Dunhuang caves totaling 4,500 pieces. In addition, many music manuscripts have been discovered in the Library. These documents provide invaluable material for the study of the history of Chinese music and of the musical exchange between China and regions to the west.

Dance is another art form abundantly portrayed in the murals; most of the wall paintings contain scenes of dances of various kinds.

▲ Pattern on the Ceiling Cave 10 of the Yulin Grottoes
The Yuan Dynasty (1227–1368)

▲ Heavenly Musicians (the western side of the ceiling) Cave 10 of the Yulin Grottoes
The Yuan Dynasty (1227–1368)

There are dancing scenes from secular events, such as dances at wedding banquets and other festivals, and scenes from court life as well as depictions of divine scene, such as dancing apsaras and other heavenly musicians and dancers. From the Library Cave, we have also found manuscripts of dance compositions. The art of dance is an ephemeral art, difficult to preserve. So we know little of the dance movements of the past. But in these caves, a large number of beautiful dancing images have been preserved. These caves can be rightly called a museum of ancient dance.

Dunhuang also offers rich material for the study of ancient architecture. There are thousands of buildings of various kinds painted in the murals dating from the sixteen kingdoms to the Western Xia. There are monasteries, city walls, palace watchtowers, huts, domes, tents, inns, restaurants, slaughter houses, beacon towers, bridges, prisons, and tombs. They have also left rich information about building components and decorative details, such as recessed beams, pillars, windows, and infrastructure. There is little record about the Chinese architecture from the Southern Dynasty to the high Tang elsewhere; Dunhuang wall paintings have captured many architectural forms of this period and helped fill gaps in our knowledge. In addition, more than 800 caves are extant, built in different periods and forms; five wooden verandahs built in the Tang and Song and the stupas are all concrete material for the study of ancient architecture.

C. Scientific and Technological Significance

There are many farming scenes in the paintings of Jataka tales,

episodes from the life of the historical Buddha, Sakyamuni, Maitreya and the Lotus S ū tra. These scenes offer a glimpse into the agricultural life in Dunhuang from the Northern Zhou to the Western Xia, a span of 600 years. The farming activities portrayed in these paintings include ploughing, seed broadcasting and planting, harvesting, thrashing, and winnowing. The tools consist of straight shaft ploughs, curved

觀音菩薩赴會
應理之寺
廣明之聖寺
天壽之寺
大佛光之寺

阿羅漢一百二十五人會
阿育王瑞現塔
東臺之頂
中天之閣
大法華之寺
河北道鎮州

◀ The Illustration of Mount Wutai (detail) (the West Wall) Cave 61
The Five Dynasties Period (907–959)

▲ Female Donors (the southern section of the east wall) Cave 61
The Five Dynasties Period (907–959)

shaft ploughs, iron plough shares, grinders, forks, hoes, spades, shoulder posts, steelyards, jars, dou (a unit of dry measure for grain, equivalent of one decalitre), sheng (a unit of dry measure for grain, e–quivalent of one liter), and hu (a dry measure, originally equal to 10 dou, later 5 dou). The most valuable is the image of a curved shaft plough, depicted in the illustration of the Maitreya S ū tra in Cave 445 of the high Tang; the depth of plough can be adjusted in this tool. It is the only picture that records the most advanced farming tool used in that period.

Dunhuang cave murals also record transportation methods used in medieval times, including oxen, horses, camels, mules, donkeys, elephants, boats, ships, carriages, sedan, chairs, and imperial car–riages. The most significant contributions ancient China had made to the field of transportation are the invention of one –wheeled vessels, horse harnesses (chest harness and shoulder harness), spurs, and horseshoes. Their images have been well preserved in the wall paint–ings at Dunhuang.

Murals in both cave 285 of the Western Wei and cave 296 of the Northern Zhun tell the story of five hundred robbers regaining eye–sight and converting to Buddhism. There are battle scenes of horsemen fighting footsoldiers (bandits).The horses in the pictures all wear armor and other protective gear for battle. The horse armor is an–cient China' s unique contribution to world military gear.

In the figures of deities from the Sui to the Western Xia, and the illustrations of Medicine Buddha Sūtra, glass ware is held in the hands of Buddhas, Budhisattvas, and disciples or placed on offering tables. There are glass bowls, cups, and trays. They are transparent, featuring different pale tones of blue, green, and brown. Their shapes, colors, and decorative patterns represent the styles of Shashan of Western A–sia and Rome. These paintings not only reflect the technical charac–teristics of early glass, but also tell the story of the glass trade between China and the west.

DUNHUANG LIBRARY CAVE

On June 22,1900 (May 26 of the Twenty–sixth year of Guangxu Reign of the Qing Dynasty) , Wang Yuanlu, a Daoist practicing in the Lower Monastery of Mogao Grottoes, stumbled upon the Library Cave 16. He discovered more than fifty thousand objects of cultural treasure including Buddhist s ū tras, assorted manuscripts, embroidery, paint–ings on silk, and other religious objects. His path–breaking discovery provide the world with a large number of materials for the study of the history, geography, religion, economy, politics, language, literature, art, and science of China and Western Asia. These documents have been affectionately called the "Encyclopedia of the Middle Ages" and the "ocean of ancient knowledge" .

▲ Ploughing and Harvesting (the north wall) Cave 25 of the Yulin Grottoes Mid-Tang Dynasty (781-847)

Ninety percent of the materials are Buddhist manuscripts. The earliest hand-written sotra found in the Library is an Avadana (parable). At the end of the book, there is an inscription indicating, "Completed on March 17 of the First Year of Ganlu." The first year of Ganlu refers to Ganlu Reign of the Former Qin (AD 259). This is also the oldest document among all the manuscripts. The Library held all kinds of Buddhist classics, including sutiapitaka, vinayapitaka, and abhidbarmapitaka. But the most valuable documents are the classics of Chan (Zen) Buddhism and the manuscripts of Three Stages Sect (a Buddhist sect in the Sui and Tang China,6th to 10th centuries). The jewel among the Chan documents is an earliest version of Analects of the Sixth Chan Patriarch Huineng, Which differs in many ways from the version circulated after the Song Dynasty. The works of Three Stages Sect of Chinese Buddhism include Three Stages Dharma, Secrets of Three Stages Dharma, and Dharma of the Three Realms. Their discovery adds new material to the study of the history of Chinese Buddhism.

The Library also held many lost Buddhist works (documents that are not collected in the Tripitaka). The discovery of these missing documents helps complete gaps in The Tripitaka published after the Song Dynasty.

Some of the manuscripts are apocryphal s ū tras written first in Chinese but given a Central Asian and Indian pedigree leading an air of

► The Master of Pounding Rice (the middle section of the south wall) Cave 465
The Yuan Dynasty (1227–1268)

▼ Ploughing in the Rain (the western section of the north wall) Cave 23
High Tang Dynasty (705–780)

▲ The Story of Five Hundred Bandits Becoming Buddhas (the south wall) Cave 285
The Western Wei Dynasty (535–556)

authenticity. This phenomenon reflects a unique feature of Chinese Buddhism. These documents are invaluable for the study of the development of Chinese Buddhism.

Among the manuscripts, many are written in other languages other than the Chinese, such as Sanskrit, early Tibetan, Hui, Yutien, and Turfan. There are also some bilingual scriptures. These bilingual documents are extremely valuable for research on the sources of Chinese translations of Buddhist classics and as a check on the accuracy of translations. Moreover, the Buddhist scriptures found in Dunhuang Library Cave, especially the calligraphic examples produced in the Sui

▲ The Illustration of the Baofen Sutra (a section of the south wall) Cave 85
Late Tang Dynasty (848–906)

► Buddha Preaching the Law in Grdhrakuta (the north wall) Cave 4 of the Yulin Grottoes
The Yuan Dynasty (1227–1368)

◄ The Story of Five Hundred Bandits Becoming Buddhas (battle scene) (the south wall) Cave 285
The Western Wei Dynasty(535–556)

◀ White Tara (the eastern section of the south wall) Cave 4 of the Yulin Grottoes
The Yuan Dynasty (1227–1368)

▼ Mahaparinirvanasutra (section) No.227
The Six Dynasties

and Tang period, were well proofread and, thus, contain few errors. They may serve as standard texts for checking on the accuracy of the scriptures printed after the Tang.

Included in the library holding are documents of local monasteries. They consist of asset records, lists of monks and nun's names, official papers, reports of religious activities, and speeches for different occasions. They are rare materials for research on monastic life in Dunhuang.

Although Daoism was not as popular as Buddhism in Dunhuang, in the early Tang Dynasty, it flourished for a short period of time because the early monarchs of the Tang worshipped Laozi, the founder of Daoism. Therefore, a large number of Daoist classics are also found in the Library Cave, There are approximately five hundred scrolls, mostly hand written. In addition to Buddhist and Daoist documents, there are

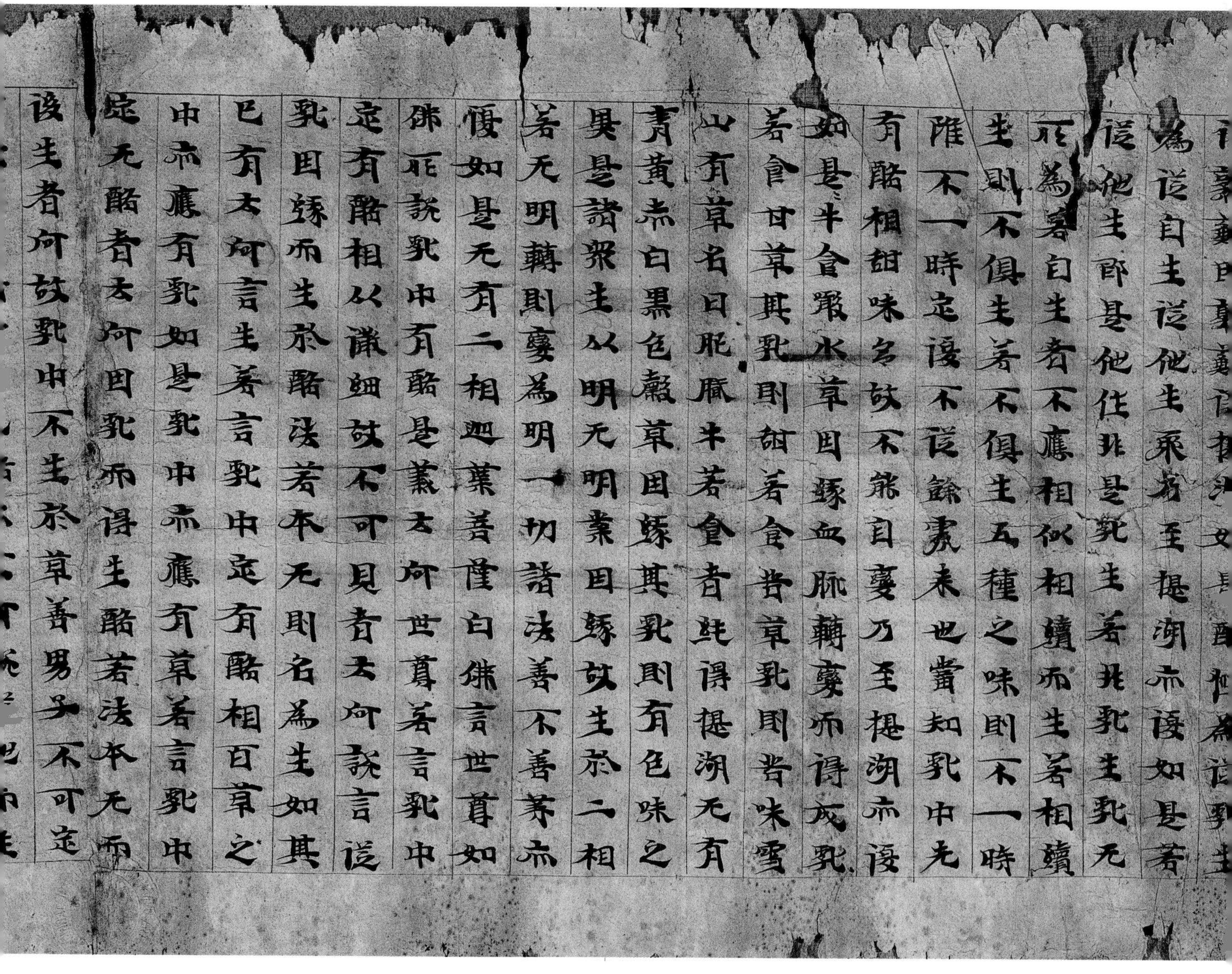

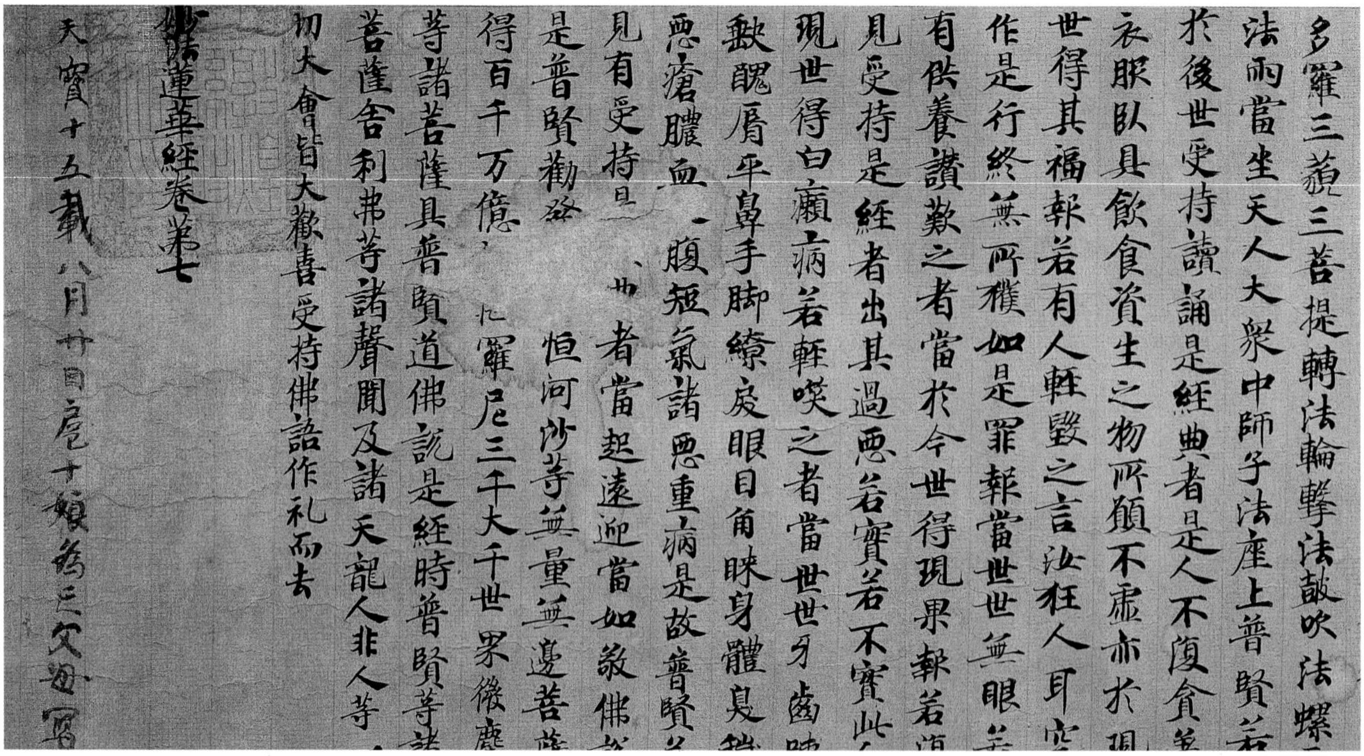

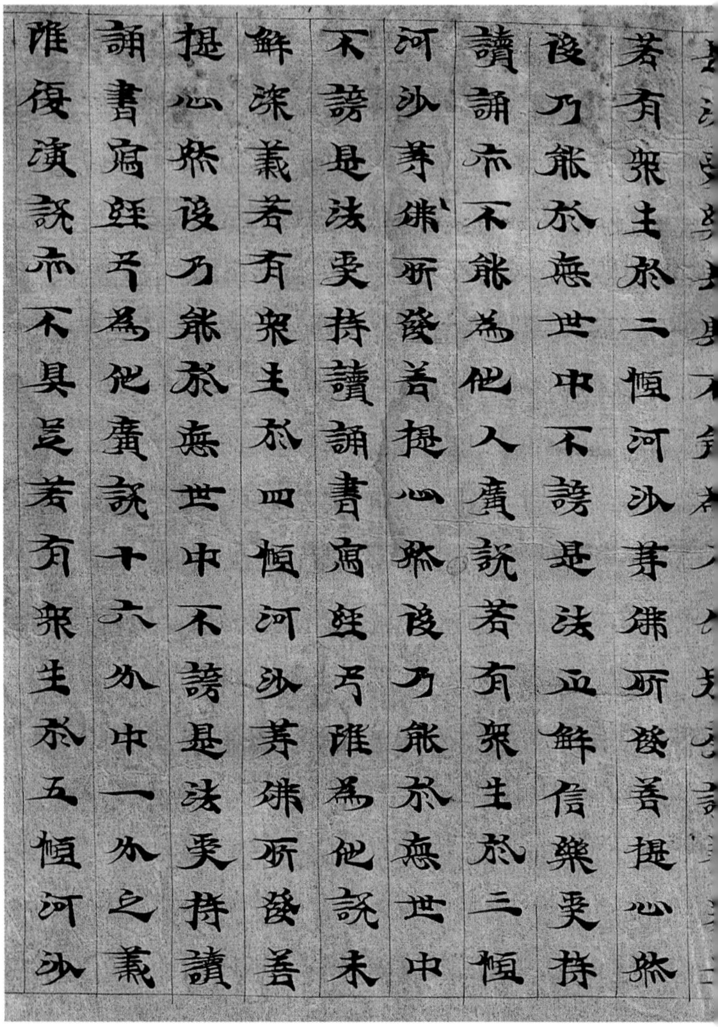

Manichean and Nestorian papers, which help us understand the cultural exchanges between China and Persia.

The works of history and geography and private and official documents in the Library are the first-hand material for the study of medieval society. Some ancient books of history, long believed to have been lost, are found in the Library collection. There are books of local history that are valuable for the study of Shazhou and Yizhou, Shouchanga County, and the Shazhou Chronicles. Some works of geography have also attracted a great deal of attention, such as Maps of Shazhou.

Little has been written about the history of Dunhuang under the rule of the Insurrection Army and what has existing literature contains many errors. There are some one hundred documents preserved in the Library Cave, which offer rich material about this part of Dunhuang' s history.

A great number of Chinese literary classics have also been well preserved. They include Confucian classics and collections of poems, lyrics, prose poems, novels, and folk drama. Most of the literary holdings in the Library are works of folk literature, and of the numerous poems found, most belong to the Tang and Five Dynasties. The importance of the Confucian classics found in the Library is their function as standard texts for editing modern versions.

The most significant finding of the literary material is bianwen, a unique literary genre that combines verse and prose component that would be spoken and sung. As a genre, it was unknown before the

◀ Saddharmapundarikasutra (section) No.674
High Tang Dynasty (705–780)

▼ Mahaparinirvanasutra (section) No.228
The Six Dynasties

discovery of the Library Cave. Its discovery fills a gap in the study of Chinese literature. There are also some important linguistic treaties found in the Library collection. They include Rhymes, Phonology and Semantics, and Lexicology.

The Library has many works of science and technology ranging from mathematics to astronomy, medicine, paper–making, and printing. Works on math include Multiplication Tables, Calculations, and Speed Calculation. They are all the earliest hand–written documents on math in China.

There are many star maps in the Library collection. These maps are evidence of ancient China' s advanced knowledge of astronomy. In ancient times, astronomy and the calendar were closely related. Dunhuang' s calendars are made by local astrologers. One calendar that is worth a special note here is the one made in the third year of Yongxi of the Song (AD 986), which used the week system of the Christian West. At least sixty volumes of medical works have been found in the Library Cave as well. There are four kinds of medical works: principles of medicine, acupuncture, dictionary of medicinal herbs, and prescrip–

tions. They offer many new materials of medical diagnosis and treatment.

Since the manuscripts cover the period from the 4th century to 12th century, they can serve as a witness to the history of Chinese paper making and printing. The Diamond S ū tras of the ninth year of Xiantong of the Tang (AD 868) found in the Library is the earliest woodblock print, evidence of the Chinese invention of this technology.

Dunhung Cave Shrines, with its large number of caves, sculptures, murals manuscripts, and other religious and artistic objects, has attracted the interest of scholars all over the world. The interest is still persistent today. The study of these art and cultural treasures has become a unique and independent discipline by itself. "Dunhuang Studies" will occupy an important place in the fields of humanities and social science and will have a splendid future.

▼ Saddharmapundarikasutra (section) No.670
The Western Xia Dynasty (1036–1226)

CHINA DUNHUANG

CHINA DUNHUANG

Publisher: Jiangsu Fine Arts Publishing House(165 Zhongyang Road, post code: 210009), a subsidiary of Phoenix Publishing & Media Group, Ltd.

Phoenix Publishing Group, Ltd. Website: http://www.ppm.cn

Distributor: Jiangsu Xinhua Distribution Group

Film Producer: Nanjing Xinhuafeng Platemaking Corp.

Printer: Nanjing Kaide Printing Company, Ltd.

Format: 889 × 1194mm 1/16

First Printing Date: April, 2006

Third Printing Date: August, 2010

ISBN: 978-7-5344-2082-5

List Price: 190 RMB